THE
BEAR
HUNTER

THE
BEAR HUNTER

SEARCHING FOR RANGERS' NINE-IN-A-ROW HEROES

BY JOHN IRWIN
WITH MURRAY SCOUGALL

First published by Pitch Publishing, 2017

Pitch Publishing
A2 Yeoman Gate
Yeoman Way
Worthing
Sussex
BN13 3QZ
www.pitchpublishing.co.uk
info@pitchpublishing.co.uk

A CIP catalogue record is available for this book
from the British Library.

ISBN 978-1-78531-288-5

Typesetting and origination by Pitch Publishing
Printed in Great Britain by TJ International.

Contents

This book is
dedicated to Debbi,
my daughter

Acknowledgements

John would like to thank:

My nephew Andy Thomson and Gemma Sneddon for their constant support and sponsorship of several of the trips.

Nuno Dias for kindly sponsoring a trip.

Kenny Miller and Madjid Bougherra for giving me their match-worn shirts to auction, David Templeton for the kind donation of a shirt and his boots, Kenny McDowall for taking the time to have the first-team squad sign his training top before donating it, and also Dale Gordon for his autographed strip.

Ally McCoist for his support and for taking the time to put me in touch with people.

Brian and Gaynor Campbell for their help and outstanding hospitality.

Scott MacKinnon, not just for being a trustworthy courier but for the memorabilia purchased from me over the years.

Colin Singh, who was a good friend throughout my time back in Glasgow and for his interest and help in searching for the players.

And my friend Ana Resende, who stressed over every foreign trip until I touched back down on home soil. I made it back in one piece!

Murray would like to thank:

John for sharing his incredible story with me, and Adriana and my parents for their patience and help during the writing of this book.

Paul, Jane and everyone at Pitch for their interest in the project and for all of their hard work in putting the book together.

Foreword by David Robertson

IT'S HARD to believe 20 years have passed since Rangers clinched nine-in-a-row.

In fact, it seems like yesterday that the squad reunited for the tenth anniversary match at Ibrox. I think the expanding waistlines and creaking legs ensure there won't be a reunion game to mark the 20th!

The past 20 years have gone by in a blur, but so did my six seasons at Rangers. That's not to say I don't remember every moment, though.

My first championship win, the 1991/92 season, was brilliant. Unfortunately I missed the title-clinching match against St Mirren due to a build-up of yellow cards, but to lift the trophy for the first time remains a great memory. The rest of the title wins, meanwhile, were more of a relief than anything else.

The pressure was never tougher than during the ninth season. We were confident we would do it, but crossing that line seemed to be put on hold for a long time. We were all set up for the celebrations against Motherwell at Ibrox, only to be defeated. Up next was Tannadice, and that was always a tough place to go, but we didn't want it to go down to the wire away to Hearts. We knew what we had to do against Dundee United and thankfully we did it.

For me, the 1992/93 season is the highlight. We won the treble, defeating my old team Aberdeen in both cup finals and holding them in second place in the league, and I played virtually every game in all competitions. It goes down as one of the most successful seasons in the club's history, and it's great to know I played a big part.

I still keep in touch with what is going on at the club, so I had become aware of what supporter John Irwin was trying to achieve.

When he got in touch with me and said he wanted to come to America to meet me and a couple of the other former players, I was delighted to welcome him into the family home. If he was making the effort to come all this way for a couple of autographs, the least I could do was show some hospitality.

What an amazing story it is. The time, the effort, the money it took to track down and meet every member of the nine-in-a-row squad – lesser men would have given up when faced with some of the problems John encountered along the way, but he remained determined to gather every signature.

As you are about to read, John had a great adventure in making his dream become a reality. The will and desire he displayed epitomises what it means to be a Ranger. Ultimately any football club is about its supporters, so it seems fitting that the 20th anniversary of nine-in-a-row is marked by the incredible achievement of one of the fans.

David Robertson
Austin, Texas
February 2017

Introduction

LIKE SO many fans, I was born a bluenose.

I came into the world in 1951, the youngest of seven, and was brought up in the Whiteinch and Yoker areas of Glasgow. From an early age I always felt I was different compared with my four sisters and two brothers. I looked at life in a different way, and I suppose I'm what some people would call eccentric.

My dad took me to my first game at Ibrox when I was eight years old, and from that moment on I was hooked and rarely missed a home match. When I was a teenager, I started going to away games. I can still remember my first away trip – and it was nearly my last. My dad allowed me to travel up to Tannadice with my friend when I was 16. Back in those days, it wasn't uncommon for supporters to run on to the park when their team scored, although the police were trying to stamp it out.

When Rangers scored, I rushed on but was quickly huckled by a policeman and taken to the back of the terracing, beside another young guy who had also been caught. There were two cops standing guard over us, but that didn't stop the other boy from trying to escape. He was quickly collared and the sergeant punched him in the gut. I couldn't believe what I was seeing.

I was escorted from the ground and taken to the local police station. My furious dad had to come through on the train to get me. It was a bank holiday weekend, so I returned to Dundee on the Tuesday for a court appearance, where I was fined £50. I thought that was the end of it, but two months later a couple of policemen came to my parents' door. They wanted to know if I had seen the sergeant punching the other boy

11

at Tannadice. I said I did, but my dad jumped to his feet and insisted I had seen nothing and sent the cops on their way. 'If you testify against a sergeant, your life will be made a misery,' he told me.

I had a habit of making the wrong choices. Another time when I was a teenager, my mate and I jumped on the boat to Belfast with no tickets and no money. Once we were in Northern Ireland, we met a couple of girls and stayed at their gran's house for a week. The problem was I hadn't told my parents, who were searching the streets back in Glasgow, frantic with worry.

I married young and had two daughters by the time I was in my early twenties. The relationship didn't work and I moved south in 1973, where I married again twice and had my third daughter. While none of my marriages went the distance, I'm proud to say I've maintained friendships with each of my ex-wives. I have to be creative when explaining to new people I meet about my Flora tattoo, though, so I just tell them it stands for 'For Love Of Rangers Always'!

I've survived all of my life by being a ducker and diver. The character of Del Boy could have been modelled on me. I would often sleep in my car overnight in order to secure the best spots at car boot sales, and I've had every job you can imagine, from painting boats to driving lorries to working in bakeries. One of my favourite occupations was when I worked as a nursing assistant in a psychiatric hospital. I also drove the bus when we took the patients on days out. One time I decided to stop by my house and invited the 18 passengers in for a cup of tea. My wife at the time wasn't best pleased.

I'm also a big royalist, so much so that I once lost a job because of The Queen. I heard on the radio that Her Majesty was visiting Chichester Barracks, which was near where I lived, the next morning. I was on the early shift at the bakery, and it was all I could think about as I brought out the rolls. I knew I would always regret it if I didn't try to see her, so I wrote on the blackboard, 'away to see The Queen, back tomorrow' and off I went. I didn't get to meet her but I did catch a glimpse, so it was worth the effort. When I went into work the next morning I was told I was fired. It was OK, though, because I got a new job in another bakery later that day.

I did, however, manage to meet Princess Diana. She was visiting a hospice in Leeds, where I lived at the time, so my youngest daughter, Debbi, and I turned up five hours early in anticipation. Unfortunately she didn't come our way when she arrived. It was the middle of winter and everyone was wrapped up, but I was wearing a Union Jack T-shirt and no jacket, so I stood out. As she was leaving a couple of hours later, I yelled at the top of my lungs, 'Lady Diana,' and she turned round and walked over to us. 'You must be very cold,' she said. I was completely gobsmacked that she had come over and I couldn't find the words to say anything. 'You're very loyal,' she added, as she smiled and walked away.

As you can no doubt tell by now, I believe in living for the moment. But the one constant throughout my life, apart from Rangers, has been darts. I was a good player and played county for West Sussex and Yorkshire B. I managed a nine-dart finish during a match at Sir Patrick Moore's local pub in Sussex in the eighties. Had it happened on television, I would have won thousands, but unfortunately I only received £300 this night. Another time in the same pub, I watched as a group of guys threw nails at the dartboard. I had never seen anyone do this before and started asking them lots of questions. They gave me a shot and all three nails hit the floor, but I was hooked and began practising for hours on end.

By the time I moved back to Yorkshire, I had become really good and fate shone on me one evening in the local working men's club. The manager of Bass Brewery was visiting, so I approached him and asked if I could have a minute of his time. I started throwing the nails and he was really impressed. At the time, Bass had a roadshow that would tour the pubs and clubs – variety acts like magicians and fire-eaters – to promote the brand, and I asked him if I could have a job.

A month later he was in touch to offer me a contract, and for the next ten years I travelled the country with Bass Brewery, challenging punters to a round of darts – they would throw standard darts while I would use nails, screwdrivers and anything else I could lay my hands on. It was a great time, and I was sad when my time as a professional nail thrower came to an end.

I returned to Glasgow in 2006 after retiring from my security role at a Butlin's holiday camp, and I was on the lookout for something that would occupy my time. It should come as no surprise that my idea of a hobby was something a little different from the norm …

Dave McPherson

TENS OF thousands of miles around the world, tens of thousands of pounds spent getting there. All to track down every man who ever played a minute for my beloved Rangers during their glory nine-in-a-row years between 1988 and 1997. I met some of my biggest heroes and found myself in cities and situations I could never have imagined when I returned to Glasgow, having previously lived more than 30 years in England. There I was, thinking I was coming home to live a quiet life in my retirement. Instead it became my greatest adventure, although it all started quite accidentally.

I moved into a house just a short walk from Ibrox Stadium, and thought I might try to gather a few autographs on matchdays since I was so close. I didn't just want the signatures on scraps of paper that would go missing, so decided to buy replica strips and use them as my canvas. I bought three identical shirts online – the white away top from the 1992/93 season. It would be easy to see the autographs on the design, and also it was the strip from one of the greatest seasons of the nine-in-a-row years, when Rangers won the treble and were a goal away from reaching the inaugural Champions League Final.

I was watching television one Friday evening when a football preview show came on STV. Their guest was ex-Rangers defender Dave McPherson. As I watched, a notion popped into my head. I'm going to go to the studio for his autograph. The STV and BBC headquarters are just a short distance from Ibrox, down by the River Clyde, so I pulled one of the strips from the drawer and made my way to the studio.

I explained at reception that I would like Dave to sign my shirt once he had finished filming. They told me I couldn't wait, but if I wanted to leave the top they would have him autograph it and I could collect it the next day. I was hoping to meet him since I had gone to the effort of walking round, but I agreed and left it with the receptionist. I returned the following morning and was pleased to see it had been signed, along with a little message, 'To John, best wishes'.

Dave McPherson, also known as Slim thanks to his lithe 6ft 3in frame, was signed by his boyhood heroes Rangers when he was just 15, arriving from Gartcosh United in 1980. He played his way into the first team within a few years – making his debut in a 1–0 League Cup win against Brechin when he was 17 – during what was a miserable time on the pitch for the club. Better times were around the corner, and the big defender won the title in Graeme Souness's first season as manager in 1986/87. But he was soon surplus to requirements as the gaffer brought in one big-name international defender after another, and he was sold to Hearts in 1987, where he was a big success and well liked by the support.

By 1992, Walter Smith was in charge at Ibrox and was actively signing the best Scottish talent as he tried to deal with the three-foreigner policy, which meant no more than three non-Scottish players were allowed to play in European fixtures. As well as being an able centre-half, McPherson could also run with the ball, so could slot in at right-back. Walter took advantage of that and re-signed Dave in 1992 for £1.3m, beating other reportedly interested clubs like Seville, Spurs, Southampton and Borussia Dortmund. He played a big part the following season, the aforementioned treble-winning campaign, and the sight of his long-haired perm bobbing up and down the touchline soon became a regular one, although it did take him a while to adjust to the role.

Dave played 34 times in the league that season, following it up with 28 appearances during six-in-a-row. Unfortunately that campaign ended on a downer for Dave, after a defensive mix-up between him and goalkeeper Ally Maxwell during the Scottish Cup Final allowed Dundee United to score the only goal of the game and end my team's hopes of a historic double treble. In the following season he made just nine appearances, his final game for Rangers coming in a 2–1 away defeat to Motherwell on 22 October. He was sold back to Hearts just a few days later.

The Tynecastle club were in financial trouble and were forced to offload their star prospect, young defender Alan McLaren, who came to Rangers in a swap deal for Dave, with Rangers also paying an additional fee. McPherson picked up where he left off in Edinburgh and was one of Hearts' most reliable players. When he had his testimonial match in 1997, there could be only one opposition – Rangers. He moved to Melbourne in 1999 to play with Carlton SC, but not before he lifted the Scottish Cup the year before, defeating Rangers in what would be the nine-in-a-row squad's final match together.

In Australia he was playing under fellow nine-in-a-row alumnus Stuart Munro, but the club sadly went out of business. Dave returned to Scotland as assistant manager and then player-manager with Morton in 2001/02, playing 16 league games and scoring four goals. He moved into sports management once he retired from playing.

I met him outside Ibrox a few years after he signed the shirt at STV. By this point I had decided to ask each player to be photographed with the strip when they signed it, so I took the opportunity to go over and introduce myself. To my surprise, Dave knew who I was and was happy to pose for a picture. Clearly word was spreading among the players about my project. But I'm getting ahead of myself. In the weeks after McPherson's signature in 2009, I met a few more ex-players outside Ibrox and had them sign the top. I realised the four or five autographs I had so far were from the nine-in-a-row squad.

How many players featured during those nine years, I wondered, and wouldn't it be great if I could have them all sign the shirt? I researched it online and found the answer – 86.

I can't explain it, but I knew from that moment on that I was going to dedicate myself to tracking down each of those men, except for the late, great Davie Cooper, of course. Little did I know it would consume the next seven years and take me on a journey I never could have imagined. This is the story of my trip around the world in 86 signatures.

Alexei Mikhailichenko

ALEXEI MIKHAILICHENKO'S Rangers career can be summed up in one word – frustrating. And that's the polite way I would describe my dealings with him when I tracked him down to sign my shirt. It led to a terrifying night in Kiev that left me convinced I was going to die and almost made me throw in the towel in my quest to meet all of the nine-in-a-row squad. People think it's just a signature on a shirt, but they don't understand the hassle, the trials and tribulations and the drama that securing an autograph often entailed. My experience with Miko was the most stressful of them all.

When Alexei signed for the Gers in 1991, he was regarded as one of the most talented attacking players in Europe. He quickly became one of my idols of the Rangers team of that era, which makes my encounter with him even more disappointing.

Born in Kiev in 1963, the gangly 6ft 1in playmaker played for his home-town team, Dynamo Kiev, from 1981 to 1990 and was instrumental in their success. He first came to the attention of the Rangers support in 1987 when Kiev played the boys in blue in the European Cup. Following a 1–0 win for the home side in Kiev, Rangers triumphed 2–0 in the second leg to win the tie. (This was the famous game where Souness reduced the width of the pitch after Kiev trained on the park the night before, in order to reduce our opponents' attacking options down the wings.)

Mikhailichenko was named the Ukrainian Footballer of the Year in 1987 and won it again the following year, during a prodigious period for Miko when he also won Soviet Footballer of the Year, came fourth in the Ballon D'Or and won Olympic gold at Seoul. After winning the league title with Kiev in 1990, he moved to Sampdoria and won Serie A with the Italian team, before Rangers came in with a bid of £2.2m – at the time a Scottish transfer record.

He made his debut at Falkirk on 7 September 1991, marking his first game with an audacious attempted shot from the halfway line. During that first season he made 24 starts in the league, with three appearances off the bench, and scored ten goals, his first coming in a 2–0 victory over Hearts at Ibrox. Alexei was a typical attacker in the sense that he ran hot and cold, one minute electrifying the crowd and the next looking like he couldn't be bothered chasing after the ball. He was regarded as lazy, and there's a famous but most likely apocryphal tale of assistant boss Archie Knox ordering him to warm up for training only to come back into the dressing room soon after to find Miko heating himself with a hairdryer!

To be fair to the player, he was often played out of position as a winger when he was best utilised as an attacking midfielder and playmaker. He certainly had his memorable moments in a Rangers jersey, such as his pinpoint cross for Gary McSwegan to score against Marseille in the opening group game of the inaugural Champions League at Ibrox in 1992. He also scored twice in the 4–2 New Year's Day Old Firm game in 1994 at Parkhead. He followed that up with another goal against Celtic in a 1–1 draw at Ibrox in April, the match where Rangers owner David Murray banned Celtic fans from the stadium.

In Miko's final two seasons in Glasgow, he made only fleeting appearances, with the signings of Brian Laudrup in 1994 and Gazza in 1995 pushing him further to the sidelines. His last league appearance, at Ibrox on 23 March 1996, was against Falkirk, the team he also faced on his debut, and he retired at the end of the season aged just 33.

After hanging up his boots, the man who earned 41 caps for the USSR and CIS and a further two caps for Ukraine became assistant boss at Dynamo Kiev, and then manager from 2002 to 2004. From there he spent four years as Ukraine under-20s boss, followed by a spell as national manager. He then returned to Kiev as sporting director in 2013.

One of the biggest hurdles when trying to locate foreign ex-players is the language barrier. What I was doing was fairly odd even when explaining it to someone who could speak fluent English, but when I went on the phone to another country and tried to explain as briefly and plainly as possible, it could become horrendous. I'm sure lots of the people I spoke with thought I was at the wind-up, but thankfully on this occasion I managed to talk to a helpful chap at the BBC in Ukraine, who said he would try to get in touch with Miko. A short time later, he called with a mobile number for him.

Alexei's English wasn't great when I called (he refused to do interviews during his time in Scotland, blaming the language barrier, although it was rumoured he could speak English perfectly well), but eventually he seemed to understand and agreed to meet me. I spoke with him a few more times while I gathered the money I needed for the flights, cobbling the cash together by selling some replica jerseys that some of the current squad signed at the gates of Auchenhowie, Rangers' training facility.

I called him to confirm when I would be flying and was delighted when Alexei said he would meet me at the airport with two other Ukrainian-based nine-in-a-row players, Oleg Kuznetsov and Oleg Salenko. This would allow me to tick off three players in one shot – great news for my limited budget.

I'll be the first to admit the timing of my trip wasn't the best. It coincided with Ukraine rarely being out of the news after civil unrest broke out, and it seemed every day there were reports of shootings and stand-offs. I was fairly confident that Kiev was far enough from the trouble spots to not be affected, but you can never tell what you'll be heading into when a country is in turmoil. Understandably, some of my family weren't keen about my plans, but I don't believe there is any point in worrying in advance. I deal with a situation as it arises. Besides, I had established contact with Miko so I wanted to act while that line of communication remained open.

I flew into Kiev at 5pm, as scheduled, via a three-hour stopover in Amsterdam, and made my way through to the main arrivals lounge, passing by intimidating security guards dressed all in black, including balaclavas. Not the most welcoming sight when entering a country, it must be said. I looked all around for Miko – I had seen recent pictures of him on the internet and he hadn't changed much, so I was confident I would recognise him. I walked around again and again, but he was nowhere to be seen. Maybe he had been delayed. I tried calling him but it rang out, so I sent a text to tell him I was here and asked if he was on his way. No response.

I took a seat and waited. I had no idea what to do. I called again and sent another text, and while I waited for a response I decided to exchange my money. To say I didn't have much would be an understatement – it was probably less than a tenner. As I mentioned earlier, I made all of the trips on a strict budget, hence flying into a country at war with no travel insurance! I didn't think I would need much cash for this trip, since Alexei was supposed to be meeting me at the airport. Once he signed it, I intended to just hunker down in a quiet spot and sleep while I waited for my flight home the following afternoon. At the most I would need just a few quid for some food and drink.

I located the bureau de change and stood in the queue. Just as I stepped up to the booth, the woman on the other side of the glass pushed the window down and walked away. I stared at her, wondering what was going on. She didn't crack a light. There were people behind me in the queue, too. 'They do that here,' said an American guy standing just off to the side of the window. 'When it's time for a break they don't care if there's someone still to serve. She'll be back in 45 minutes.'

While I waited I tried calling Miko's number again and sent him yet another text. I was becoming increasingly concerned at the lack of response. The teller with the thunderous expression returned 45 minutes later and I exchanged my few pounds into the local currency, hryvnia.

By now my nerves were jangling – I needed a smoke. I walked out of the terminal and across the road, making sure I was a good distance away from the building since I didn't know what the smoking laws were in Ukraine. I had just put a cigarette to my mouth when I felt a presence beside me and all of a sudden the fag was slapped from my lips. I looked up, shocked. In front of me was a stern-faced policeman. He began speaking in a raised voice and, although I couldn't understand a word, I knew this wasn't a friendly 'hello, welcome to our country'. The last thing I needed was a fine. Then another two officers arrived – one stood in front of me and the other behind. They were making sure I was going nowhere, not that I intended to run. I could only assume I was in a no-smoking area, but this seemed a rather intimidating reaction.

I tried to explain in a few words why I was there but I don't think they understood. One of them said 'passport'. I handed it over and they examined it, then looked at me as I stood before them in my Rangers top. One of them pointed towards the terminal. It looked like I was being dismissed, so I didn't hang around. As I walked across the road, shaken and annoyed at the way I'd just been treated, I looked over my shoulder and saw one of the cops lighting up a cigarette.

I went inside and waited. My flight home left at 2.30pm the following day. By now it was 9pm, four hours after I'd landed. Just then a text came through. It was Mikhailichenko.

'Where are you?' it read.

'I'm still at the airport.'

A few minutes later and another text pinged.

'Get a taxi into the city centre.'

That was it, end of communication. I didn't know how far it was to the city centre or how much it would cost, but I felt I didn't have any other option. I went outside and got into one of the waiting cabs, but of course I couldn't tell the driver where to go. 'Centre, city centre,' I said, but he didn't speak any English. He dropped me off at the train station, maybe because I was foreign and he thought I was continuing my travels. Thankfully the fare was the equivalent of pennies, so it didn't eat too much into my very limited funds.

I texted Miko again to tell him I was at the station. I stood outside, near what I suppose could be termed a taxi rank, except it seemed to be a long line of private cars, where the drivers bartered with customers over the fare. My stomach rumbled while I waited, and I realised it had been hours since I'd eaten. I went into a café on the outskirts of the station and ordered by pointing at whatever I could see, so I ended up with French fries and a Coke. I sat at an empty table and tried to relax for a moment as I ate. Just then a text came through from Mikhailichenko. My heart sank as I read it. I was miles away from where I needed to be. He gave me an address for Kiev's training complex.

I finished eating and stood up, a million thoughts swirling around in my head. I was about 50 yards along the street towards the taxi rank when I froze in realisation at what I'd done. I had left the bag containing my nine-in-a-row strip under the café's table. I rushed back as quickly as I could, praying someone hadn't picked it up and walked off with it. Years of work could be gone in a moment of absent-mindedness. I went straight to the table where I'd sat and thankfully the bag was still there. I gripped it tightly in my hands and let out a relieved sigh.

I returned to the taxi rank. By now it was nearly midnight. This is crazy, I thought. A driver approached me, 'Taxi, taxi?' he asked. I nodded and showed him the text from Miko with the address. I managed to knock the price down by around 50 hryvnia (the fare was the equivalent of about £4) and sat down in the back seat of his beat-up old Lada with more than a degree of trepidation. As we set off I tried to speak to him – 'How long will it take? Where do we go from here?' – but he never said a word. We drove in silence for what seemed like forever.

Sometimes the mind remembers things at the most inopportune times and, while I sat in the car, my teeth rattling as we struck giant pothole after giant pothole, I suddenly recalled the stories I had read weeks before about two separate instances of men being kidnapped in Kiev while taking taxi rides.

The worry only increased as we seemed to drive farther out of the city. There were no street lights, so we were enveloped in darkness, but through the night sky I could distinguish the outline of trees all around. We appeared to be driving into a forest. Maybe it was the long day or the isolating feeling of being in a strange country, coupled with the uncertainty and confusion I had faced since arriving, but as we drove deeper into the wood I convinced myself I was going to die. I stared at the back of the driver's head and wondered how he was going to kill me and where he was going to dump my body. Would I ever be found? Could I try to escape? I'll admit I have never been as frightened in my life as I was at that moment.

We had been driving for more than an hour when the car headlights shone on a sign at the roadside. From the quick glimpse, I was certain I recognised it from a picture I'd seen online while doing my research. It was for Dynamo Kiev's training complex! Thank God, I thought, he is taking me to the right place after all. He pulled up outside the gates and I hurried out, making sure I lifted my bag, and gave the driver a nod as he pulled away. By now it was after 1am, and I wondered why on earth Miko was at the training ground at this time of night.

I walked over to the gates, where there was a security box with two armed guards sitting in the dark inside. I explained I was there to meet Alexei. I knew they wouldn't understand, so I brought out an old picture of him from his Rangers days and pointed at it and then at myself. One of them spoke into a walkie-talkie and I prayed they understood. A few minutes later I saw a figure approaching from the opposite side of the gates, which began to open. As he came closer I realised it was Miko. Thank you! I smiled and said hello, and brought out the shirt.

'Where's your taxi?' he asked.

I couldn't believe it. Those were his opening words. Not 'Hello, John' or 'How was your journey?' or 'Sorry for messing you around earlier.' Three abrupt words.

'I let it go. I wasn't sure how long I would be here, so he's gone.'

He didn't say anything as I handed him the shirt and a pen. As he signed it I asked where Kuznetsov and Salenko were, since he'd told me all three would meet me at the airport.

'Call this number,' he said, digging into his pocket and pulling out a scrap of paper that was no more than a couple of inches long. It had a phone number scribbled on it which, I presumed, was for one of the men.

He clearly wasn't waiting around to chat, so after he posed for a picture I reached into my bag and brought out two more Rangers tops for him to sign, which I intended to auction off for my next foreign trip. But he refused to sign them.

Just then a car drove towards us from within the grounds, with a middle-aged man and woman inside. Alexei spoke to them briefly, then turned to me and said to get in and they would take me back to the airport.

'I don't have any money to pay them,' I explained, but he told me not to worry. With that, my time with him was over. The meeting had lasted no more than 30 seconds.

As I drove away with the two strangers, I couldn't help but feel let down by what had just happened, although I was relieved to have secured the signature. I attempted to talk to the pair in the car but didn't receive any reaction. I assumed they did not speak English. I had no idea if they were part of the Dynamo Kiev staff, visitors or Miko's friends or family, and I wasn't likely to find out. We spent the next hour or so in silence while bouncing back through the crater-like potholes and navigating pitch-dark roads.

As the man pulled up at the airport, the woman put her hand out and said 'money'. She said it with such forcefulness that it shocked me.

'I'm sorry, I don't have money,' I explained apologetically, reaching into my pocket for the remaining loose change. I placed it in my palm and said, 'This is all I have.' The woman snatched every last one of the coins from my hand. I hesitantly thanked them for the lift and stepped out, wondering what could possibly happen next. Those few coins, however little they might have been worth, were my lifeline. Now I had absolutely nothing.

I was approaching the terminal's main entrance when I spotted what appeared to be a full bottle of water sitting just outside the door. I picked it up, checking for police in case they gave me any more hassle. The night had been hellish enough already. The seal wasn't broken, so I pushed the bottle into my pocket and went inside. I don't enjoy the best of health – I've suffered multiple heart attacks, among other complaints – so I have a lot of important medication I need to take every day. I required that water to swallow my tablets, because I was wary about drinking the water from the taps in Ukraine, what with the spectre of Chernobyl lingering three decades on. I also knew the water was the only thing that would pass my lips between now and my flight the following afternoon. Once inside, I found a quiet spot and settled down for the night. It was after 2am and I was exhausted.

I shifted around in the seat, uncomfortable and irritable, for a few hours. And then, at 8am, came the last kick in the teeth. A group of men came walking through the terminal, wearing tracksuits that I recognised to be those of Dynamo Kiev. It was the team. And then I spotted him. Mikhailichenko. He had been coming to the airport all along. The bother, worry and strife I had gone through the night before could have been avoided if he had just told me to sit tight until the morning. He was just yards from where I stood. I don't know if he saw me, but I was furious and had to bite my tongue as he walked past me and into departures.

When I felt it was an acceptable hour I called the number on the scrap of paper he had given me at the training complex. It seemed I was calling Oleg Kuznetsov. I explained to him what I was doing, that I was in Kiev and expected to meet him, Miko and Salenko at the airport the night before. Oleg was apologetic, but said he knew nothing about it and that 'we' were in Poland right now. I wasn't sure if by 'we' he meant him and Salenko or him and the team of Ukrainian youth players he was coaching. He said I could keep in touch and arrange to meet him the next time he and the team were in a place that was a little easier for me to reach.

I've never been so glad to board a plane as I was that afternoon. Due to the stopover in Amsterdam and the connecting flight, it was late before I finally made it home to Ibrox. It had been a hell of a couple of days, and, if I'm being honest, the experience left me totally sickened, so much so that for a few weeks I seriously considered abandoning my quest. My previous experiences with the players had all been so positive, but this encounter left me wondering if it was all worth it. What made it worse was the expectation of picking up three signatures on the journey and coming back with just one – barely. But my nephew, Andy, who was my biggest supporter and helper through the adventure, soon talked me round and it wasn't long before I was planning my next trip.

Little did I know, years later, that Oleg Salenko would prove to be the final piece needed to complete my nine-in-a-row jigsaw.

Neil Murray

NEIL MURRAY made more appearances than most of the lads who came through the youth ranks during nine-in-a-row.

After joining Rangers when he was 16 in 1989, he picked up a full set of medals – the Premier League, League Cup and Scottish Cup – and made 63 league appearances across seasons five, six, seven and eight. He made his first start on 20 February 1993 in a goalless draw away to Dundee United and never missed another game until the end of the season, also featuring home and away to Marseille and Club Brugge in that memorable Champions League campaign.

A handy utility player – he could fill in at full-back or midfield – Murray started the first four games of the following season, but only made fleeting appearances until he had a run in the team over the festive period, starting ten games on the bounce between the 1 December 2–0 home win over Aberdeen and the 5–1 Ibrox destruction of Partick Thistle on 5 February, with the cracking 4–2 New Year's Day triumph at Celtic part of that fixture list. He played 20 games and made two substitute appearances that season.

In seven-in-a-row, he started 14 games, including the opening-day contest against Motherwell on 13 August, which we won 2–1, and had six run-outs from the bench. It was during one of those cameos that he scored against Aberdeen in a 3–2 win at home on 8 April. It was one of just three goals he scored in a Rangers shirt. The most famous was also against Aberdeen, in the 1992/93 League Cup Final triumph, and the third was a strike at Arbroath in the Scottish Cup.

His final game was a start away to Raith Rovers in a 2–2 draw on 28 October 1995, one of just five league appearances he made that term.

Murray moved to Swiss side Sion for the 1996/97 campaign and won the country's league and cup double, making 35 appearances. From there he signed for L'Orient in France, before returning to Scotland briefly to play for Dundee United. He was then on his travels once more, this time to German side Mainz 05 for two seasons, although he spent part of that time on loan to Grimsby Town. He signed for Falkirk in 2002 and finished his playing career at Ayr.

Neil, who graduated in accounts from Glasgow University while at Rangers, worked with Kevin Drinkell in a sports management company for a while and was also a commentator for Setanta's Bundesliga TV coverage. He was appointed chief scout at Rangers in 2011, but left in mysterious circumstances in March 2013, during the period when there was bad news and as-yet unsolved mysteries coming out of Ibrox on an almost daily basis.

I met him outside the stadium briefly while he was still under employment. He was one of my earliest signatures, and it was before I decided to photograph the players with the strip. While I managed to catch up with most of the others who I failed to take a snap with first time round, I never did track Neil down again due to the sudden circumstances of his exit, and I feel he's the one who got away. If you're reading this Neil, let me know when I can arrange that picture!

Fraser Wishart

IT WOULD be fair to say Fraser Wishart had a journeyman's football career before and after his stint at Rangers.

He began his professional career as an 18-year-old with Motherwell in 1983 and spent six years at Fir Park before moving on to St Mirren for three years. He played a couple of games for Dumbarton in 1992 and then went to Falkirk for a season. Walter Smith came in for him in 1993 as full-back cover, and Wishart must have been on cloud nine when he started the first three games of the six-in-a-row season, beating Hearts 2–1 at Ibrox on 7 August, playing his part in another 2–1 victory at St Johnstone the following Saturday and then holding firm in a goalless draw at Parkhead. He next played in the 2–1 Ibrox win over Hibs on 25 September, but didn't feature in the league again until the penultimate game of the season, a 1–0 loss at Kilmarnock.

His first game of the 1994/95 campaign was at Parkhead on 30 October, and we left with a 3–1 win. He played the following week against Partick Thistle at Ibrox, a game that finished 3–0, and also started when we hosted Aberdeen on 25 November in a 1–0 victory. His final appearance came from the bench in a 3–2 win at Falkirk on 14 January. He was sold to Hearts for £50,000 in March, where he played nine games in the league run-in. He returned to Motherwell in the summer, then switched to Clydebank, where he played for four years. His final move came in the 2001/02 campaign, turning out on a handful of occasions for Airdrie.

Fraser had been working as players' union assistant while he was still performing, and he took this on full-time when he retired, firstly becoming secretary of the Scottish Professional Footballers' Association and later the chief executive of the Professional Footballers' Association Scotland. He also works as a pundit on Radio Clyde's football coverage.

My mate's son plays football, and he told me Fraser Wishart's boy was the same age and competed at Overlee playing fields in Clarkston, a short distance from Glasgow, on Sunday mornings. One of my sisters lives in Clarkston, so I was familiar with the area. My mate said Wishart would always attend the games, so I took a drive over one weekend in time for the 11am kick-off. As I approached the pitch I spotted Fraser standing on the touchline, one of a handful of spectators scattered around the park's edge.

I went over and explained I was trying to track down every nine-in-a-row player. He was more than happy to sign the shirt and pose for a picture. I stood with him for around ten minutes afterwards and watched some of the match, and then thanked him and returned to my car. I would meet Fraser on several more occasions over the years at various venues, and he remembered me from that day on the playing fields. He would ask who I was still searching for and said he would let me know if he heard of their whereabouts, but nothing ever came of it. Wishart was an easy one on a list that was throwing up a fair number of puzzles.

Paul Gascoigne

WHAT ELSE can be written about Gazza that hasn't already been 100 times or more?

Setting aside the personal demons that have gripped his life more and more over the years, the man was simply a football genius and Walter Smith's audacious signing of him is one of the greatest moments in Rangers' recent history. Who can forget 10 July 1995, when a bleach-blond, slimline Gazza arrived at Ibrox to sign a contract and hundreds of fans were there to greet him?

Not only was it the costliest transfer in Scottish football history at the time at £4.3m, but it was also one of the most surprising. Few would have thought one of the most famous footballers in the world would find himself in the Scottish league, but that was the clout of Rangers, before football went money mad due to the television deals and England raced away from the pulling power of Ibrox.

Walter Smith had visited Gazza at his plush villa in Lazio a short time before to sell him the move and persuade him to end his injury-laden time in Italy. But before Walter had the chance to give him the sales pitch, Gascoigne told him there was no need. He was signing, and so began one of the most exciting summers for Rangers fans as we awaited the chance to see the midfielder pull on the blue jersey and run out on to the Ibrox turf. What an eventful season that turned out to be for Gazza, not that we expected anything less.

From the pre-season friendly when he was fooled into pretending to play a flute by Ian Ferguson, to his stunning display on the penultimate day of the campaign when he scored a hat-trick against Aberdeen to clinch eight-in-a-row, there was rarely a dull moment. He scored a stunning first league goal in a classic breakaway in his debut Old Firm match in a win at Parkhead, found himself in a running battle with referees which reached a low point – for refereeing – when he was booked by killjoy Dougie Smith for humorously flashing a yellow card at the ref after the whistler dropped it, and was also a joker in the dressing room. His teammates were often his victims, none more so than Gordon Durie, who was forced to write off a car after Gazza hid two fish in the inner workings.

But it was that title-clinching performance against Aberdeen on 28 April that remains the defining moment of Gazza's Rangers career. After falling a goal behind, the Gers equalised in the first half with a beautiful finish from the number eight after he picked up the ball outside the box from a corner. But the score remained in deadlock as the minutes ticked down, and it was beginning to look like the league – in which Celtic had managed their most sustained push in years, losing just one game all season – would go to the last day. Defender Alan McLaren pleaded with an exhausted Gascoigne to produce just one more piece of magic, but Gazza told him he was knackered. Yet he found inspiration and strength from somewhere, maybe the roar of the fans in the packed ground, as he picked up the ball in his own half with just ten minutes to go and powered towards the Aberdeen goal. Brushing defenders away, he curled a left-foot shot into the top of the net, leaving the goalkeeper stranded. It was a piece of magic, and Gazza was to get his rewards a few minutes later, when Gordon Durie won a penalty and Gascoigne converted it, giving him a memorable hat-trick.

His form saw him win the end-of-season awards, and he starred for England in Euro '96 as the team reached the semi-finals in their homeland, scoring a peach against Scotland on the way to the last four. He played another important role in the nine-in-a-row season, scoring 13 goals in 26 league appearances. Among the strikes was a memorable goal in the first Old Firm game of the season at Ibrox. Holding on to a 1–0 lead, Rangers rode their luck in the last minute when John Hughes powered a header off the crossbar. The ball bounced out and was collected by Gazza, who rushed out and fed Albertz. The German raced down the left, he sent a cross into the six-yard box, and there was Gazza, who had kept running, to twist his neck and send a diving header into the back of the net to clinch the victory.

But Gazza's demons were beginning to show themselves, and he spent an increasing amount of time occupying the news pages of the tabloids. Matters on the football field hit a bump when he picked up a serious ankle injury in a meaningless six-a-side tournament in Amsterdam in January, as Rangers competed in the mini tournament against Ajax, AC Milan and Liverpool. He was out for three months.

Gazza's downfall coincided with Rangers' ill-fated attempt at ten-in-a-row, and in March 1998, with the team still very much in the title hunt, Walter Smith had had enough of the troubled genius and sold him to Middlesbrough. Some have argued that had Gazza not been sold Rangers would have won the league, but that's a hard one to judge. What is certain is that Gascoigne wasn't the player of the previous two seasons. Leaving Ibrox was the beginning of the end for his football career, and although he had a solid first season with the north-east side, he never again reached the heights of his first two years in Glasgow and would move to Everton to be reunited with Walter, followed by short spells at Burnley and Boston United and in China, before he called it a day in 2004.

Unfortunately, without football in his life, Gazza was unable to cope and went completely off the rails. His long periods of sobriety are punctured by life-threatening falls from the wagon, and it was during one of the times when he wasn't doing so well that I turned my attention to trying to meet him. I read he was in a rehabilitation centre, The Providence Projects, in Bournemouth, so I wrote a letter to the recovery centre, explaining what I was doing and asking whether it would be possible to travel down and meet Paul for five minutes to get his autograph. I didn't receive a reply. To be honest, I didn't expect one, but it was a rare occasion when I knew for certain where he was located, so I thought I would try my luck. I toyed with the idea of driving down to Bournemouth in the hope I might see him around the town, but I decided it was too far away for such an unlikely chance.

I left it for a couple of months while I tried to track down some other players, but I was desperate to add Gazza's name to the jersey and so I decided to go back to basics – the phone book. Gazza's best mate for years was Jimmy 'Five Bellies' Gardner, and I thought he might be able to help. I made my way down the list of Gardners in the Newcastle area and eventually found his dad. Jimmy still lived with his parents at the time, and his dad was good enough to pass the message on when I explained what I was doing. A short while later, I spoke to Jimmy and he said he would speak to Gazza for me. Weeks passed and I never heard anything, so I tried calling Jimmy again but he never answered. I called Jimmy five times after that first conversation, but never heard another word from him.

Realising I'd hit a dead end down that route, I switched my attention to Paul's family. I knew he was originally from the Gateshead area, and I remembered watching a documentary where it was revealed he bought several houses in the same street for some of his relatives, so I was on the lookout for similar addresses under the family name. As it transpired, there were only eight Gascoignes in the area. The first three I called claimed they had no connection, but I had better luck with the fourth. It was his niece, who put me on to Paul's sister, Anna-Marie. She was really pleasant and down to earth and took the time to listen to my story. I could have been a reporter posing as a fan just to try to get some information on Paul, which I'm sure must have happened over the years, so to trust me and agree to help says a lot and I'm indebted to her.

Anna-Marie said she would speak with him and get back to me. Unlike Five Bellies, she was true to her word and called me a while later to say there was no need for me to go down south to meet him, because he was coming to Glasgow to host one of his Q&A evenings soon. Anna-Marie told me I should go along to the host venue, the Thistle Hotel, prior to the event starting and speak to reception, who would be aware of my attendance and would take me to a private area to meet Gazza.

I had gone to events like this in the past and knew they could become hectic affairs, with fans and autograph hunters hanging around trying to grab a glimpse of the big name. I wanted to blend in with those attending, so put on a shirt and tie and tried to stay away from the autograph hunters, many of whom I knew. I knew if I told any of them I was meeting Gazza they would ask me to try to get him to sign lots of their items, and I didn't want him being pestered.

I made my way to the reception and explained who I was. They looked at a list and seemed to be aware that I would be attending. I could feel the butterflies in my stomach as a concierge asked me to follow him and took me along a corridor and into a private room.

As the door opened, I caught a glimpse of him straight away, one of the greatest players Britain has ever produced. I noticed there were lots of different shirts laid out on tables and a few men were in discussion with Gazza. I presumed these were memorabilia dealers and he was negotiating a price with them for his signature, but I would require no such conversation.

He seemed fit and healthy as I shook his hand and introduced myself. I don't think he knew who I was at first, but once I explained I had been in touch with Anna-Marie and she had organised for me to come along, he made the connection and seemed to remember. I explained to him about my quest and the Facebook page I had set up, just in case he wanted to take a look later. He happily signed my shirt and also agreed to autograph an Italia 90-era England strip for my nephew, and then posed for a photo with me. I'll be honest, he wasn't the same sparkling and quick-witted Gazza I had come to know from seeing him on TV over the years. His character seemed more subdued and muted, but I suppose in that sort of situation it's to be expected. He had just come through a tough spell and now he was in a hotel surrounded by people desperate to meet him, so I was just happy to have my moment.

I left the Thistle Hotel beaming about seeing Gazza in the flesh and adding his signature to the shirt, but as I walked along the street I also hoped one of the greatest players I've ever seen in a Gers top could find peace of mind, overcome his demons and live a life that made him happy and healthy.

That's a hope I continue to have to this day.

Mel Sterland

MEL STERLAND'S time at Ibrox was brief, but he still had a moment to remember when the right-back scored two first-half goals on the day Rangers clinched the first title of the nine-in-a-row run. The opener came from a free kick, which he fired low to the keeper's left, and he followed that with a header at the back post from a neat Mark Walters cross.

The England cap had also scored on his league debut against Hamilton on 11 March 1989 and featured in all nine games of the run-in to the championship, including that title-winning match on 29 April. Despite only arriving in March, his last match was in the Scottish Cup Final defeat against Celtic in May, turning out just 13 times for the club.

Manager Graeme Souness later described Sterland as a 'quick fix', buying him for £800,000 from Sheffield Wednesday and selling him to Leeds for £700,000. That loss was just a little more than the £90,000 Sterland claimed he lost on a house he had to quickly sell in Glasgow after learning he was being sold by Souness, according to an interview he gave two decades later. He said he'd come to Glasgow to play in Europe, but he was gone before the European Cup campaign even got under way.

One of nine children, Mel was born in Sheffield in 1961 and signed for Sheffield Wednesday as an apprentice in 1978. He made his debut the following year and played under esteemed managers like Jack Charlton and Howard Wilkinson. He spent 11 years at Wednesday, being lured from his home-town team to Ibrox for that brief period before heading back south to Leeds, where he stayed for five years, and then he became player-manager at Boston United for two years.

He was forced to retire due to an ankle injury that was operated on four times, although he did turn out for non-league Denaby United and was also briefly manager of Stalybridge Celtic.

Sterland's story is an eventful one and the title of his autobiography – *Boozing, Betting and Brawling* – tells you a little about his life after he was forced to give up football. He became something of a lost soul without the game in his life, turning to heavy drinking for a period, and life became very dark. He was a football agent for a while and did various jobs including labouring and working for local radio. He even had a part in the Sean Bean football movie, *When Saturday Comes*, as the captain of Sheffield United, his rival team in real life, and was also accused and cleared of robbing a post office in 1995. Then in 2004 he tried to sell the league medal he had won with Rangers on eBay, but it failed to reach the £3,500 reserve price.

Just like Mel's eventful life, my attempts to meet him were far from straightforward. I knew Sheffield Wednesday were his club, so when I saw the fixture list for the weekend and spotted that they were playing at home, I took the chance and drove down to Hillsborough in the hope I could meet him. I didn't know if he worked in hospitality or would even be at the game, but I thought it was worth a try. Time was against me, and I arrived at the ground just on full time. By the time I had parked the car and made my way through the crowds that were coming in the opposite direction, it was probably another ten minutes or so before I reached the main entrance. I caught the eye of an official and asked him if Mel Sterland was around. He went away to check, and I unfolded the shirt in anticipation. But he came back with bad news – Mel had just left. I couldn't believe it. What an absolute sickener. I had come all that way and missed him by a couple of minutes. The return drive to Glasgow was a long one.

I wrote about my mishap on Facebook, and a little while later I received a message from a guy called John Bell, who said he was friends with Mel and gave me his number. Mel couldn't have been nicer when I called, and we arranged a new date for me to come down. When that Saturday arrived I drove down, content in the belief it was going to be a productive journey. When I got to Hillsborough, though, I was told he hadn't turned up. A club official told me his wife had surprised him days before with tickets for a cruise to mark his 50th birthday. Clearly the shock of being whisked away on a last-minute holiday meant he had forgotten to let me know he was no longer going to be at the match.

I gave it a few weeks and then made contact with him again. He was apologetic for missing me the last time, and we made fresh arrangements that I would go down for Wednesday's next home match. Once more I made the familiar drive to Sheffield, and thankfully it was third time lucky. I was taken into the stadium by an official and waited at reception. A few minutes later I saw him come through a door at the far side. I made my way over and introduced myself, although my accent and my Rangers top probably gave me away. Mel greeted me like a long-lost brother, with a huge smile and even bigger hug, and called me 'love' over and over again in his thick Yorkshire accent. We had a quick chat about his time at Ibrox, and then he signed my shirt and I took a picture. It was shortly before the match was due to begin, so we didn't have much time, but I was just happy to finally meet him.

Never did I think it would take 1,500 miles to track him down – longer than some of my European trips – but with Mel being the character that he is, it seemed somewhat appropriate that it hadn't gone exactly to plan.

Trevor Steven

TREVOR STEVEN is one of only two players to have had two stints at Rangers during the nine-in-a-row years. In a squad full of genuinely world-class players, the right-sided midfielder was up there with the best. He featured in every season except for the first and showed his worth by starring for England at two World Cups and two European Championships. The man from Berwick-upon-Tweed's skill and finesse made him a stand-out, and only injuries hampered him from becoming a true Rangers great.

He began his career with Burnley in 1980 and was part of a promotion and relegation in his three seasons there. He was sold to Everton for £300,000 aged just 19 and won the FA Cup in his first season on Merseyside, playing in the final. Trevor developed a great partnership down the right with full-back Gary Stevens, a tandem that would be replicated in the national side, and was part of the legendary Everton team that won two league titles, the European Cup Winners' Cup and the aforementioned FA Cup. He spent six years at Goodison, but was tempted to move north not only to have the opportunity of European football during the ban on English sides, but also to renew his partnership with Stevens, who had joined Rangers a year earlier.

He signed for the Gers in 1989, the same summer as Mo Johnston, but Trevor remained long after Mo had left. He made the number seven shirt his own and only missed two of the 36 league games that season, the goalless draw at Hibs on 30 December and the final match away to Hearts on 5 May, which finished 1–1. He had a great presence, was a really intelligent player and also chipped in with a few goals. His first came at Tynecastle on 2 December in a 2–1 win, and the next came at

Ibrox against Motherwell on 14 April, which also finished 2–1. But there's no doubting his most memorable and important goal of the season. It was against Dundee United at Tannadice on 21 April. His header from a Stuart Munro cross gave Rangers a narrow 1–0 win and secured the league title.

The three-in-a-row campaign saw his influence curtailed by injury. Trevor made just 19 starts and scored two goals – one against Hibs in a 4–0 home win on 3 November and the other coming in his final appearance of the season, a 2–1 home victory against Hearts on 9 March. Trevor was back in the starting line-up for the opening two games of four-in-a-row in 1991, against St Johnstone in a 6–0 demolition on 10 August and three days later against Motherwell, in which he scored in the 2–0 triumph. That was to be seemingly his final game for Rangers, because French giants Marseille came in with a £5.5m bid – a £4m mark-up on what Walter Smith had paid for him – and the club felt it was too much money to turn down. Indeed, it was a joint record fee for a British player at the time, with only David Platt's move from Aston Villa to Bari earlier that summer equalling it.

It quickly became evident that Marseille were struggling financially, and after just a season in France, in which he won the league title (the third country where he lifted the championship trophy), Trevor made a cut-price return to Ibrox for £2.4m the following summer. Injuries were to hamper his five-in-a-row season, during which Rangers were drawn against Marseille in the inaugural Champions League, and he managed just 24 starts from the 44-game league campaign. He scored five goals, against Dundee United, Partick Thistle, Hibs, Falkirk and, most memorably, Celtic. It was the only goal in the 2 January Ibrox clash, and it was a well-worked one. In the 34th minute, John Brown played a short free kick from inside the centre circle to Ian Ferguson, who floated a pinpoint ball to Mark Hateley in the box. He had the vision to cushion a header across the area to the on-rushing Steven, who met the ball with a bullet header on the penalty spot, and it landed in the left-hand corner of the net. Trevor described it after the match as one of the greatest moments of his career, no small boast when you consider what he had already achieved.

Six-in-a-row was better for him with 32 starts from 44, with goals home and away to Hibs, along with strikes against St Johnstone and Partick. But it was to go downhill from there. His first appearance in seven-in-a-row came from the bench away to Falkirk on 14 January in a 3–2 win, and he managed ten starts in the remainder of the campaign.

The following season he played in the opener, a 1–0 home victory on 26 August against Kilmarnock, and then didn't feature again until 10 April, a 2–0 defeat at Hearts. He came on as a sub the following week and then started the final three games, no doubt wishing the season could go on longer now that he was fit. He played in the opener of nine-in-a-row on 10 August against Raith Rovers and scored the only goal. It was his first in two-and-a-half years. Unfortunately injuries were his downfall again. He managed a run of five games in December, the first two as a sub, and then started against Hibs on 23 February at Ibrox, which we won 3–1. His final appearance was as a sub when Dundee United won 2–0 at Ibrox on 12 March. With nine-in-a-row achieved, Trevor decided to retire at the end of the season. In addition to his league successes, he earned four League Cup and two Scottish Cup medals in Glasgow, quite the haul to end his career. He also played 36 times for England, often vying for that right-hand berth with Chris Waddle, and scored four goals.

Trevor not only moved into the business world after football, but also wrote a weekly football column, became a football agent and does lots of media work, especially for RTE in Ireland. I met him during one of his punditry jobs. During Rangers' administration, the club was barely out of the news as the media reported on our troubles almost constantly. I happened to be watching one of those broadcasts when they went to a live interview with Trevor Steven outside the ground. I jumped out of my chair, grabbed the shirt and rushed along to the stadium as quickly as I could. I walked by the John Greig statue and past the Main Stand, straining my eyes to see if I could spot him. The interview had been filming at the other end of the Main Stand, at the Broomloan Road end, and as I got closer I saw the TV crew packing away the equipment.

Then I spotted what looked like the figure of Trevor walking towards the car park at the back of the stand. I caught up with him just as he was opening his car door. It was a windy, miserable day and he looked keen to be back inside, but he was kind enough to sign the shirt and take a picture before driving away. He was probably halfway home before I got my breath back!

Ally Maxwell, David Robertson and Paul Rideout

WHEN I became serious about finding all of the nine-in-a-row squad, I realised there was going to be some travelling involved. Many of the players had returned to their own countries, while others had emigrated in search of a new life.

Through online research I discovered a trip to America was a necessity, since four ex-players had made the United States their new home after hanging up their boots. Marauding left-back David Robertson, back-up goalie Ally Maxwell, short-term striker Paul Rideout and former youth striker John Spencer had all crossed the Atlantic to continue their careers in football, or soccer as they would have to get used to calling it.

I began planning my journey. Robbo, Maxwell and Rideout all lived fairly close by each other in the Scottsdale area in Arizona, so I presumed I'd be able to meet them in one swoop. As far as I could tell, Spencer was by this point in Dallas, Texas, having left his management position with Portland in the north-west of the country. The distance between Scottsdale and Dallas was around 1,000 miles. That was enough miles to warrant another flight, but I knew I was going to struggle just to get to America and back without taking additional internal flights to Texas. I decided I would hitch-hike between the cities instead. I'd seen it in the movies a million times and was pretty confident I would find enough truckers and kind-hearted strangers to get me to where I needed to be.

I'm not sure my loved ones thought it was the best idea I've ever had – but, as it turned out, I wouldn't have to go to Texas after all. During one of my stints outside the main entrance at Ibrox I chatted with Kris Boyd, who had played under Spencer at Portland, and he told me John was back in the UK, in London he thought. So that made it a little easier to plan.

Even booking well in advance and taking the cheapest flights was still going to be very expensive, not to mention accommodation, so I sold, saved and scrimped wherever I could over a matter of months. I auctioned a few signed strips, and people were kind enough to give me their unwanted items, which I then took to car boot sales to make a few more quid. Every penny counts in these situations, and I'm grateful to everyone who gave me something to sell or who bought one of the strips, not to mention the players from the 2014 team, who also donated strips and a pair of boots for me to sell. Finally I was in a position to book flights, so I contacted David Robertson, thanks to one of his ex-teammates who I was in touch with. He seemed a lovely guy and said he'd be happy to meet me, and we discussed dates. David gave me Paul Rideout's number, and Paul gave me Ally's number. All three were going to be available during the dates in October I was looking to book, so it was time to gather every penny and pound and make it official.

I flew from Glasgow to Amsterdam and then into America, touching down at Minneapolis–Saint Paul Airport in Minnesota. From there I took a connecting flight to Indianapolis and finally on to Phoenix, Arizona. It took 18 hours in total, but it was the cheapest route I could find. I was knackered by the time I arrived at my hotel in Scottsdale, so I spent my first night, a Saturday, resting and attempting to freshen up for the next couple of days, which were shaping up to be pretty hectic.

Ally Maxwell was the first of the trio to meet me, coming to my hotel on Sunday morning. We had a chat about his new life in America, where he's lived since 2008. He's the goalkeeping coach at an organisation called SC Del Sol, which is a youth football programme in the area, with more than 800 male and female players from the ages of four to 18 making up 50 teams, coached by a staff of full-time ex-pros from home and abroad. He was responsible for more than 50 keepers aged between seven and 19, so he'll never be short of something to do! He seemed to have made a good life for himself in Arizona, where the weather was just a little brighter than in his home town of Hamilton, where he was born in 1965.

He was signed by neighbours Motherwell from Fir Park Boys' Club in 1983 and went on to establish himself as the number one. Undoubtedly the finest moment of his career came in the Scottish Cup Final of 1991, known as the Family Final due to brothers Tommy and Jim McLean being managers of the opposing teams, Motherwell and Dundee United respectively. In one of the most memorable Scottish Cup finals in history, Motherwell won the trophy 4–3 after extra time in a remarkable contest. Adding to the drama was the fact that Maxwell played on after suffering what turned out to be a ruptured spleen and broken ribs following a second-half collision, toughing it out for an hour while seriously injured. The fact he tipped over a goal-bound shot in the final two minutes of extra time only added to his legend among the Motherwell fans.

He fell out with Tommy McLean during the summer due to a contract dispute, and was farmed out to Bolton on loan, where he didn't play a game, until Rangers came in to sign him in 1992 as back-up to Andy Goram. Ally didn't get off to the best of starts, losing his debut league match in a shock 4–3 defeat at Dundee in August, and he never played another league game until March, ultimately turning out ten times in the five-in-a-row season. However, he did go on to play more often for the Gers than probably he or anyone else expected, due to Goram's frequent bouts of injury. Maxwell became the de facto number one in the turgid six-in-a-row season, making 32 league appearances in what was a terrible campaign for injuries across the squad. Rangers only won half of their 44 league games yet still triumphed in the end. He made 11 league appearances during seven-in-a-row before he was sold to Dundee United in 1995. It seemed almost fate that he ended up at Tannadice, because not only were Dundee United the opponents in the game where he made his name, but also when Rangers appeared in the Scottish Cup Final of 1994, where a win would have given us a historic double treble. But Maxwell's part in a defensive blunder with Dave McPherson allowed United to score the only goal of the game and dash our dreams.

Maxwell spent three years with United and then another three years with Morton, where he also spent a brief time as manager, before retiring in 2001 and eventually emigrating to America.

It was good catching up with him and, after he'd signed my top and posed for a picture, we said our goodbyes and I waited for Robbo to pick me up from the hotel at 2pm. When it was confirmed I would be travelling over, he insisted I come to his house on Sunday afternoon for a roast dinner. It was unbelievable hospitality from the big man, and to insist on picking me up was the icing on the cake. America had obviously been kind to David. He arrived in a beautiful car with a personal registration plate, 'Robbo', and took me to his stunning house. This was a place you can only dream of, absolutely gorgeous, located out in the desert of Arizona. In Scotland, I would estimate a similar house would cost £1m. His wife, Kym, was just as friendly as she welcomed me inside. We sat and had a chat about football and his great six years at Ibrox, and he told me he really was a Rangers fan.

David was barely a teenager when he knew he was going to become a footballer. Sir Alex Ferguson used to show up at Robbo's youth games to scout him, and the youngster was signed when he was just 13. He then had to see out another three years of school impatiently until he could go full-time. The marauding right-back made his debut with Aberdeen when he was 17 and went on to play 44 games that season. He won a League Cup and Scottish Cup at Pittodrie and came perilously close to clinching the league, only falling on the last day when Rangers won the famous game that secured three-in-a-row. A few weeks later, Walter Smith signed Robertson for £970,000.

He missed just two league games in his debut season, and the following year was even better. Arguably the greatest in Rangers' nine-in-a-row campaign, the team went 44 games unbeaten, won the domestic treble and enjoyed that incredible run in the inaugural Champions League. Robbo played 58 games that season, only one fewer than John Brown, and was first choice throughout the remainder of the nine-in-a-row years.

He chipped in with a few goals each season, but probably his most famous strike for the Gers was one that didn't count – although it should have done. In an incredible Old Firm game at Ibrox in November 1995 during eight-in-a-row, Robertson scored what was regarded as an equaliser only for it to be ruled offside. In the midst of the typical Old Firm chaos it had looked such a perfectly good goal that the TV commentators and the stadium scoreboard didn't realise for around ten minutes that it had been chalked off.

The match eventually finished 3–3, but the offside decision and failure to give a penalty after Jackie McNamara handled inside the box meant referee Hugh Dallas's first Old Firm game wasn't without controversy.

Just days after nine-in-a-row was clinched, Robertson departed from Rangers. His form had sparked interest from clubs in Spain and Italy, but he chose Leeds and signed a four-year deal, citing his boredom with facing the same players year after year in Scotland as his reason to quit. Unfortunately injuries meant he only played 26 league games at Elland Road, and he ended his career at Montrose, a team he went on to manage. He was also boss at Elgin City, and later he and his family moved to America, where he was manager of Phoenix FC for a time in 2013. When I met up with him he was director of boys' coaching at Sereno Soccer Club.

Davie was back on the pages of Scottish newspapers – front and back – when he recommended Rangers to American tycoon Robert Sarver, the owner of basketball team the Phoenix Suns, in 2014, during the period when our club was in the wrong hands. Sarver's offer of £20m to the board was rejected, and David spoke out against the decision and backed the businessman as being trustworthy and good for the club. While it didn't come to anything, it showed Robbo was still thinking of Rangers and keeping an eye on our situation from afar.

Joining us for dinner was the third of the players I'd come to America to meet, Paul Rideout. He lived nearby and was a fellow coach at Sereno Soccer Club, having previously had a similar role at Kansas City Wizards. Born in Bournemouth in 1964, the striker made his debut for Swindon Town at 16 and went on to play for a number of clubs including Aston Villa, Bari in Italy, Southampton and Notts County, the team Walter Smith paid £300,000 to bring him to Ibrox. He was intended as back-up to Ally McCoist and Mark Hateley after Mo Johnston was sold to Everton, and made his debut at home to Hibs in a 2–0 win in January 1992. His only league goal came as a substitute against Airdrie in a 5–0 battering on 29 February, and in total he made seven starts and five sub appearances in the league. His final game was in the first league match of five-in-a-row, a home win against St Johnstone, before he too was sold to Everton. It was there that he enjoyed the greatest moment of his career, scoring the winner in the 1995 FA Cup Final against Manchester United. He had spells in China and America and finished his career at Tranmere in 2002, before moving back to the States to coach.

We enjoyed a great meal as we chatted about their lives over there and I told them some of my stories about meeting other players. Before he went home, Paul signed the top and had his picture taken with it. Afterwards, the three of us sat down in front of the telly to watch David and Kym's eldest son, whose college soccer match was being shown live. Sitting with proud parents watching them cheer on their boy as he scored two goals is one of my favourite memories from my trips. Seeing their beaming faces and sharing in that moment at their home was unbelievable, considering I used to sit in my house and watch Robbo do the same thing 20 years earlier. Once the game was finished, we went out to a bar and then David gave me a quick tour of the town, before they dropped me off at my hotel. Kym told me I should have been staying with them, but they had been more than hospitable already.

But my night wasn't over quite yet. In a demonstration of the global fanbase of Rangers, a fellow fan who lived in Orange County, California, had been in touch with me through Facebook in the weeks leading up to my trip and said he would arrange to meet me while I was there. His name was Brian Campbell, and he insisted he and his wife, Gaynor, would show me around. He admitted he was also desperate to see the famous shirt and all of the signatures. Brian drove 370 miles from Orange County to Scottsdale, while Gaynor flew and met him in Arizona. Once he'd studied the strip, he and Gaynor took me to a Wild West bar up in the mountains. It was just like I'd seen in the movies, with the live band playing banjos and everyone decked out in cowboy gear. It was a little different from a typical night in my local! We had a great time and stayed out late. By the time the lovely couple had driven me back to my hotel, I still couldn't believe they had come all that distance to meet someone they didn't know. But when you're part of the Rangers family, you're never a stranger.

I had another unusual meeting lined up for the next day, Monday. While organising the trip, I had not only contacted some newspapers in Arizona to publicise my adventure but also the mayor's office. I explained to Mayor Jim Lane's secretary why I was coming to their city and asked if it would be possible to set up a meeting. I had no agenda – I just thought it would be an interesting thing to do. I heard back from his people a while later and a time was confirmed. We enjoyed a great one-hour chat in his immaculate office. American state flags stood in the corner and a massive floor-to-ceiling map of his city was hanging on a wall, alongside various pictures of him with dignitaries and family. For the first half an hour we spoke about American and British politics, and then the chat turned to what had brought me to the States. He seemed impressed by what I was doing and called me an inspiration for not giving up. When it came time to take a picture before I left, he asked me if I wanted to wear a cowboy hat. He was wearing one and

I was in desert country, so how could I say no? As well as providing me with a memorable photo, Jim also gifted me a lovely pen with his insignia on it and a couple of pin badges. Just like everyone else I'd met in America so far, he was extremely warm and hospitable and I was glad I had acted on my whim to contact his office. Afterwards I made my way back to the hotel. On the way I spotted a sign for a garage sale, so I decided to take a look. When I turned on to the street I was stopped in my tracks by police tape cordoning off the road. Flashing lights from numerous police and ambulance vehicles farther down the street indicated something serious had happened. I looked around and saw a lady out in her front garden, not being nosy but actually tending to her flowerbeds while this was all going on just yards away. I asked her if she knew what it was about and she told me matter-of-factly that a woman had just been shot dead by her husband. I was now experiencing the side of America that we hear so much about on the news. Despite it having just happened, this lady seemed unperturbed, although maybe that said more about her attitude than anything else. I made my way back to the hotel and packed my belongings in anticipation of my return home the next day.

It was to be another long one. Not only did I follow the incoming route of Phoenix, Indianapolis, Minneapolis–Saint Paul and Amsterdam to see me back to Glasgow, but some of the flights were delayed. I made it home eventually, exhausted. But there wasn't time to rest and recover from the jet lag, because I had been tipped off that another member of the nine-in-a-row squad had unexpectedly turned up in Glasgow. I would have to act fast or else I might miss out – but what was I going to do about the important appointment I already had booked for the next day?

Sebastian Rozental

THE DAY before I came home from America, I was online and chatting with a fellow autograph hunter. He tipped me off that Chilean striker Sebastian Rozental was rumoured to be in Glasgow. He showed me a picture that had been posted on Facebook of big Seb in a restaurant, and the two of us sat, on opposite sides of the Atlantic, examining the décor in the background trying to determine if it was a Glasgow establishment he was eating in.

Andy Goram was usually in the know and I had his mobile number, so I sent him a text and asked him if he could confirm that Rozental was in town. The following day, just before I began my journey home, I received a response from The Goalie, confirming Seb was here for just 48 hours and would be visiting Rangers' facility at Auchenhowie the next morning.

This gave me a dilemma.

It just so happened that the day after I came home from America, I had an operation scheduled at the Southern General Hospital to take care of a long-standing issue that was causing me a lot of pain. It wasn't life or death, and you know what Bill Shankly said about that, but I also didn't want to mess the NHS around. I was in a real quandary and spent the flight home flipping back and forth over what to do. Rozental was one of the players on the list who I feared would be a tough one to track down and, even if I did, I wasn't sure I would ever be able to afford the flights to Chile. Now here he was on my doorstep. By the time I touched down in Glasgow, I knew what I had to do.

Sebastian Rozental was signed by Walter Smith in January 1997, halfway through the nine-in-a-row campaign, for around £3.5m. He was just 20 years old and the first South American to sign for Rangers. He caught the eye of scouts after netting 39 goals in just 75 league appearances for Universidad Catolica in the previous four seasons, winning Player of the Year in 1996. He made his debut as a sub at Motherwell in a 3–1 win, before making his first home appearance in a cup tie against St Johnstone. He scored after latching on to a pass from Gazza, but tragedy was to strike later in the match when he went off seriously injured. It was to signal the beginning of a years-long battle with fitness, and unfortunately his Rangers career was, in effect, over before he barely got his jersey dirty.

Seb never featured again that season, requiring a knee ligament operation which was performed in America. However, an infection set in on the bone, necessitating a second procedure back in his homeland.

He made just four league appearances the following season and only three from the subs' bench in the next, 1998/99, amid more injuries. He scored no goals. It prompted a loan return to Universidad Catolica, where he appeared to regain full fitness, firing home 22 goals in 27 games, and a spell with Independiente in Argentina. His work permit to play in Scotland expired in November 1999, and he was forced to go to a panel to fight for another. His goals and form in Chile secured the permit, and he was granted leave to play for Rangers again in January 2000. The decision was even made to lengthen his contract – it was due to end in 2001 but was extended to the summer of 2003.

This was to mark Seb's most successful and prolonged period at Rangers, making 13 appearances under Dick Advocaat and scoring five goals – two against Ayr in a 7–0 cup drubbing, home and away versus Dundee and a penalty against Motherwell. But he was soon off on loan again, this time to Colo Colo back in his homeland.

Seb's Rangers career finally came to an end in the summer of 2002, after he had endured four knee operations, several loan spells and just six full games. It's often forgotten just how long he was at Rangers and it seems remarkable that Jorg Albertz, Kenny Miller and Giovanni Van Bronckhorst left Ibrox before him, while Allan McGregor made his first-team debut when Rozental was still on the books. He joined Grasshopper Club Zurich after leaving Glasgow and won the league title in his first season in Switzerland. He played for a further six teams before retiring in 2008.

Rozental's sole contribution to nine-in-a-row was that 13-minute sub appearance at Motherwell on a cold January day, but it was enough to qualify him for the elite squad, and that's why I knew I had to cancel my operation. I'm not proud to say I called the hospital and told them my flight back from America had been delayed and I wouldn't be able to make the surgery. I then informed my family that the hospital had called to say the procedure was being postponed. I knew if I told them the truth they would lose the head.

I was familiar with the security personnel at the training ground because I'd been there so many times for autographs. They seemed to be expecting me this time and waved me on through – perhaps Goram had mentioned it to Ally McCoist, who was manager at the time. I spotted Seb out on the training pitch standing alongside Ally, Ian Durrant and Walter Smith. I kept my distance and waited until they returned inside before approaching them. Ally greeted me with his trademark big grin and said he had just saved me £3,000 in flights. I told him it was the thousands of miles of travel I no longer had to endure that I was happiest about!

It was a great morning. I chatted with Walter, who I had met previously outside Ibrox. Back then he probably thought I was just an autograph hunter, but as we stood in the foyer at Auchenhowie, Ally told him what I was attempting to do. Walter told me I was crazy. Seb was perfectly polite but didn't seem to speak much English, so I thanked him for signing the strip and had my picture taken with him. To top off a perfect trip, one of the staff then gave me a tour of the complex.

I read in a press interview a while later that Seb had taken the opportunity to visit Glasgow after travelling to Newcastle for work. He was employed by an agency that helps South American players settle in a new country.

I felt I had made the right decision, but my lies weren't slow in catching up with me when I posted the pictures on Facebook later on. My daughter Debbi called and asked if I was sure the hospital had cancelled the operation. There was no point giving me a hard time – she knew how much this meant to me. At the end of the day, I was willing to put up with a little more pain in order to tick off another of the nine-in-a-row.

As usual though, Walter was probably right!

John Spencer

THANKS TO Kris Boyd tipping me off outside Ibrox, I knew John Spencer was no longer living in America. Boydy had given me John's number, and I called to explain what I was doing and ask if we could possibly arrange a meeting. I expected I would have to travel to London, where he was based with the family business, but he told me he was coming home to Glasgow for a few days and it just so happened to be the weekend after I returned from America. He said I should call him when I came back from the States to work out the details.

Wee Spenny is the only player I met from the nine-in-a-row squad who was smaller than me, but that didn't stop him from making a great career for himself in the game. He signed with Rangers as a schoolboy, and the story made headline news. A bit strange, you would think, except the media jumped on the fact that he was a Catholic who had been to St Ninian's. John later said in interviews that he received a fair amount of hassle for deciding to join Rangers, with some members of his family refusing to talk to him ever again. But he overcame all of that and worked his way through the ranks, and ultimately the striker made 13 league appearances during the nine-in-a-row years.

First he went to Morton on loan for a few weeks during the 1988/89 season, and the following campaign he went to Hong Kong team Lai Sun and scored 20 goals in 24 games, earning him the Foreign Player of the Year award. That was enough to provide his breakthrough into the Gers' first team, and he started three games and made two substitute appearances during three-in-a-row. His first start was on 9 February 1991, at home to St Mirren in a 1–0 win, and he also started away to Celtic in a 3–0 defeat on 24 March. He came off the bench the following week, away to Dunfermline in a narrow 1–0 win, and also came on at home to Hibs in a goalless draw on 6 April. He started the following week at home to St Johnstone and scored a goal in the 3–0 victory.

The following season he made eight appearances – four from the start and four off the bench – and scored in the 4–0 home win against Dunfermline on 24 August. But his time at Ibrox was coming to an end. With Ally McCoist and Mark Hateley's partnership in full flow, he knew his chances would be limited, so moved to Chelsea in a £450,000 transfer. He spent five years at Stamford Bridge and made more than 100 league appearances, but in his final season he was loaned to Queens Park Rangers, where he scored 17 in 25 league games. It was enough to earn him a permanent move and he found himself teaming up with Mark Hateley, who by that point had also moved to the other Rangers. After a loan spell at the end of the 1998/99 season with Everton, he made the move to Merseyside permanent the following campaign and was reunited with old boss Walter Smith. But his time there didn't go so well and he found himself on loan yet again, this time back up the road with Motherwell, which again led to a permanent deal. Bothered by injuries, he left Scotland behind and began a new life in America, enjoying three years with Colorado Rapids. With the injury lay-offs mounting up, he retired and moved into coaching, first as an assistant with Houston Dynamo and then as manager of Portland Timbers until 2012.

John and I met early one Sunday morning at a hotel in the Shawlands area of the city. He was a friendly guy and we talked about my trip to the States and meeting the three ex-players over there. I told him I had been planning to hitch-hike to Texas, where he had been living, until Boyd told me he was back in Britain. The hitch-hike would have been around 1,000 miles, not a huge distance in America, but John just laughed when I told him. He probably thought I was crazy.

He signed the shirt and posed for the picture in the hotel foyer. He had somewhere to be, so I thanked him and let him carry on with his day. I was chuffed to have met him and it brought to an end a very productive week. Not only did I meet Robbo, Rideout and Ally Maxwell in the States, but I also unexpectedly met Seb Rozental and now John Spencer. Five players within days of each other was great news, and it gave me a boost for continuing my search for the remaining players.

Greg Shields

GREG SHIELDS was another of the players I thought I would have to meet in America. While I was researching my trip to the States for the other three players, I looked him up online and saw he was part of the coaching set-up for Carolina Railhawks, a team based in Cary, North Carolina. That was not good news, because Cary, on the east coast, was more than 2,000 miles from Phoenix, where Robertson, Rideout and Maxwell lived. It was a 32-hour drive or, more sensibly, yet another flight. It might even work out cheaper to make it a separate trip at another date.

I acquired Greg's number from a contact and called him. This was soon after Dunfermline, another of his former clubs, had entered administration in 2013. He told me he was actually coming back to Scotland soon for a fortnight's visit, so would meet me there. That was a huge relief because I really had no idea how I would be able to afford the journey to North Carolina. He told me when he would be home and asked me to call his British mobile number within those dates to arrange a meeting.

Greg relocated to America in 2009 after a decent career in British football that began with his boyhood team, Rangers, in 1993. The right-back from Falkirk had been picked up from Gairdoch United when he was 16 and came through the youth ranks. His debut for the Gers was about as tough as you could imagine. He was thrown into a Champions League match against Ajax in 1996 and told to track Marc Overmars.

He played 11 times in total for the Gers and eight of those were in the nine-in-a-row campaign.

His first match came in the final encounter of eight-in-a-row, a 3–0 win at Kilmarnock on 4 May 1996. He played a bigger part in the pivotal ninth season, starting seven league matches. The first came on 19 October in a 2–2 home draw against Aberdeen. His next appearance was against the same opposition, this time at Pittodrie, on 1 December, and we returned to Glasgow with a 3–0 win. He played the following match, a 4–3 home win against Hibs, and was part of the Boxing Day 4–0 win against Raith. He played against Hibs again, this time at Easter Road, in a 2–1 triumph on 4 January, but his last two appearances were both defeats – a 2–1 loss to Kilmarnock at Ibrox on 22 March and the final game of the campaign at Tynecastle, when Hearts won 3–1 on 10 May.

He moved on to Dunfermline that summer and enjoyed two good seasons there, winning a move to Charlton in 1999. After loans to Walsall and Kilmarnock in 2002, he made his move to Ayrshire permanent after the close season. Two years later, he returned to Dunfermline, where he spent a further five years, before deciding to try his luck in the American league. He spent a loan term at Partick after that first American season finished and eventually retired in 2012, moving on to be assistant coach and head of the Railhawks' development programme.

I arranged to meet Greg at Dunfermline's ground, East End Park, and a friend (a fellow autograph hunter) and I drove through to meet him. Greg was staying with his sister during his trip home, and had come to Dunfermline's ground to catch up with his former colleagues while the club went through a tough time. I could empathise with him, considering where Rangers found themselves at the time thanks to our financial issues. We chatted about that catastrophe as well as his new life in the States. I told him about my recent visit to America and who I still had to meet. We only spent a short time together, but I appreciated him taking the time, because a trip over the Forth was a much simpler and cheaper journey than another flight across the Atlantic.

Steven Boyack

VERY FEW of the players were still playing when I tracked them down, but Steven Boyack signed the jersey at the side of the park after he had just fired in an impressive hat-trick.

He joined Rangers as a 14-year-old schoolboy, and the midfielder was one of many promising youths who just couldn't break into the first-team ranks at a time when the pressure to pick up every point was never greater. He had the best part of a decade at Ibrox and is one of the single-match men from the nine-in-a-row squad.

He had just turned 20 when he came off the bench at Hibs on 12 October 1996. It wasn't the best of days. In fact, Steven's single appearance was in an infamous 2–1 loss where Brian Laudrup missed two penalties. Bad luck continued, as Steven broke his leg a week later in an Old Firm reserve match and was out for ten months. He went to Hull on loan and then moved to Dundee on a permanent deal in 1999, signing for £25,000. He spent two years there, including a loan at Ayr, and then switched to Hearts for three years. From there he moved to Livingston and then brief spells at Boston United, Blackpool and Stirling Albion, taking him through to 2006. Steven moved to the juniors, first with Bathgate Thistle and, when I tracked him down through Facebook, later playing for Stirling City.

His dad, David, had also been a footballer, turning out for Raith Rovers, where he was best known for scoring a hat-trick of headers in one match.

Steven tells a great story from his time at Rangers, where he was used as Paul Gascoigne's body double. Gazza had found himself in a spot of bother and the press were at Glasgow Airport waiting for him to come off a flight. But club officials smuggled him away and sent Boyack towards the press, giving them a glimpse of blond hair to make them think he was Gazza. They followed his car all the way to Ibrox, only to find it was Boyack they had been chasing since Paisley. They weren't impressed.

When I sent him a message through Facebook asking if he would mind meeting me, he replied that he would be playing for Stirling City the following week if I wanted to meet him there. I took the bus up and then a taxi from the station to the ground. I enjoyed the match and was even more impressed with Steven's performance. This was in September 2012, when Rangers had just begun their long road back to the top and were playing in the Third Division. At the end of the game, I approached him as he walked off the pitch and introduced myself. He greeted me with a smile, and told me to go into the clubhouse for a drink and said he would come out and speak with me once he had showered and changed.

By the time I had finished my pint, the former under-21 cap was ready and came over for a chat. He told me he had his own employment agency these days for builders, labourers, electricians and other tradies, securing them with short-term and long-term work throughout the Central Belt. When he realised I had come by bus, he told me to jump in the car and gave me a lift to the station. On the way I told him I thought he'd turned in a great performance in the match, and, knowing where Rangers were at the time and our need for players, I said to him that he could obviously still do the business and did he not think he was fit enough to do a wee turn for the Bears? He had just turned 36 and was an experienced head, but Steven said he was a long way off the level of fitness required for that and was quite happy doing what he was doing. For Steven and others in the youth squad, he was maybe with Rangers at the wrong time, when youngsters had little chance of being given a shot. On the other hand, who wouldn't want to say they featured in the famous nine-in-a-row team? Steven is one of the 86 and that can never be taken away.

David Hagen

STEVEN BOYACK said he thought David Hagen was working with car dealership Arnold Clark in Stirling. There were three branches in the city, so I looked up the numbers and began to call. The receptionist at the second one I tried confirmed he worked there, but said he wasn't in that day. I asked if he would be working a couple of days later and she confirmed he would, so a mate and I drove up, only to be told he was on another day off. It was a wasted journey. One of his co-workers said he would definitely be there the following day if we wanted to come back.

David signed for Rangers from Bonnybridge in 1989 when he was 16 and went on to make nine starts and seven substitute appearances during nine-in-a-row.

He made his league debut from the subs' bench in a 2–0 home win against Hearts on 19 September 1993, during the historic five-in-a-row season when we came so close to reaching the first Champions League Final. He came on as a substitute again in the 2–2 draw with Airdrie at Ibrox on 13 February 1994, but it's the game on 13 March that's more significant for Hagen. Not only did he make his first league start, but he opened the scoring against Hibs in front of a home support. He cut in from the right, chipped the ball over Tortolano, chested the ball down and slotted it away. It was a dream goal for the youngster, and it inspired the team on to a 3–0 win.

It was enough to give him another start in the next match, an Old Firm game at Parkhead which ended in a 2–1 defeat. He started and scored at home on 17 April against Partick Thistle in a 3–1 win, started another two games and came on as a sub in the final three matches of the season.

Six-in-a-row began well for David when he scored in first-half injury time in a 2–1 home win against Hearts. The following week he wore the number nine jersey against St Johnstone in another 2–1 victory. He came on as a sub the next week in a goalless draw at Celtic and started on 25 September against Hibs, in a 2–1 win. His final league start came on 6 October at Ibrox in a shock 2–1 defeat to Motherwell. He didn't feature again until 7 May, when he came on in a 1–0 loss at Kilmarnock.

He made two substitute appearances during seven-in-a-row, away to Motherwell on 22 October in another 2–1 defeat to the Lanarkshire team, and away to Celtic eight days later when we won 3–1. Walter Smith told him he wasn't going to be a regular and was free to find another team, so David moved to Hearts, where he spent a season. He then switched to Falkirk, where he played for five years between 1995 and 2000. Livingston was next and then three years at Clyde, followed by two years at Peterhead. The Scotland under-21 cap then moved to the juniors for a season with Bo'ness United, before retiring in 2007.

My mate and I drove back to Stirling the following day and were told, thankfully, that David was in. One of his co-workers took us over to him and I explained why I was there. He wasn't a very talkative guy and seemed quite embarrassed about posing for a picture with the shirt – although perhaps that was because there were customers in the sales yard and he didn't want to look unprofessional. My mate took a quick snap, David signed the shirt, we shook hands and I left him to carry on with his work. Job done!

Darren Fitzgerald and Paul McKnight

I DON'T think I fully appreciated just how many air miles I would rack up in order to meet all of the nine-in-a-row fraternity when I took the first plane ride of the mission in January 2013.

That initial flight was a short trip across the water to Belfast – less than an hour in the sky and certainly not a sign of the lengthy journeys to come. I was meeting two Northern Irish lads who had been signed up by Rangers as youths, Darren Fitzgerald and Paul McKnight. I contacted Darren, or Mucker as he was more commonly known, thanks to Steven Boyack, who gave me his number. Mucker then gave me Paul's details once I explained what I was doing and that I would like to come over and meet them. Paul was fine about it too, so I made arrangements for when I could travel across. Both would be working, but said they could spare a few minutes to meet with me.

Darren signed for Rangers in the same week as a much higher-profile forward, Duncan Ferguson, in July 1993. Darren was just 15 but had caught the attention of scouts by scoring 102 goals in one season for his school team, Lisnasharragh. He went back to school – the same one George Best attended – until he was of leaving age, and then came back to Glasgow to begin his professional career.

Striker Paul McKnight signed the following month, and the 16-year-old slotted into the youth set-up. Both youngsters looked to have bright futures, and Darren won four under-21 caps while Paul earned three, but they just couldn't fight their way into contention at

Ibrox during a time when there was no margin for error as the club chased the nine titles.

They each made just one substitute appearance in the league. Paul was first, coming on against Partick Thistle in the final game of seven-in-a-row. The match at Ibrox on 13 May 1995 finished 1–1. Darren's big moment came two seasons later, in the fraught home stretch as the club came ever closer to that ninth title. He too came on as a sub, in the 2–1 home defeat by Kilmarnock on 22 March 1997.

Both players left Ibrox in 2000, after reaching an age when they had to be playing first-team football.

McKnight went to St Mirren and made his debut against Airdrie. The following week he had a fairy-tale call-up to the Northern Irish international squad. In his next match for the Buddies, he came on as a sub and scored a late winner versus Falkirk. A fortnight later he scored a last-minute winner at Ayr, which prompted a pitch invasion. Paul's decision to move on seemed to be an astute one, but unfortunately his progress was curtailed by injuries and he was released by the Paisley club in 2002. He moved back home to Linfield, but continued to spend lots of time on the treatment table. Unfortunately that had often been the case while he was at Rangers, too. He returned to St Mirren in the summer of 2003 but only lasted until November, injuries again causing his downfall. Back in Northern Ireland, he played for Glenavon, Larne, Newry City, Distillery and Ards, where he was also assistant manager from 2010 to 2012. His manager at Distillery described him as possibly one of the unluckiest players to ever play the game.

Darren, meanwhile, moved to Glentoran after leaving Ibrox and won the Irish Cup with them in 2001. He later moved on to Ards, Ballymena and back to Ards.

I touched down in Belfast before the sun had come up on a cold winter's morning and hopped on the bus that would take me to the Shankill Road. I had decided against hiring a car to take me between my stops, thinking back to a previous trip to Belfast when I had driven. That time, I took a wrong turn and found myself on the Falls Road, not a place you wanted to be if you were wearing Rangers colours, especially during the Troubles, and had the missus and kids in the car!

I had arranged to meet Darren, or Mucker, at the library on the Shankill. He was working as an engineer fitting security alarms, but had taken five minutes out of his shift to meet me. He was a nice bloke and we had a quick chat, but he seemed a little embarrassed or shy when it came to taking a photo with the shirt. Maybe it was because we were in the middle of a library! I thanked him for his time and made my way back to the bus stop to carry on my journey to the Cliftonville area. I always wore my Rangers colours when on trips to meet the nine-in-a-row players, but on this occasion I made sure to cover up while I sat on the coach, as the locals wouldn't have been so accepting of seeing a Rangers strip as they were on the Shankill.

Paul was a physical education teacher at a high school there, but was able to nip out of class for a few minutes to meet me. I gave him a call as I was approaching the academy, and he came out to meet me. I think he had a class at the time, so I only had a few minutes with him. We stood in the corridor, where he was happy to pose for a couple of pictures and sign the shirt.

With that, I was on my way back to the bus stop and down into the heart of Belfast. Once I saw the kerbstones change back to red, white and blue, I unzipped my jacket and knew I didn't need to worry any more about my colours being seen!

It was time to return to the airport and, after a quick bite to eat, I was on the 6pm flight bound for Glasgow with another two signatures added to my growing collection.

John Morrow

WHILE I was in Northern Ireland meeting Paul McKnight and Darren Fitzgerald, I spoke with Paul about other players I had yet to meet, and he mentioned that his brother was best friends with John Morrow.

John was another of the Northern Irish boys from that era signed by Rangers as a youth. Born in Belfast in 1971, the winger spent a season with Linfield, impressing not just Rangers but also Manchester United. He had a trial at Old Trafford in October 1987, but it was Glasgow he ended up in the following summer.

John spent eight years at the club and played 15 matches, including a European tie against CSKA Sofia. He made five league appearances, beginning with three starts in the number seven jersey in October of the four-in-a-row season: away to St Johnstone and at home to Hearts and Falkirk with 3–2, 2–0 and 1–1 results. He started twice in the six-in-a-row season – a 1–1 draw at home to Partick Thistle on 11 September and a 2–1 defeat to Motherwell at Ibrox on 6 October.

He moved to Oldham for the 1996/97 season and then returned north to Morton for two campaigns. He went on trial at Linfield during the 1999 close season and played in a number of pre-season games, but just when it looked like he would re-sign with his first club, there were reports that he had come back to Scotland to consider his future.

Paul gave me John's number, and I spoke to his wife. He was on shift at the oil rigs up north when I called, but she told me when he would be home in Bothwell, Lanarkshire, and we arranged a date for me to visit them. They had their hands full at the time with a newborn baby, so it was lovely of him to invite me into their beautiful house for coffee. We had a chat about Northern Ireland, and I told him about my recent trip to meet Paul and Darren, also sharing stories about some of the other places where I had met players in the UK. We spoke briefly about football, but I didn't want to outstay my welcome, especially when he had a baby to be doting over during his off-time from the rigs. So I thanked him and made my way home, turning my attention to the next name on the list.

Colin Scott

PERSISTENCE PAID off when it came to tracking down ex-youth player Colin Scott, who I had been told lived in the southside of Glasgow. I went through the phone book and, as you might imagine, there were plenty of listings under that surname. I narrowed the search by highlighting postcodes for that area of the city and began calling. It would be no exaggeration to say I spent hours on the phone, calling the numbers one after the other.

'Does the Colin Scott who used to play for Rangers live there?' Over and over and over again. And every time I was told the same thing – I had the wrong number.

But one of those people added that he knew who I was looking for, because Colin lived at the top of his street. What were the odds? That piece of good fortune allowed me to pinpoint the search, and finally I located the ex-Ger.

Colin was one of the nine goalkeepers to play for the Teddy Bears during nine-in-a-row. He signed from junior side Dalry Thistle in 1986 when he was just 16 and made his way through the youth system until he reached the first-team squad. He was third choice, in effect the back-up to the back-up, so first-team appearances were hard to come by. Colin made 11 league starts and two sub appearances during the nine-in-a-row years, having to bide his time until the sixth campaign.

With Andy Goram out due to a long-term injury, Colin was ready to deputise for Ally Maxwell, and his chance came in 1993 when he replaced the temporary number one in a match on 2 October at Stark's Park against Raith Rovers. The game finished 1–1. He started the following game, on 6 October, at home to Motherwell in a 2–1 defeat.

He stepped back in for the final four games of the season, the first being that unique match against Celtic on 30 April when the away support was banned from Ibrox by David Murray. John Collins scored first, but Mikhailichenko equalised and the game finished 1–1. Three days later, and with the title already won, Hibs beat us 1–0 at Easter Road, and it was the same result at Kilmarnock on 7 May. The final match of the season was a goalless draw at home to Dundee.

His next match came on Boxing Day during seven-in-a-row, and finally he was on the winning side, the team securing a 2–0 home win over Hibs. He then played on Hogmanay away to Motherwell, with Rangers winning 3–1. Up next was a home match against Celtic on 4 January, with Ian Ferguson scoring a screamer from the edge of the box in a 1–1 share of the points. Three days later he came on as a sub when the returning Goram broke down injured in a 1–1 draw away to Partick.

Eight-in-a-row would be Colin's last season at Ibrox, and he played three times – a 2–0 home win against Falkirk on 4 November, a similar result at Kilmarnock four days later, and a 3–2 win over Falkirk at Ibrox on 23 March.

Having already been on loan to Brentford in 1990 and Airdrie the following year, Colin decided it was time to move permanently and secure regular first-team football in 1996 after so many years behind Woods, Goram, Maxwell, Thomson and Ginzburg. He spent brief spells at Hamilton and Raith Rovers, but it was at Clydebank where he established himself. After two years there, he signed for Queen of the South in 2000. He played 115 league games over the next seven years and found himself once again battling with a veteran Andy Goram for the starting jersey. Unfortunately injury forced him to retire in March 2007, and the club thanked him for his service with a special presentation in the final league game of the season.

Colin trained to be a driving instructor while playing lower league football, and when I called him he said he was happy to stop by my house the next time he was in the area with a learner. A week or so later he turned up at my door. He was a massive guy and still looked like he was in playing condition. He had a learner waiting in the car, so I didn't want to take up too much of his time. He signed the shirt and posed for a picture in my living room before heading back to work. It was bizarre having one of the nine-in-a-row squad turn up at my door to pose for a picture, but he wouldn't be the last.

Gary Bollan

I WAS in the BBC Scotland building so many times over the years that I had my own seat in reception where I would wait for celebrities and athletes to come and go. Most of the people I met there weren't part of the nine-in-a-row squad, but were stars who I would ask to sign another shirt or piece of memorabilia that I could then sell to fund my next overseas trip. I met everyone from Amy Macdonald and Gary Lineker to a winning *QI* team there, and during the Commonwealth Games in Glasgow in 2014 I spent most days hanging around the building and collecting a massive number of signatures.

But on this occasion I was actually there to meet a nine-in-a-row player. When I lived in Glasgow I listened to Tam Cowan on *Off the Ball* every Saturday, and on this particular Saturday afternoon in 2012 his guest was Gary Bollan. I realised he was one of the home-based players I had yet to tick off the list, so I immediately threw on my jacket and shoes, grabbed the shirt and my camera, and made my way over to the BBC. I checked with the reception staff, all of whom I would eventually know well, if Gary was still in the studio. He was, so I was invited to take a seat and wait.

I must admit he was another of the fringe players I didn't know so well, having missed so many of the games when I lived down south during the nine-in-a-row era. He came from Dundee and was signed by United when he was a teenager from a local boys' club. The defender progressed to the first team at Tannadice and caught the eye of Walter, who had been tracking Gary and his teammate Alec Cleland for a while. Gary tells the story of Jim McLean, the United chairman, approaching the two of them at training at 11am one day and telling them they were signing for Rangers and to get through to Ibrox for 1pm. Gary, understandably, was gobsmacked.

Unfortunately the £750,000 move didn't work out for Bollan, who spent much of his time at Rangers injured. He made five starts and an appearance from the bench during seven-in-a-row in 1994/95. His debut came in a 2–0 away defeat to Aberdeen on 12 February, and he played three games in March – draws against Hibs and Falkirk and a 2–1 loss at Tynecastle. He came on in the 2–0 win at his old ground, Tannadice, on 1 April and started the 1–0 win at Kilmarnock on 20 April. The following season, he played every game in November except for the 3–3 home draw with Celtic, racking up three wins and a draw. He went on loan to Wolves in 1997, and played one game in 1997/98 for Rangers before moving on to St Johnstone, where he spent three years. He then played for two years at Livingston and returned to Dundee United for a spell. Brief turns at Motherwell, Clyde, Brechin and Albion Rovers followed, before he moved to the juniors with Carnoustie Panmure from 2006 to 2008. He moved into management, first with Livingston from 2009 to 2012, shortly before I met him, and later with Airdrie and Forfar.

I was given the nod that he was on his way down the stairs from the studio, so I was on my feet and ready for the big guy as he made his way to the exit. I quickly explained what I was doing and then took a picture and he signed the shirt. He didn't have much to say and I didn't know much about him, but I was happy to have another easy one ticked off.

Gary McSwegan and Charlie Miller

GARY MCSWEGAN and Charlie Miller were two Glasgow boys who came through the ranks, played for the club they loved and became internationals, and now they coach ordinary young lads – just as they were 25 and 30 years ago – in the hope that football will also give them a good life.

I read a newspaper article about Gary working as a youth development coach on behalf of Glasgow Housing Association, and during the press promotion for Charlie Miller's autobiography it was reported he was doing similar. I contacted the housing association, which directed my call to the sports facility at Petershill Park in the north of Glasgow, where McSwegan was supposed to be coaching. The person I spoke to didn't know who McSwegan was, and said numerous different groups trained there, but when I gave him more information about who he worked for I was told I would have the best chance of finding him there on a Friday evening.

Gary McSwegan is not only in Rangers' record books but also those of European football. He was 22 when he came on as a substitute during the first night of Champions League group stage action on 25 November 1992, when Rangers were 2–0 down to French title holders Marseille at Ibrox. As the clock ticked down, the game seemed to be slipping away from the Gers. But in the 78th minute, Durrant played a ball down the left to Mikhailichenko, who fired a pinpoint cross to McSwegan, standing just inside the box. His perfectly guided header went into the corner of the net, and the joyous young striker ran to the bench to celebrate, having scored with his first touch. It was the first goal by a British player in the Champions League. The goal inspired Rangers, and Hateley levelled soon after. There was the feeling that had the game gone another ten minutes, Rangers might have snatched the win, but the result still goes down as a famous one in our European adventures.

That goal was McSwegan's most famous, but he actually made his debut in the 1987/88 season. He would also make a single appearance during the first title triumph the following campaign, appearing as a sub on Hogmanay away to Hamilton in a 1–0 win. He failed to make an appearance the following year, but made one start and twice came off the bench during three-in-a-row. He came on in a 2–1 home defeat against Dundee United on 10 November and in a 3–0 Ibrox victory on 13 April against St Johnstone. He then started the following week in a 1–0 away win at St Mirren.

By now Gary was showing his worth in the reserve league, firing in goal after goal, but it was just unfortunate for him that he came to the fore at the same time as one of the club's greatest striking partnerships, Ally McCoist and Mark Hateley, was hitting its peak. During four-in-a-row he made four appearances from the bench: wins against St Johnstone, Airdrie and Hearts, and a 1–0 defeat at St Mirren on 23 November.

Five-in-a-row was his most successful season at Ibrox, but it was also his last. Not only was it the year of his goal against Marseille, but he also made eight starts and one sub appearance, and scored all four of his Rangers league goals. His first appearance came the weekend after his European goal and he started – and scored again – against Partick Thistle in a 3–0 win on 28 November. He also started a few days later in a 1–1 draw away to Airdrie on 1 December and then enjoyed a strong end to the season due to Ally McCoist's leg break while on Scotland duty. He started in a 3–2 away win at Hearts on 14 April, scored two in a 3–1 home win three days later against Partick and scored the only goal in the game that won the league, away to Airdrie on 1 May, when Broomfield was taken over by Rangers fans. He started in the 3–0 loss at Partick on 4 May, the squad no doubt still recovering from their celebrations, in the 1–0 Ibrox win against Dundee United on 8 May, as a sub in a 1–0 loss at Pittodrie and in the starting line-up again in the 2–1 away win against Falkirk in the final league game. After the Airdrie match, Walter Smith revealed that Gary had decided it was best for him to move on and find first-team football elsewhere, but The Gaffer said if he didn't find a team to his satisfaction he would be welcome back at Ibrox.

He did find a team, choosing to move south to Notts County in a £400,000 deal. He played two seasons there, scoring 21 league goals, and moved back up the road in 1995, playing three seasons at Dundee United. He then transferred to Hearts, with his form in the capital earning him a Scotland call-up. He came on as a late substitute in the Euro 2000 qualifier against Bosnia and started the match four days later against Lithuania, scoring the second in a 3–0 win. Towards the end of his time at Tynecastle he had two short loan spells at Barnsley and then Luton. He next moved on to Kilmarnock and Ross County for two years each, but his time in Dingwall was ruined through injury. He won a move to the Premier League with Inverness Caledonian Thistle and finished his career at Clyde, where he played for a season and a half. Gary moved into sports agency work and has also done some scouting, as well as being involved in youth coaching in Glasgow.

I went along to Petershill Park one Friday evening, more in hope than expectation that I might see Gary or Charlie. There were kids playing and practising across lots of pitches, and coaches in high-visibility vests worked with them on their ball control. I walked round the perimeter until I spotted a guy who looked like McSwegan, wearing a Glasgow Housing Association bib. As I got closer I realised it was him, so I waited for a lull in the action and then approached.

'Not a problem,' he said with a smile when I asked if he would sign the jersey. After taking his picture with the shirt, I inquired if Charlie Miller was also there. Gary told me Charlie was working that night, but at another park a mile or two along the road. I thanked Gary and went back to the car. I would have enough time to see Charlie as well.

Like Gary, Charlie also has his own place in Rangers folklore. He set up the goal that won nine-in-a-row – a moment that has been immortalised in song and can still be heard in the stands today. As the lyrics state, 'The year was '97 up at Tannadice, We were going for number nine, Charlie Miller crossed the ball into the box, and Laudrup headed over the line.' The unlikely header from the Great Dane was matched only by right-footed Charlie Miller's rarely seen left-footed cross to set the goal up.

The ultra-talented midfielder had just turned 21 when that historic goal was scored, but had already been in the side for three seasons previous to the ninth. Huge things were expected of the boy from the tough Castlemilk area of Glasgow, so much so that Walter Smith went along to a Rangers Boys' Club match when Charlie was 14 and told him he would be fine if he kept working hard. And he did go on to have a fine career, but it could have been a great one.

Charlie made 115 appearances for Rangers and scored 16 goals. Of those appearances, 83 came in the league – 60 during nine-in-a-row, 47 from the start. His league debut came at 17, playing in the number nine jersey away to Aberdeen on 18 September 1993 in a 2–0 defeat. He was a sub in the 2–2 home draw with Raith Rovers on 13 November and started the final game of the season, a 1–0 loss at Kilmarnock, on 7 May.

Seven-in-a-row was the teenager's breakthrough season. He won the SPFA Young Player of the Year award after starting 21 games and scoring three goals. Those came in home victories against Kilmarnock, Partick Thistle and Hearts, winning 2–0, 3–0 and 1–0. In his debut Old Firm league game, he robbed Tom Boyd and set up Hateley to score one of the striker's two goals in a 3–1 victory at Parkhead on 30 October. Over the years Charlie would start six games against Celtic and come on in six more, and was never on the losing side.

The following season he featured more often, starting 17 and coming off the bench six times, again scoring three goals. Those came in the demolition jobs of Raith (4–0) and Hibs (4–1), and that famous 7–0 victory over Hibs on 30 December. Charlie only made seven starts and six sub appearances in the ninth season, scoring a single goal in the 3–0 away win at Aberdeen on 1 December, and didn't feature much in Walter's final campaign in 1997/98. There were stories that Charlie was failing to make the most of his talents due to off-field behaviour and had previously become too close to the departed Gazza, who of course had his own much-publicised issues.

When Dick Advocaat took over as boss in the 1998/99 season, Charlie became a firm part of his plans and played 22 times – just one game short of his best season with the Gers in 1995/96. He also had a four-game loan at Leicester during that campaign. With Barry Ferguson making his mark too, the future looked sparkling for both Rangers and Scotland in the heart of the midfield. But Charlie was to fall foul of the Little General and was sold to Watford in 1999. His spell there was brief and he came back north to join Dundee United, where he recovered some of his best form, despite battling a gambling addiction that came to a peak while at Tannadice. It was during his time in Tayside that he won his solitary Scotland cap in an away match against Poland in April 2001. The game finished 1–1 and is notable for also being the international debut of Kenny Miller.

After leaving United, Charlie became a footballing nomad, playing with SK Brann in Norway, Belgium's Lierse, and Brisbane Roar and Gold Coast United in Australia, ending his career at Clyde before becoming involved with community football projects. I spotted him working with some youngsters when I arrived at the second park, and once he was finished talking with the boys, I went over to him.

He was a lovely bloke, down to earth and happy to sign the shirt. He told me if he could assist in finding any other players in the future I should just give him a call, and he gave me his number. It was too dark to take a decent picture, but I saw him in future years at Ibrox and asked for a photograph then. He recognised me from our first meeting and always had time for a smile and a quick chat. Charlie is a part of our greatest league title triumph, and hopefully he can go on to coach and unearth plenty of local lads who will follow in his talented footsteps and help Rangers win more titles in the future.

Terry Butcher

TERRY BUTCHER was the lynchpin of Graeme Souness's Rangers Revolution.

The capture of the England captain in the summer of 1986, soon after the manager had taken over, in a £725,000 deal, was a massive statement of intent. He led by example, literally bleeding for the cause. The rock at the heart of the defence, he guided the Bears to their first title in nine years when he scored the goal at Pittodrie that clinched the 1986/87 title. Many consider Butcher's leg break the following season as the primary reason the team failed to retain the title. Had he remained fit, perhaps we would be celebrating eleven-in-a-row instead.

Born in Singapore in December 1958 and brought up in Lowestoft in East Anglia, Butcher played schools football but was never approached by a senior club until he started on a three-year course to be a quantity surveyor. Both Norwich and Ipswich invited him for trials, and he signed for Ipswich, his childhood heroes, in August 1976. He spent ten years there and won the UEFA Cup in 1981.

His move to Rangers was a big deal, and he went on to wear the number six jersey with pride. Tel made 73 starts during nine-in-a-row and scored five goals. In the first campaign, 1988/89, he missed just two games – a 2–0 win over Dundee United at Ibrox on 2 May and away to Dundee four days later in a 2–1 victory. He scored a memorable header in a 4–1 demolition of Celtic at Ibrox on 3 January and struck again at home on 21 January in a 3–1 triumph over Dundee.

Again he missed just two games during two-in-a-row – a 1–0 win away to Dunfermline on 27 January and a 3–1 home result against Dundee United the following week. He scored three goals that season, another header against Celtic in the opening Old Firm game of the campaign, which was a 1–1 draw at Parkhead on 26 August, against Dunfermline in a 3–0 Ibrox win on 25 November, and versus Motherwell on 9 December in another 3–0 win at home.

At 31 years old, it looked like he might finish his career in Glasgow, but things change in a hurry in football. He played only the first five games of three-in-a-row before he was dropped by Souness. He scored a strange own goal at Tannadice, a back-header from a Dundee United goal kick that looped over Chris Woods and into the net. It was by no means Butcher's first own goal at Rangers, but it was his last. There were rumours of a knee injury bothering him following Italia '90, and the manager dropped him for the League Cup semi-final against Aberdeen four days later. Manager and player had fallen out, and nine times out of ten in that scenario the boss is the winner. Butcher never played for Rangers again and was eventually sold to Coventry in a £400,000 deal in November 1990, also becoming the Midlands club's manager.

He stuck mostly to the sidelines, only playing six league games, but his time in charge didn't work out and he was sacked in 1992. He signed for Sunderland and played 38 league games, but would soon take on managerial duties again, being appointed boss there in January 1993. He was sacked in November of the same year. Tel then played three games with Clydebank at the end of the year before hanging up the boots.

Butcher was out of the game, and he and his wife, Rita, ended up running a hotel in Bridge of Allan for a few years as he searched for a way back into football. Three years passed before he was given a youth coach role at Raith Rovers. He then became assistant manager at Motherwell and took over full gaffer duties in 2002. In 2006 he moved Down Under to become boss of Sydney FC. A year later he was back in Scotland as caretaker boss at Partick, followed by a brief stint as Brentford boss. He became George Burley's assistant with the Scotland national team in 2008, a controversial appointment in some circles due to his image as Mr England when he was a player. In 2009 he became Inverness Caledonian Thistle gaffer, and he enjoyed a good spell in the Highlands, which was punctuated by him leaving the Scotland set-up when Burley was let go. He would have been better staying with Inverness rather than taking on the Hibs role in 2013, as his season in charge led to relegation and the loss of his job. He had a brief spell at Newport County in 2015 and was in negotiations to join Filipino club Global towards the end of 2016.

Sadly Butcher is no longer held in as high regard as he once was with a section of Rangers fans, having made several comments in the media about the club over the years which riled many supporters. Considering he was so in love with Rangers that he claimed to have named his third son after Ally McCoist and Ian Durrant, and was voted into Rangers' greatest-ever team, it's sad that one of the club's captains perhaps doesn't have the legacy other great skippers continue to enjoy.

I met him when he went back to his old club, Motherwell, with Inverness Caley. I waited outside the main entrance after the game, keeping my eyes peeled for the big man to emerge. There were a number of other fans hanging around, so I knew I would have to be on my toes. When he came out of the door to make his way to the team bus, I pounced and got to him first before the others rushed round. He signed the shirt and paused for a picture, but I had no chance to tell him about my search for all of the players as other autograph hunters waded in.

Living down south for the entirety of nine-in-a-row, I saw more of Tel than I did of the rest of the team, due to his high-profile role in the England squad. When I think of Butcher even now, it's that wild-eyed image of him from the Sweden game in 1989 I like to remember him by, a head bandage failing to stem the blood from streaming down his face and turning his white strip a deep shade of crimson.

He was a warrior on the pitch, and his contribution to the early years of nine-in-a-row won't be forgotten.

Dale Gordon

I WAS in a taxi being driven through streets that looked like something out of a science fiction movie. My surroundings were like nothing I had ever seen – they were stunning and awe-inspiring. I felt like I had stepped far into the future.

What had started out as a hopeful drive to Great Yarmouth in search of another ex-player had led me here, Dubai, and a cab ride that I was sure was taking me in the wrong direction. Admittedly I had only just arrived in the country, but when I was booking my hotel online I specifically chose accommodation that was only a five-minute drive from the airport. We drove for 25 minutes before the driver finally pulled up outside a hotel. I looked at the name above the entrance.

'This isn't my hotel, mate,' I told him.

The driver's English was limited, but I understood that he said this is where I'd told him to go. I looked at the sign again and then checked my hotel name. It was similar, too similar for someone who couldn't articulate the local language properly. My mispronunciation had cost me 50 dirham, the currency in the United Arab Emirates, rather than just 5 dirham. As we made our way to the hotel by the airport, the correct hotel, the driver handed me a card.

'Call if you want massage,' he said, thrusting the card towards me.

'No thanks mate, I'm OK,' I replied, declining with a wave of my hand.

I looked around the lobby of the hotel as I checked in, and while it wasn't swish by Dubai standards, it was more lavish than most places I had stayed during my search for the nine-in-a-row squad. It was also one of the most expensive, costing me £800 for a two-night stay and a return flight from Glasgow with Emirates Airlines. The trip hadn't gone well so far. Not only had the taxi taken me on a half-hour detour, but the litre bottle of whisky I bought in duty free before I boarded was probably rolling around the floor of the plane after I forgot to lift it. I like to have a couple of drinks before I go to bed every night, not so easy in a dry country, so I thought I was being smart by preparing in advance.

I was here to meet Dale Gordon, the winger who played for Rangers for around 18 months in the middle of the nine-in-a-row campaign. Born in Great Yarmouth and making his name at nearby Norwich City, where he played from 1984 to 1991, more recently he had been working with budding professionals at the Glenn Hoddle Academy near London, before branching out and opening his own academy in his home city. And he was – until a few days before I turned up in the south-east hoping to meet him. After researching his whereabouts on the internet, I called the facility and asked if it was possible to speak with him. I was told he wasn't around, so I asked when would be the best time to come down to meet him and was told various dates when he would be there. It's a long drive from Glasgow to Great Yarmouth, but I picked my daughter Debbi up from her home in Leeds to give me company for the second half of the drive and that made it a little easier.

But there was bad news awaiting us. Just a few days earlier, Dale had flown to Dubai to follow up a job offer. His colleague was kind enough to give me Dale's mobile number, so I called him once I was home. He told me he was going to be staying in Dubai, where he had accepted a job to run a kids' football academy, but was happy to meet me if I wished to come over. A few months on and here I was.

It had been a long day and I was in need of a nightcap, so I had a quiet word with one of the hotel workers and asked if he knew of anywhere I could buy a drink. He directed me to a bar only ten minutes' walk from my lodgings. It was a little dingy and felt seedy, but I took a seat at the bar and ordered a whisky from the South American bartender and people-watched as I drank. I was surprised at the number of Arabs in the bar drinking. I had another couple of whiskies and made my way back to the hotel, more than ready for my bed. Unfortunately the guests through the wall from me included a troop of six or seven kids whose parents didn't seem to mind letting them run riot. Sleep was fitful.

Dale and I had arranged that he would stop by my hotel the next morning, but he called first thing and asked if I could come to his hotel instead. I took a cab downtown and was dropped off outside a seven-star establishment. It was absolutely stunning, ridiculously beautiful and opulent. As I walked through the lobby, Dale came towards me, spotting my Rangers clothes. He looked good, not all that different from his time at Ibrox, except his trademark moustache was gone. He was wearing a T-shirt and shorts and explained he had just come from a coaching session. We found a spot, ordered coffee and began chatting about his time in Dubai so far. He told me his knees were playing up and he was preparing for an operation. He had been known as Disco Dale in his playing days due to his love of the nightlife and for having a good time, and it seemed he was still enjoying himself now, sailing on luxury yachts in Dubai and staying in this amazing hotel while making a good living teaching kids.

The conversation soon turned to Rangers and we reminisced about his time at Ibrox, which began in November 1991 when Walter paid Norwich £1.2m for the 24-year-old right-winger. He made a dream debut away to Dunfermline on 9 November in a 5–0 victory. He set up the opener for Richard Gough, scored in the 23rd minute, teed up Mark Hateley and finished off the scoring in 72 minutes. His performance was so impressive that Walter later joked that for the first 25 minutes he thought Dale was a different player from the one he signed.

He made 23 starts over the remainder of the four-in-a-row season, scoring five goals, including strikes away to Motherwell, at home to Dunfermline and against Hibs in a 2–0 win at Ibrox on 11 January. The following season he made 18 starts in the league and four substitute appearances, scoring just one goal – in his first match of the campaign – against Airdrie in a 2–0 home win on 4 August. He left at the end of that season, despite admitting that Walter wanted him to stay, when an £800,000 offer came in from West Ham United. He was swayed by the offer of better wages and being closer to home. He later said he regretted leaving so soon – he was only 18 months into a four-year contract – and felt he had made the wrong decision.

He scored West Ham's first goal in the Premier League, against Coventry in August 1993, and spent three years at Upton Park, which included loan spells at Peterborough and Millwall. The four-times-capped England under-21 finished his playing career with a season at Bournemouth before moving into coaching. He also had spells as manager of non-league teams Great Yarmouth Town and Gorleston and was the head coach at Ipswich's youth academy. Working with youngsters eventually led him to the seven-star hotel where two Brits sat in our football gear, reminiscing about the good old days. As I looked around the grand lobby of the complex on our way out, I decided the present day wasn't too bad for Dale either.

I asked if there was anywhere he would recommend I visit, and he suggested the world's tallest building, the Burj Khalifa, which measures an incredible 2,722ft. He said he had a meeting to go to and would drop me on the way. It was a nice gesture, and I thanked Dale for taking the time to meet me as he pulled up near the incredible sight. It's hard to describe just how tall it is. It's a feat of construction and I don't think I've ever felt as small as I did when I stood in the shadow of this shiny, monster skyscraper and looked up at its tapered peak. I went inside for a nose around and was considering taking the ride to the top, but I was put off. Not by the height – I've no problem with that – it was the price that changed my mind. They were looking for around £80 to go all the way up. The height in the mall section of the building was good enough to give me a view over the city, so I made do with that.

Afterwards I went for a wander and found myself down by a vast river, where lots of vintage boats were docked. They must have been hundreds of years old and provided sharp contrast to the futuristic-looking buildings all around. I asked a guy who was standing by the docks about the boats, and he told me they were still in use, often setting sail to Iran.

Skyscrapers are constantly being built in Dubai, and I watched one construction site as men worked at great heights on these huge buildings. I was horrified to see them standing on slim ledges 500ft or more up, risking life and limb for a day's wage. They were so high up, they looked like ants from the ground.

Not too far from my hotel, I spotted a jewellery shop and decided to go in for a look and maybe pick up a gift for my friend Ana. As I browsed, I noticed there were lots of gold items on display on top of the cabinets, on the near side of the glass, and no members of staff to be seen. I looked around in case the shopkeeper was bending down behind a unit or had gone through to the back of the store, but no one appeared. I went outside and approached a guy selling fruit on the street corner and asked if he knew where the shop's staff were. He told me the owner had gone to prayers and would be back later. I couldn't believe it. He had left the shop unattended and the door unlocked. I decided to make a sharp exit in case something went missing and the bloke from the western country was blamed.

I wasn't a fan of the food in Dubai. Even the meals I thought I would be familiar with, like in the KFC fast food restaurant I visited, were different. I don't know what they do to the chickens over there, but the meat tasted terrible. I ended up with a hot dog and fries and then made my way back to the seedy bar run by the South Americans for a nightcap.

The next morning, I took a taxi to the airport and headed to the lost and found. It was a long shot, but I thought I would check if my bottle of whisky had been handed in. I was shocked when they brought it out. Once I had filled in a form, I was given the bottle back. Of course, I forgot I couldn't take the liquid on to the flight because it was in my hand luggage, so minutes after the whisky was returned to me I was forced to throw it in the bin! That left a sour taste but it was soon forgotten when I took my seat on the plane and began chatting with a couple of Muslim guys who, it transpired, were good friends of Bilel Mohsni, a Rangers player at the time. We spent the journey home talking about the Rangers and my crazy mission, and, by the time I touched down in Glasgow, I was already plotting my next epic trip.

Ray Wilkins

IT WAS a pleasure and a privilege to see Ray Wilkins grace Ibrox in a Rangers strip. In an era of magnificent players who the Rangers support were proud to watch, Wilkins is up there with the elite members of that squad of greats. He might only be 5ft 8in, but he was head and shoulders above every one of his opponents in Scotland.

From a football family – his dad George was a professional and his three brothers, Graham, Dean and Stephen, all played – the Londoner began his career at Chelsea in 1973 and was made captain at 18. After six years at Stamford Bridge he transferred to Manchester United, where he spent a further five years. Butch moved to AC Milan in 1984 and at the start of the 1987/88 season he moved to Paris Saint-Germain. But his time in France was brief. After just four months, Graeme Souness came in for the majestic midfielder and he was on his way to join the Revolution out Govan way. He made his debut at home to Hearts in a 3–2 victory on 28 November 1987, two months after his 31st birthday, helping to knock the Edinburgh side off the top of the league.

Wilkins made 45 league starts and one substitute appearance during nine-in-a-row, scoring one goal. And what a goal it was. One of the most famous from the nine campaigns, perhaps even in Old Firm history, was Butch's blistering volley on the sunny afternoon of 27 August 1988 when Rangers battered Celtic 5–1 at Ibrox. Gary Stevens launched a long throw into the box and the ball was flicked on by Butcher. Celtic headed it out, but it was met by Wilkins, who struck it in the air first time, and it fizzed into the back of the net. Thirteen years later, during an Auld Old Firm Challenge match, he scored an eerily similar goal into the same end, proving natural talent never fades.

Wilkins, with 84 England caps to his name between 1976 and 1986, played the first 15 games of two-in-a-row in 1989/90, but his time in Glasgow was to be cut short when his family wished to go back to London after ten years away. It was a huge loss to Rangers and the support, but we gave him a great send-off in his final game, a midweek match against Dunfermline at Ibrox on 25 November 1989. He demonstrated his sublime talents by setting up the first goal in the 3–0 victory, with a beautiful long pass that landed perfectly on Mo Johnston's foot inside the box. As the fog came down in the second half, the fans stuck around to wish Ray all the best. He admitted afterwards he wasn't sure how the fans would respond since he had only been at the club for two years, but admitted the warm reaction would live with him forever. It's been said often but once a Ranger, always a Ranger.

Ray moved to Queens Park Rangers, where he spent five years, and then on to fellow London club Crystal Palace as player-coach, but he broke his left foot on his debut. It was his only league appearance for Palace, and he was soon back at QPR as player-boss in what turned out to be a turbulent introduction to management. He left in 1996 and turned out once for Wycombe before coming back north to play 16 times in the league for Hibs. When he featured against Rangers, the Bears showed him he hadn't been forgotten. After leaving the capital club, he returned south to play a handful of matches for Millwall and then Leyton Orient, finally hanging the boots up in 1997, in his 41st year.

After a spell as Fulham boss, he became Chelsea assistant for two seasons and then deputy for Watford, Millwall and the England under-21s team. In 2008 he returned to Chelsea as assistant before being let go two years later. He went back to Fulham as assistant in 2013, was Jordan's international boss in 2014/15 and was Aston Villa's assistant during a troubled time for the Midlands club.

It was in 2012, when he was out of the game during the period between the Chelsea and Fulham roles, that I had the opportunity to briefly meet Ray. I was waiting around outside the main entrance at Ibrox before a match when a taxi was allowed to pass through the closed road by the police. I knew if that was being allowed to happen it must be someone of note, so I crouched down and looked in the window as the cab pulled up. I spotted the bald head and realised it was Wilkins. There were still scores of supporters milling around the front of the stand, so I knew I would have to act quickly.

I brought the jersey out of the carrier bag and waited for him to emerge from the car. I never liked pouncing on the players; I always tried to show them respect and give them space. I was a step ahead of most of the others waiting around who hadn't yet noticed who was inside the taxi, so I was the first to approach him. He signed the shirt, but already there were fans swarming around us, pushing items towards him to sign, so I considered myself lucky that I was able to negotiate enough space to take a picture of him with the strip. He did it without a grumble and was an absolute gentleman – not that I expected anything less from Ray Wilkins.

Stephen Wright

STEPHEN WRIGHT signed for Rangers in the same week as Paul Gascoigne's incredible transfer in July 1995, and left Ibrox in the same week as Gazza in March 1998. Unfortunately, due to injury, the promising right-back didn't experience anything like the success the English midfielder enjoyed during his spell in Glasgow.

Born in Bellshill, Lanarkshire, in 1971, Stephen was a Rangers supporter as a kid, but was signed as a youngster by Aberdeen and trained in Glasgow, where Alex Ferguson or Archie Knox would come down once a week and watch him and the rest of the boys being put through their paces. He made the breakthrough at Pittodrie and secured the right-back position. He picked up 15 under-21 caps for Scotland and two full caps for the national team as Rangers monitored his progress.

Walter signed him in July 1995, and he slotted into the side for the season opener against Kilmarnock on 26 August with a 1–0 win kicking off the eight-in-a-row season. He played in six of the first eight league games, but the Rangers injury jinx struck again in November during a Champions League match against Juventus at Ibrox, when he suffered a cruciate ligament injury. His Rangers career was more or less over before it had really begun. Even after he returned to fitness, Alec Cleland had made the right-back role his own, and Stephen would play only one match in the nine-in-a-row season, the final game against Hearts on 10 May at Tynecastle, when we were defeated 3–1.

With a barren season the following year, Stephen went on loan to Wolves within days of Gazza heading south to Middlesbrough. He failed to win a contract at Molineux but signed with Bradford, where he spent two seasons, and then had two seasons back in Scotland with Dundee United. His career finished prematurely due to injury during a brief spell at Scunthorpe.

Stephen looked to become involved in coaching, and that's where I tracked him down. I'd read in the newspaper that he was one of a clutch of former players attending Hampden the next day for their coaching badges. I turned up bright and early at the stairs to the national stadium's entrance to await Stephen's arrival. There was only one problem – I had no idea what he looked like. Having been in England during his Rangers career, and with Stephen having played so few times, I couldn't recall seeing him turning out for us, and I had forgotten to look up a picture of him online before leaving the house. Thankfully there were a few autograph hunters also waiting and they pointed him out.

I called him over as he reached the top of the stairs and asked if he would sign the shirt. There was no time to explain what I was doing as he was heading inside, but he still took a moment to pose for a picture, giving a big smile for the camera, and I thanked him for his time. That was one of the briefest meetings I had with a nine-in-a-row player.

Stephen worked with the Rangers youths and then moved on to Dunfermline. He became head of football at the Fife Elite Football Academy, which covers Cowdenbeath, Raith Rovers, Dunfermline and East Fife, and has received plaudits for his work there.

Alec Cleland

ALEC CLELAND was a steady and reliable right-back for two-and-a-half seasons of nine-in-a-row. Signed as a squad player alongside teammate Gary Bollan from Dundee United, Cleland quickly made the position his own.

He played 68 league games during the glory run, making his debut away to Aberdeen in a 2–0 defeat on 12 February 1995 during seven-in-a-row. He started ten of the final 12 games that season.

His first full season at Ibrox followed, and he started 21 games, came on four times and scored his solitary nine-in-a-row goal (he would also score a Scottish Cup hat-trick that season in a 10–1 demolition of Keith). That single effort was a memorable one, coming at Parkhead on 30 September, opening the scoring in a 2–0 win over Celtic with a header. A minute before half-time, Gascoigne passed to Oleg Salenko – who had one of his best games that day – and he hit a perfect cross to Cleland, who guided it into the net.

Alec played 32 of the 36 games during the historic ninth season, continuing to link well with Laudrup on the right, and played one more season at Ibrox before following his gaffer, Walter Smith, to Everton. But a calf injury months into his Goodison career ultimately led to his retirement and Cleland, capped 11 times at under-21 level, turned to coaching.

He was assistant manager at East Stirling and became youth coach at Livingston, where he also had spells as caretaker boss. He worked with the kids at Rangers Academy and became youth coach at Inverness Caledonian Thistle and then St Johnstone, where he also stepped in as temporary manager.

It was while he was working on his coaching badges that I met him. It was the same day that fellow right-back Stephen Wright, whose long-term injury opened the door for Cleland to claim a regular starting role, signed the shirt at Hampden.

A short time after seeing Wright, my friend pointed Alec out as he walked up the steps to the stadium's main entrance. I was deep in conversation with someone at the time and rushed over just as he was going inside. There was no chat as he quickly signed the picture and posed for a photograph, but I was quite happy because it was a bonus autograph. It wasn't often I managed to meet two players in one day, after all.

Stuart McCall

STUART MCCALL is the only nine-in-a-row player whose 40th birthday party I attended.

That was in the summer of 2004, five years before I began my nine-in-a-row quest. I was living in England, and wee Stuart, believe it or not, was still playing football at a decent level, turning out week after week for Sheffield United and running the show in the middle of the park. Harrogate True Blues, a Rangers supporters' club, put on a birthday night for him in their social club, and Stuart came along. It was a great night, a crazy one, but I'd better leave it at that for risk of embarrassing anyone! I had some pictures from that evening and decided to dig them out to show Stuart when I turned my attention to securing the wee man's signature.

It was January 2013 and Stuart was manager of Motherwell. I called the club and found them to be very helpful. The woman I spoke to said I should come to the stadium any day they were training and I could meet him then. She said he left at 10am each day and would be in a black Mercedes. A few days later I drove over to Fir Park and waited in the car park for Stuart. When he came out, I chatted to him about my project and mentioned I had attended his 40th birthday at Harrogate years earlier.

He laughed when I brought out the photographs from the evening and told me his wife had some similar pictures of him up on stage from the do. He said he would put them with the others, then signed my shirt. We chatted for a couple of minutes about football, particularly the unbelievable Rangers situation, as at that point we were down in the Third Division.

Stuart was born in Leeds to Scottish parents and followed his dad Andy's career path by becoming a professional footballer. His trademark tenacity and determination were there early doors, with one story I read recalling how he scored the winning cup final goal in a schools competition after coming off the bench with his arm in a sling. He played for several youth clubs before he joined Bradford City in 1982 and spent six years there. He helped them win the Third Division championship, an achievement overshadowed by the tragic stadium fire that killed 56 and injured nearly 300 more, including his dad.

McCall's form won him a transfer to Everton in 1988. Like so many of that era, his next destination after Goodison was Govan, with Walter signing him just hours before the European transfer deadline in August 1991. The Gaffer admitted he had targeted him early and felt he grabbed a bargain at £1.2m. In 1998, reflecting on his managerial tenure, Walter said Stuart was his third greatest signing, after Goram and Laudrup. The box-to-box midfielder quickly became a fans' favourite too, his never-say-die attitude and abundance of skills and intelligence proving a winning combination befitting the blue jersey. He gave his all for the Gers and made 159 league starts and four substitute appearances, contributing four goals in our run to the nine.

His Rangers career didn't get off to the best of starts, though, with his debut coming in a 1–0 defeat away to Hearts on 17 August, but it was a small blip on the way to four-in-a-row. He started 35 games in that 44-match season and made one substitute appearance. His only goal came in a 3–1 win away to Falkirk on 14 December. He made 35 starts and one run-out as a sub the following season too, but this time scored five goals. Those came in a 4–1 win at Partick on 12 September, a 2–0 home win over Hearts the following week, a 3–2 victory against Dundee United at Ibrox on 5 January, a 3–0 home win over Dundee on 27 March and a 3–2 triumph against Hearts again at Tynecastle on 14 April.

Injury curtailed the start of his six-in-a-row campaign, and he only played three games in the first three months. He made his comeback in the home defeat to Celtic on 30 October and only missed one more game all season, giving him a total of 34 starts from the 44 matches. He scored three times, against Partick at Ibrox in a 5–1 win on 5 February, in a 4–0 victory at home to St Johnstone on 19 March and in a 1–1 home draw with Aberdeen on 2 April. He was ever present until the final six games of the seventh season, starting 30 games and scoring two goals, away to Motherwell in a 3–1 win on Hogmanay and at Falkirk in a 3–2 win on 14 January.

Injuries were once again a factor during eight-in-a-row, as he made just 19 starts and two appearances from the bench. He scored three times – the only goal on the opening day against Kilmarnock on 26 August, in the 5–0 Ibrox demolition of Partick Thistle on 13 April, and the following week in a 3–1 win at Motherwell. The ninth season was a disappointing one for Stuart. He started the first seven games, but then suffered an injury and didn't feature again for the rest of the campaign. His final game of nine-in-a-row came in a 2–0 Ibrox win over Celtic on 28 September, so at least it was a good note to end on.

Despite still having a year of his contract to run when Dick Advocaat arrived in the summer of 1998, Stuart moved on, returning to his first club, Bradford, where he enjoyed another four years. Combined with the six seasons he spent during his first stint, this meant he was due for a testimonial in 2002, and there could only be one club he would ask to provide the opposition. A team of his nine-in-a-row brothers turned out for Rangers one more time in April of that year, and an incredible 10,000 Rangers fans travelled south for the match, surely the greatest indication possible of the high regard in which they held the flame-haired warrior. Stuart left Bradford a couple of months later, aged 38, but he wasn't finished yet. He joined Sheffield United and played with them for three years – and celebrated the aforementioned 40th birthday while on their books – finally retiring shortly before his 41st. Rangers were never far from his thoughts, though, and he was spotted in among the Rangers fans in May 2005, better known as Helicopter Sunday, when we famously won the league at Hibs on the final day of the season.

With 40 caps to his name – and a World Cup goal for Scotland in a 2–1 win over Sweden at Italia '90 – Stuart enjoyed a great career, and he had already begun planning for its next stage while still playing. He was made assistant manager at Bradford in 2000 and appointed caretaker boss while the club was in the Premier League. His first match as temporary manager just so happened to be against Everton, and his adversary in the opposite dugout was The Gaffer, Walter Smith. Everton won the game 1–0. He was later made first-team coach and was also coaching while at Sheffield United, guiding the reserve team to the second-string title, and then serving as assistant manager.

His first full managerial role came in 2007, and once more he returned to Bradford, where he remained until 2010. He came back north to take over at Motherwell later that year and turned the

Lanarkshire team into a decent side considering his budget. Two years later he took advantage of Rangers' downfall by claiming our Champions League qualifier place after we were barred from playing in Europe due to administration, the spot falling to Motherwell in third position. With the Teddy Bears out of the top league, Stuart guided 'Well to a second-place finish in the season when I met him for the autograph, giving the club another brief bite at the Champions League. A poor start to the 2014/15 season led him to walk, and he was working as a pundit until the call came from Dave King to come in as interim Rangers boss, relieving caretaker Kenny McDowall of his duties, as we tried to stumble over the line and back into the Premier League via the play-offs. While he did succeed in having the team play a little better, it still wasn't enough and a major clear-out was required in the summer of 2015, which also included McCall.

After more punditry, Stuart was given another crack at management in 2016 and it seemed inevitable that it would be with Bradford – it was his second spell in charge of the club and his fourth time there overall, a connection stretching back almost 35 years. Whether or not Stuart is ever lucky enough to return to Rangers one more time, we all know his heart will always belong here and he'll forever be a true blue who gave everything to the cause.

Chris Vinnicombe

CHRIS VINNICOMBE is one of those players who was at Rangers longer than I realised.

Signed from his home-town team of Exeter when he was just 19, he remained at Ibrox until the end of the six-in-a-row season, meaning he was at the club for five of the historic campaigns. Although he didn't play too many games, he always stuck in my mind as I watched from afar down in Leeds, I think because of his unusual surname.

It was that surname that helped me to easily track him down through Facebook in 2013. His page was set to private, but I was able to contact him via his wife Paula's profile. I arranged to fly down to Exeter on a Saturday, where I would meet him at Witheridge FC, the team he managed in the South-West Peninsula Premier Division.

I flew from Glasgow to Exeter, then took a bus to Tiverton, where the Vinnicombes lived. I dropped my bag at the bed and breakfast I had booked and then took the bus to Witheridge, only around ten miles away. I called Chris when I arrived at the tiny stadium, and he came out to meet me. He was a lovely guy and led me into the ground's one small stand to introduce me to Paula and their two teenage daughters. I had taken down a few pairs of Rangers gloves to thank the family for their hospitality, which I gave to Paula and the two girls before the match started, and while Chris went to work, the four of us sat together to watch the home side secure a victory.

Chris met Paula at an Exeter game in April 1989, seven months before their lives were turned upside down when a transfer bid from Graeme Souness, one of his heroes growing up, was accepted by the club. Having made his debut at 16, the left-back was making an impact in the south-west of England, but he had no idea word had spread to Scotland's top team. Rangers paid £150,000 for his signature in November, and Chris and Paula relocated to Glasgow to begin a new chapter of their relationship.

He debuted as a sub in a 3–0 home win against Motherwell on 9 December and came on again a fortnight later at Ibrox in a slim 1–0 win over St Mirren. His third appearance, again as the number 14, was an entirely different prospect when he was thrown into the wild atmosphere of a New Year's Old Firm game. Rangers came away from Parkhead with a 1–0 win thanks to Nigel Spackman's goal. Four days later he came on as number 14 once more, this time during a 2–0 home triumph against Aberdeen. His next league appearance was his only start of the season, a 3–1 victory at home to Dundee United on 3 February. Chris made two more substitute appearances that season, in a 2–2 draw at Dundee in March and in the final game of the season at Tynecastle, which finished 1–1.

The following season, three-in-a-row, was Chris's most successful for the Teddy Bears. He started ten matches, including a best-ever four games on the bounce, which was enough to earn him a league medal as the Gers pipped Aberdeen to the title. He made just one start, against St Mirren in April when we won 4–0 at Ibrox, and a sub appearance in a 4–2 home win over Hibs in October, during four-in-a-row. He didn't feature at all in five-in-a-row but made two starts, against Partick in September and St Johnstone in December, and two sub run-outs – away to St Johnstone in August and at home to Hearts in December – during the sixth title win.

It was in November of that season that Walter Smith placed Chris on the transfer list, alongside fellow fringe players Brian Reid, Sandy Robertson, John Morrow and Steve Watson. His time in Scotland was coming to an end, and he left Glasgow for Burnley in June 1994 for £200,000. Chris made 23 league appearances for Rangers and was never on the losing side, which is an impressive record.

He stayed with Burnley until 1998 and then moved to Wycombe, where he was part of their memorable run to the FA Cup semi-finals in 2004. He left the club the same year and spent a season at non-league Tiverton, a season back at Exeter and two more years at Tiverton, then moved on to Witheridge, where he was also manager for two seasons. He spent a brief spell as Tiverton boss, moved to Elmore and returned to Witheridge, where he remained until the summer of 2016. Chris suffered lots of injuries during his career, which curtailed his progress, but he has 12 England under-21 caps and that Rangers league winner's medal, which is more than most footballers can boast about.

After the match we went back to the clubhouse and chatted about his time at Rangers over a dinner of pie, chips and peas. He and Paula lived in Shawlands during his time in Glasgow, and both said they loved it in the city and at the club. Obviously Chris wished he had played more games, but being plucked from Exeter by Graeme Souness to come all the way to Scotland when they were still kids was an adventure, and he had nothing but good things to say about his time at Ibrox.

As the evening wound down, Chris asked how I was getting to the airport the next morning. When I said I would be taking a bus, he insisted on driving me. I think we had converted a few more locals into bluenoses by the end of the night after regaling them with stories about the Rangers! I went back to my B&B and had my regular whisky nightcap to end a long but successful day.

Chris picked me up and took me to the airport, as he had promised, the following morning. After waving goodbye to Chris, I approached the first taxi I saw outside the terminal and gave the driver an almost full bottle of whisky. I just remembered I couldn't take liquids on in my hand luggage, so the cabbie got a great tip for doing nothing!

Paula and I still keep in touch through Facebook, and she was always interested to read about my trips to meet other players. The Vinnicombes are a genuinely nice family, and rarely have I felt as welcome on a nine-in-a-row trip as I did during my day in Devon.

Andy Goram

THERE MIGHT have been nine goalkeepers to wear the jersey during nine-in-a-row, but there was only one Goalie. Walter Smith called Andy Goram his greatest signing, no small compliment when you consider some of The Gaffer's international buys. It wasn't all smooth sailing during his seven years at Ibrox, but in a club rich with great number ones in its history, Goram might just be the best of them all.

The son of goalkeeper Lewis Goram, who played for Leith, Hibs, Third Lanark and Bury, Andy was born in the latter town in 1964 and spent his youth career with West Bromwich Albion. His first professional club was Oldham, where he played between 1981 and 1987, before following in his father's footsteps and joining Hibs. He had been there four years – and even scored a goal – when Walter made him one of his first signings after taking over in 1991. It was a surprise £1m transfer, especially considering Chris Woods was the England number one at the time. But the introduction of the three-foreigner rule in Europe, which regarded English players as foreign, forced Walter to bring in more Scots. Despite having been born in England, he qualified for Scotland through his dad and had first played for the national side six years prior to joining Rangers. He was also an international for the Scottish cricket side, just like former Rangers manager Scot Symon decades earlier, although this second sport came to an end when Goram came to Govan.

Andy had a shaky start for Rangers, conceding poor goals against Sparta Prague and Hearts, but he eventually found his form and began to show his worth. The manager stuck by him, and he played all 55 games in that debut season, achieving 26 clean sheets. He became an outstanding keeper the following campaign, the five-in-a-row season. He played every match in our famous 44-game undefeated streak, including all ten European games, during which he let in just seven goals.

His performance in the second leg of the Battle of Britain tie at Elland Road, when Leeds tried desperately to fire their way back into the contest, was an incredible display of shot-stopping. He played 34 times in the league that season and conceded just 18 goals. Perhaps his greatest game came at Pittodrie on 2 February 1993, when he refused to allow the ball to go past him no matter what Aberdeen threw his way. Rangers won 1–0. His displays over the campaign were rewarded with the SPFA and Scottish Football Writers' Association Player of the Year awards.

Unfortunately Goram became beset by injuries, primarily to his knees, and he was a virtual spectator during six-in-a-row. He played in only eight games, which came in a block between Hibs on 12 February and the goalless draw with Dundee United on 5 April. The team never lost a game in the matches he played. He was a shock addition to the transfer list by Walter at the end of that season, a disagreement about his recovery from injury coming to a head. It was enough to make Goram knuckle down and lose a stone, and a few months later he signed a four-year contract.

Seven-in-a-row looked to be going better, and he played in the first 17 games, but injury struck again and he only started one more match that season. Between 7 January 1995 and the final match away to Partick on 13 May, when he came on as a substitute, he didn't play. Season eight was another improvement. He started 30 of the 36 games and kept an incredible 20 clean sheets in those. In the classic 3–3 Old Firm game at Ibrox on 19 November 1995, he made a quite incredible save from Van Hooijdonk, a point-blank stop from a volley six yards out. He then kept eight clean sheets in a row between the 2 December away match against Hearts, which finished 2–0, and the shock 3–0 home loss to Hearts on 20 January. Included in that shut-out run was another spectacular display against Celtic, this time at Parkhead on 3 January. The game finished 0–0 despite numerous attempts from Celtic, particularly a point-blank header from Thom and a 20-yard shot from Phil O'Donnell. It was the performance that prompted Celtic manager Tommy Burns to say afterwards that 'Andy Goram broke my heart' would be written on his tombstone and called him the greatest goalkeeper he had ever seen.

The ninth campaign saw Goram make 26 league starts, a decent return again, and he kept ten clean sheets, including a pivotal one at Parkhead on 14 November, when he saved a penalty from Van Hooijdonk in the dying moments of the match to ensure we left with three points in a narrow 1–0 win. Sadly he missed the last seven league games due to injury. Like so many, he left at the end of the following season, with a record of 107 clean sheets in 258 games. He then pulled out of the 1998 Scotland World Cup squad, citing the many tabloid stories about his love life that were splashed across the front pages as the reason. Unfortunately Andy was prone to self-destruct, and articles about his personal life would often be found on the front pages of the red tops.

He was 34 when he left Ibrox, and perhaps that contributed to him not sealing a move to a club worthy of his talents. He played one game for Notts County and a handful for Sheffield United, before signing for Motherwell later in 1998 and establishing himself there. There was a fairy-tale end to the 2000/01 season, when Sir Alex Ferguson took him to Old Trafford due to a series of injuries to his goalkeepers. From playing in front of a few thousand at Fir Park, Goram was back in the big time at Old Trafford and played two league games for the Red Devils. The following season, he played a game for Hamilton and then moved to Coventry. He played a few games for old team Oldham in 2002 and then signed for Queen of the South, winning the lower-league Challenge Cup with the Dumfries side. His playing career, which included 43 Scotland caps, ended with a few appearances in Elgin City colours as he approached his 40th birthday.

Since retiring, he has worked as a goalkeeping coach on many occasions, including at Motherwell, Clyde, Hamilton, Ayr, Dunfermline and Airdrie twice, most recently in 2016. He continues to attend Rangers matches, and it was before one of those games at Ibrox that I met Andy and had him sign the shirt. Even if he had simply signed it The Goalie, everyone would know exactly who it was, and that's one of the greatest of all time.

Brian McGinty

MANY A time, I had typed a player's name into the internet and become deflated when I saw where he was now located. My next thought was usually, 'How am I going to afford this?', but that wasn't the case with Brian McGinty.

When I did an online search for him I saw he was playing for Pollock Juniors. I was staying round the corner in the Shawlands area of Glasgow at the time, so this couldn't have been easier. I looked at the fixture list, noted when their next home match was and set a reminder to go along.

McGinty came through the youth ranks at Rangers, but his career was hampered by illness and injury, with everything from a broken leg to Bell's palsy holding him back. He made three league appearances for the club. His debut came with a start against Partick Thistle at Firhill on 7 January 1995 in a seven-in-a-row fixture that finished 1–1. He then played away to Hibs during eight-in-a-row on 25 November, winning 4–1, and the following week at Tynecastle, when we defeated Hearts 2–0.

He was signed by his former teammate Mark Hateley, who was Hull boss, in 1997 and played there for two years. He then had brief stints at Scunthorpe, Airdrie, Portadown and Dumbarton, and then slipped down to the juniors with Cumnock. But then St Mirren came in for him and he was back in the professional league for six years, including a loan spell at Dundee. Brian returned to the juniors in 2007 with Irvine Meadow, where he spent four years, and then had three years with Pollock, where I spotted him. After that, he turned out for Bellshill Athletic for a season and then became their boss, leading the club to promotion from the West of Scotland Super League First Division. He left afterwards, but was back in management in March 2016 at Rossvale.

Back to 2011, and I turned up at Pollock Juniors' ground with around 20 minutes of the game remaining. I had looked at a picture of Brian online to make sure I was familiar with him and quickly spotted him marauding up front. I sought out a Pollock official and asked if it would be OK if I spoke with Brian at the end of the match; the man said just to grab him as he was coming off the pitch.

When the final whistle sounded and the players trooped off, I walked across the pitch and approached Brian. I explained what I was doing and asked if he would mind signing the shirt and taking a picture. Some of his teammates overheard the conversation and gave him some good-natured stick, especially when he held up the Rangers top for the photo. I asked if he happened to be in touch with any of the other guys I was still searching for, but he wasn't. I thanked him and let him carry on into the changing rooms. That was the only autograph from the nine-in-a-row boys that was actually signed on the field of play, which made it one to remember.

Gary Stevens

AN IMPORTANT nine-in-a-row milestone belongs to Gary Stevens – he scored the first goal on the road to glory. Another 673 would follow over the next nine years.

The right-back scored the goal just before half-time on the opening day of the season at Douglas Park, as Rangers won 2–0 against Hamilton Accies on 13 August 1988. It was also Gary's debut, having signed from Everton during the summer in a £1m transfer. He was just 25 when he came to Glasgow, but had already enjoyed incredible success at Goodison.

Originally from Barrow-in-Furness in Cumbria, he signed with the Toffees when he was 14 and broke into the first team in 1981 when he was still a teenager. He won two league titles, the FA Cup and the European Cup Winners' Cup as part of one of the club's most successful teams – the last to win the league for the blue side of Liverpool. He was also an English international, yet another one who was persuaded to come to Ibrox during the Souness Revolution.

Stevens' speed up and down that right wing was something to behold, and he was a model of consistency. He made 35 starts in the league in his debut season, missing only the last game against Aberdeen. It was the same the following year, only missing the 14 April home clash against Motherwell, which we won 2–1. In three-in-a-row, a campaign where we suffered more than our fair share of injuries, Gary topped his previous two seasons and was an ever-present, scoring four goals along the way – a double against Motherwell in a 4–2 away win in November, a strike at Ibrox in a 4–1 hiding of St Johnstone and the only goal of the game away to Dunfermline on 30 March. He carried on in this vein, playing 43 matches in the revamped league, missing the penultimate match on 28 April, a 1–1 draw at Hearts.

But then the injuries started. A stress fracture on his foot, a fragment of bone detached from his knee. He had an operation, came back, and then broke his fibula. He made just nine starts out of 44 in the five-in-a-row season, and the following year he managed 28 starts and one substitute appearance. At the beginning of the 1994/95 season he was sent to Tranmere on loan, and it was made permanent a few weeks later. It seems a real shame that injury affected him so much, because it seemed that his consistency, energy and pace could lead to him being involved for the entirety of nine-in-a-row.

The 46-times-capped defender stayed with Tranmere for four years until an ankle injury forced him to retire at 35.

He went to university and graduated with a degree in physiotherapy in 2002. He worked in the stroke unit at Ellesmere Port Hospital on the Wirral, and then moved on to Bolton's Academy and worked as a coach at Chester. But he had big plans, as I found out one Saturday afternoon outside Ibrox. A fellow autograph hunter told me in the spring of 2011 that he'd heard Gary was moving to Australia to take up a physiotherapist role. I didn't want yet another of the players to move to the other side of the world (Ian Ferguson, Stuart Munro and Craig Moore were already in Oz) before I had met him.

I decided decisive action was required. No phone calls or emails or tracking people down on Facebook. I checked the fixture list and saw Everton were next playing at home on 16 April against Blackburn. Stevens was a legend at Everton and I believed he still lived on Merseyside, so I took a punt and drove down for the match and hoped that not only would he attend the game, but I would manage to see him.

I drove down on the morning of the game. I lived in the area many years ago and knew just how hard it was to find a parking space around the ground on matchdays. I knew the places to avoid and the streets where residents would charge over the odds to give you a space, similar to how it used to be around Ibrox, when the young blokes asked if they could 'watch your car, Mister'. Good fortune shone down on me, hopefully a sign of things to come, when a woman saw me driving slowly along her street and said I could use the space outside her house. 'Your car will still be there when you come back, I promise,' she told me. I thanked her and explained I would be back before the game started.

I walked round to the stadium, the streets becoming narrower and narrower on the approach. It didn't take me too long to locate the autograph hunters. I had come to know what they looked like by now. At this time of year they tended to still be wrapped up well to combat the long hours waiting outside the grounds. But a bigger giveaway was the backpacks they all carried. These were generally packed full of books, photos and other memorabilia. These guys aren't like me – they're doing it to sell the signatures and make money. Part of me wishes I'd known about the culture earlier in life, so I could have become involved and made some cash, but on the other hand I'm thoroughly embarrassed when I see them in action. I was uncomfortable approaching the players and asking them for one autograph for my shirt, but then the professionals would pull out 20 glossy pictures and have the player sign them. You would see the footballer wasn't happy and I didn't blame them.

I knew by sticking beside these guys that I was in the right place, and now it was just a case of hoping Stevens turned up. I chatted to one of the other guys and he told me Stevens did still come to the games. Hopefully today wouldn't be one he missed. I had been waiting for maybe an hour when I heard an autograph hunter shout that he saw him approaching. By the time I spotted Gary, a few people had pushed ahead of me, but I managed to force my way in and he signed his name just before disappearing through a door into the stadium.

I was annoyed that I didn't manage to take a picture of him with the shirt or tell him what I was doing. It was one of the briefest meetings I've had with the nine-in-a-row heroes, but it least it wasn't a wasted trip. I walked back to the car and drove over to the local Rangers supporters' club, which I used to visit years before. I ended up chatting away to an old friend and slept on his couch for the night, before driving home the next morning.

Shortly afterwards, Gary and his wife moved to Australia to begin their new life. I met nine-in-a-row's first goalscorer not a moment too soon.

Kevin MacDonald

KEVIN MACDONALD was that rare thing at Rangers during nine-in-a-row – a loan player.

The midfielder was brought in during the first season by Graeme Souness on a month-long deal from Liverpool and made his debut as a substitute in a 1–0 home win against Aberdeen on 26 November 1988. He followed that up with starts in a 1–0 home defeat to Dundee United and a 2–0 loss away to Hearts over the following two weekends. And with that Kevin was on his way back to Merseyside.

His appearances for Rangers were his only professional games in Scotland, even though he was Scottish. Born in Inverness in 1960, MacDonald featured for Inverness Thistle in the Highland League, where he was picked up by Leicester in 1976. He spent eight years there before signing for Liverpool in 1984. He fought his way into the team and featured in the run-in to the First Division title triumph in 1986 and also the FA Cup Final the same year, winning the derby against Everton. But a broken leg the following season meant he was never a first-team regular again. He went back to Leicester on loan for three games in 1987 and then came to Ibrox the following year. He moved permanently to Coventry, had a loan spell at Cardiff and finished his career at Walsall.

He moved into coaching and management, becoming caretaker boss at Leicester in 1994, before taking charge of the Aston Villa reserves from 1995 to 2012. He was briefly the caretaker boss of the first team in 2010 and was the Republic of Ireland's assistant manager in 2006/07.

In February of 2013, Kevin was appointed manager of Swindon Town, and it was then I decided to make him my latest nine-in-a-row target. I checked the fixtures and saw they were playing away at Sheffield United on 13 April. I left home early on the Saturday morning and arrived at Bramall Lane in plenty of time. I waited outside the main entrance, watching for the Swindon team bus to arrive. Time passed and still there was no sign of the coach. I was beginning to worry that I had arrived after the team or they had entered from another way, but I asked the guy on the door and he told me the bus was delayed.

While I was hanging around, the Sheffield United chairman, Dave Green, came out, and when he saw me in my Rangers top he walked over and spoke to me. He was a really nice guy. After telling him why I was there, he said he would sort it out for me. The Swindon bus didn't arrive until 2.05pm, less than an hour before kick-off, so there was no chance of being able to stop Kevin for a couple of seconds when they were already well behind in their preparations. Instead Mr Green took my strip and camera and disappeared inside. A little while later he came back out with both, job done. He invited me in to watch the game but I declined as I was heading to Leeds to see my daughter. The meeting hadn't worked out quite how I'd hoped, but at least I left with the signature and photograph.

As for Kevin, he departed Swindon in the close season and ended up back at Villa, first as assistant and then once again the caretaker manager in 2015.

Graeme Souness

GRAEME SOUNESS'S on-the-field influence was minimal by the time nine-in-a-row began, but the same thankfully can't be said for off the pitch. The manager had swept into Glasgow like a hurricane on 8 April 1986, thanks to a visionary move by majority shareholder Lawrence Marlborough and chairman David Holmes. They knew something big was required to shake the club out of its long slumber. Souness was all that and more. He was a genuine world-class player, one who had yet to celebrate his 33rd birthday when he was unveiled. These were genuinely exciting times, and he more than lived up to his billing, kicking off the Rangers Revolution by signing what felt like half the England international squad and also playing his part on the field as he guided us to the championship in his first season.

He played 25 times in the league in that 1986/87 season, 32 games overall, and scored three goals. He would have played more had he not incurred a three-match ban and a £5,000 fine for his challenge on George McCluskey of Hibs on the opening day. The following season he made 18 league appearances, 30 in total, and scored two goals. But by 1988/89, the first of the nine, he was affected by a calf injury and made just six appearances from the bench. Those came in the goalless home draw against Hibs on 20 August, the famous 5–1 demolition of Celtic at Ibrox the following week (many observers felt he slowed the game down, when fans were clamouring for more goals), the 2–1 away win over Hearts on 17 September and the 2–1 home victory against St Mirren the next Saturday. His other appearances were at home to Hibs in the 17 December 1–0 win and in the 2–0 Ibrox triumph against Dundee United on 2 May. During two-in-a-row he made just one sub appearance, in the 2–0 home win over Dunfermline on 28 April 1990.

It brought an end to a long and triumphant playing career that began with North Merchiston and Tynecastle boys' clubs in his home city of Edinburgh. He was signed by Tottenham Hotspur and moved to London when he was just 17, but in his two years there he only made one European appearance, although he did have a successful loan spell in North America with Montreal Olympique. He moved to Middlesbrough, where he established himself as a truly gifted midfielder in his six-year spell, which included a short loan move to Australia with West Adelaide. His form earned a move to Liverpool, where he became an all-time great for the Anfield side, lifting trophies galore in one of the club's greatest teams. After six years on Merseyside, he moved to Italy with Sampdoria in 1984, where he remained until he took over at Rangers in the summer of 1986. Before he turned his attention fully to his new challenge, however, he had the small matter of a World Cup to play in, his fourth finals in a Scotland career that included 54 caps and four goals.

Graeme might no longer have been pulling the strings in the middle of the park, but he continued to be as similarly combative in his management style. Jan Bartram, Graham Roberts, Terry Butcher and Derek Ferguson were some of the big names who clashed with the boss and found themselves looking for new clubs, while the likes of Scott Nisbet and Ally McCoist barely held on. As written about elsewhere in this book, his signing of Mo Johnston in 1989 was the biggest in Scottish football history.

He often fell foul of the officials too. On 11 February 1989, he lost the head when Dundee United scored an equaliser deep into injury time, and clashed with a linesman. He was fined £100 and banned from the touchline for the rest of the season. When he was then spotted running down the tunnel twice to pass on instructions during the Scottish Cup semi-final clash with St Johnstone two months later, he was fined £2,000 and banned from the touchline until the end of the following season. It seemed over the top and was compounded when Walter was also given a year's ban for an argument with a linesman.

Six weeks before he left the club, Souey had an argument with St Johnstone's tea lady, Aggie Moffat, who said the team had left the away dressing room in a mess. It was yet another story that made the front pages and must surely have made him feel like everyone in Scottish football was out to get him. He was at breaking point by then and, when the Liverpool job became available, he decided to escape the goldfish bowl of Scottish football and return to his old club as boss. David Murray told him he was making the biggest blunder of his life and the chairman was proved right.

During his three years at Liverpool, he only managed to win one trophy, the FA Cup. He also underwent triple heart bypass surgery a year after leaving Ibrox. After a spell out of football, he became manager of Galatasaray in 1995, and during his one season in Turkey he guided them to the cup, beating Fenerbahce on their bitter rivals' own pitch and almost causing a riot when he planted a Galatasaray flag in the centre circle after the game. He moved on to Southampton for a brief spell and then had an even shorter time at Torino, before bossing Benfica from 1997 to 1999. He returned to England again to take over at Blackburn in 2000, staying there for four years, and finally managed Newcastle United between 2004 and 2006.

He was snubbed for the Scotland management job and has since said he will never become a manager again. Instead he has shaped himself into one of Sky Sports' most respected and in-demand football analysts. He did try to become involved in the Rangers takeover during our dark days, teaming up with Scottish businessman Brian Kennedy in May 2012 to launch a bid. If they had been successful, he intended to come back as director of football, but as we all know it didn't work out. He continues to keep an eye on affairs at Ibrox and comes north occasionally for events.

It was during one of those occasions that I met him. I read he was going to be attending the Rangers Hall of Fame dinner at the Hilton, so it was just a case of turning up at the venue and biding my time. The foyer of the Hilton is fairly large, but it's square-shaped, and the lifts, three of them, are against the back wall, so it's relatively easy to keep an eye on comings and goings. As always when I attended these functions, I dressed a little more smartly to blend in. Security and management at the hotel is pretty tight compared with some places, so there weren't a lot of autograph hunters swarming around. I still needed to have my wits about me to ensure I didn't miss him in the crowd, though.

I didn't have too long to wait. He emerged from a lift with a youngster who appeared to be his son, and I quickly approached him. Others saw him too, so it was all over in a flash – a signature, quick photograph, thanks, and off he went to speak to someone else who had called his name. I made my way out of the Hilton happy and proud to have met the man who revolutionised the Rangers, brought back the glory years and kicked off the march to nine-in-a-row.

Mark Walters

DURING ONE of my many 'wait and see' vigils outside Ibrox on matchdays, I was lucky enough to meet Mark Walters, one of the most skilful players to wear the jersey during nine-in-a-row.

I had no idea the Birmingham-born ex-winger was coming to the game, but as soon as I saw him stepping out of the taxi a few yards from where I was standing, I was glad I had turned up early with the shirt. My alertness saw me at the front of the crowd that quickly formed around him, and I was first to get his signature and a photograph.

Mark spent the first six years of his career at Aston Villa before joining the Gers as a 23-year-old on Hogmanay 1987. He was pitched into action just days later in the derby at Parkhead. Rangers lost the game 2–0, but the result paled into insignificance compared with the treatment meted out to Walters. Monkey noises could be heard coming from the stands housing the home support, and the second half had to be delayed while the bananas that had been thrown were cleared from the park and pitchside. It was disgraceful. Two weeks later, at Tynecastle, it was arguably even worse. Walters showed he was made of stern stuff by not letting the horrendous racist abuse get the better of him, and he quickly became a fans' favourite thanks to his runs down the wing, which invariably included a double shuffle and ended with a cross whipped into the box.

He didn't just set up the strikers. Averaging a goal nearly every three games, Walters played a big role in the first three title successes on the road to nine. He made 83 league starts and five sub appearances during the nine-in-a-row years, scoring 25 goals.

In the first season, 1988/89, he started 30 matches, came off the bench once and scored eight goals – half of which came against Celtic.

The first was in the 5–1 demolition at Ibrox on 27 August; he then scored the goal in the 3–1 defeat at Parkhead on 12 November and netted a double in the 4–1 win at home on 3 January. His others came in two matches against St Mirren, and versus Dundee and Hearts, all at home. He made 27 starts in two-in-a-row and struck five goals, netting against Dundee, Hearts, Aberdeen, Dundee United and Celtic again, slotting one away in the April Fools' Day game at Ibrox. Mark provided his best goal return in season three, scoring 12 from 26 starts and four substitute appearances. His first was on the opening day of the season in the 3–1 defeat of Dunfermline on 25 August, and he struck doubles against St Mirren and St Johnstone. He scored in two Hearts games, struck against Hibs, Motherwell, Dundee United, and St Mirren again, and put away a famous goal on 2 January against Celtic, scoring direct from a corner kick at the Broomloan Road end of the ground. Perhaps his most important contribution came in the winner-takes-all final match against Aberdeen, when he set up Mark Hateley's opening goal with a high, swinging left-foot cross from deep.

It would be his final great contribution to the Rangers cause. Shortly after he won his only England cap (although he already had a B cap and nine under-21 caps) in June 1991, he left Rangers to follow the recently departed Graeme Souness to Liverpool. He spent five years at Anfield, although this included loans to Stoke and Wolves. Following a brief spell at Southampton, he moved down the leagues to Swindon Town, where he played for three years, and then switched to Bristol Rovers for another three years, only retiring in 2002 at 38 and bringing to an end a great 21-year professional playing career.

Mark began coaching kids the following year at Coventry Preparatory School and also at Aston Villa's Academy. He gained teaching qualifications and became head of languages at the Academy, worked with various groups trying to eliminate racism from football and also turned his hand to being a property landlord. From time to time he also dazzled Rangers fans once more in the Masters seven-a-side indoor events, showing age hadn't robbed him of his trademark shuffling skills.

Lee Robertson

I HAD just spent the night in a place I never thought I would end up – a homeless hostel.

Not that I knew it was for the homeless when I booked the room, I hasten to add. I'd quickly made the reservation online when I saw how cheap it was and its prime location. It was only when I arrived at the hostel that I was informed of the plight of most of my new neighbours. The manager who checked me in told me it was also used as homeless accommodation and I shouldn't leave anything unattended in the kitchen, because it would be gone as quickly as I could blink. One look in the kitchen and I knew I wouldn't be spending much time in there anyway – it was nasty. I wasn't impressed at only finding this out upon my arrival, but the other blokes seemed decent enough – nothing worse than you would encounter from earthy guys in Glasgow – and my room was clean enough. It was just for one night and I managed to get a decent sleep, so I couldn't complain too much. But never let it be said I make these trips in luxury!

I was in a town called Haugesund in the south of Norway, and I was here to meet the next name on my list. I'd told him in advance where I was staying and my room number, so he said it would be easier if he came to me. Just then there was a knock on the door. I opened it and there was a well-built guy with long dark hair and a bushy beard standing in the doorway.

'Yes?' I said.

'John?'

'Yeah.' I still had no idea who this was. Who are you and how do you know my name, I was thinking.

'It's Lee,' he responded.

Never in a million years would I have guessed this was Lee Robertson, who I'd last seen as a fresh-faced youth trying to break through from the youth ranks into Rangers' first team. Like so many of the young players coming up through the system at the time, Lee found it nearly impossible to make it at Ibrox. The pressure that Walter Smith and the rest of the management team found themselves under to deliver nine-in-a-row meant very few opportunities were presented to the young guys, and instead established talent from across Britain and Europe was brought in.

Edinburgh boy Lee was signed from well-respected Salvesen Boys' Club in the capital, and the midfielder was on the fringes of the first-team squad for several years. In total he made two league starts and a substitute appearance for Rangers. The first was in the second-last game of the four-in-a-row season, on 28 April 1992, in a 1–1 home draw with Hearts. His second start came in the exact same period the following season, this time in a 1–0 defeat away to Aberdeen on 12 May 1993. His final appearance saw him come off the bench away to Kilmarnock on 20 April 1995, the fourth-last match of seven-in-a-row, and saw him finally experience a league win in a narrow 1–0 victory.

Just before the nine-in-a-row season began, in the summer of 1996, Walter Smith came to Lee and told him there was interest from Norway and recommended he make the move. Lee was about to turn 23, and it was time to be playing first-team football regularly. He left on a free and joined IK Start, then moved on to Molde and joined his third Norwegian club, Glimt, in 1997. Two years later he had a week-long trial back home with St Johnstone, but due to heavy snow he wasn't able to take part in a bounce game and returned to Norway unable to showcase his talents. He re-signed with IK Start and then moved to Australia briefly, before finishing his career with a single appearance for Morton in a 2–1 win against Albion Rovers in January 2003.

The five-times-capped Scotland under-21 player had met his Norwegian wife, Ann, in his adopted homeland, and so remained there after he retired. He worked as a greenkeeper on a golf course for a while, but by the time I spoke to his mum, Sheila, he was working as a kindergarten teacher for kids with learning disabilities. Sheila had read a newspaper article about me and noticed Lee was still on my list of players to track down. She got my number from the paper and called me up, telling me exactly where her son was and that he would be happy to meet me.

It was the winter of 2013 and I managed to book cheap return flights through Ryanair from London for just £57. All had gone well, despite the revelation about the living quarters, and Lee, who turned out to be an absolutely cracking bloke, was here to see me. We had a chat, and he signed the top and took some pictures and then said he was taking me out for dinner. Although he's fluent in Norwegian, he told me he enjoyed being able to chat to a fellow Scot for a change. We talked about his time at Rangers, and he showed me a prized picture of him on the park with Goughie, clutching the league trophy.

Lee had to work the next morning but insisted that Ann come by the hostel and take me to the airport so I wouldn't have any hassle getting there. She was really nice too, and I noticed she had picked up Lee's Edinburgh accent when speaking English. Ann dropped me off at the tiny airport, where there is only enough space for four aeroplanes, and I went inside to check in.

I wasn't too concerned when I saw on the information screen that the flight was delayed. I waited and waited until finally the screen was updated. The flight was cancelled. An announcement was made over the tannoy, but it was in Norwegian, so I had no idea what was going on.

The fact that everyone around me stood up and began to leave wasn't a good sign. I went over to the information desk and asked what was happening.

'The plane can't come in to land because it's too windy,' the lady told me.

'Other planes have been landing and departing while I've sat here,' I replied, but she told me Ryanair had decided the weather was too severe.

'So when's the next flight?'

I could barely believe the response.

'Tuesday,' she said.

It was currently Wednesday.

I could feel myself beginning to sweat and my heart was racing. I was panicking. I only had enough medication for the one day and I wouldn't be a well man if I missed days and days of my tablets.

'What's the alternative?' I asked. 'There must be another flight company travelling to the UK before next Tuesday.'

She checked the computer and there was a flight with Norwegian Air to London via Oslo the next day. Thank God, I thought, that's not too bad.

And then she hit me with another hammer blow. 'It will cost £600.'

I didn't have that sort of money. I had spent less than £100 in travel and accommodation up until this point, and now I was looking at a bill six times that amount just to get home a day late. And I had no travel insurance.

I broke out in a cold sweat. This was a nightmare. The only thing I could think to do was call my nephew, Andy, my biggest supporter when it came to the nine-in-a-row mission, and explain to him. He immediately said he would pay for it and told me to go back into the town centre and find a room for the night. I caught the last bus from the airport and then walked through torrential wind and rain back to the hostel. I had barely any money and I didn't know where else was available so cheap, so although I had no wish to go back to what was effectively a homeless shelter, I felt I didn't have a choice. It was the same receptionist from earlier, who I had given a half bottle of whisky to because I knew I couldn't take it on the flight. Once I explained and he booked me in for another night, he asked if I wanted my whisky back. Damn right I do, after the day I've had.

The next morning I returned to the airport and was relieved to find the flight was on schedule. As I stood in line at security, I put my hand into my pocket for my passport. It wasn't there. What have I done with it? I felt myself beginning to panic again. Had I left it in the hostel? Had I dropped it or had it been stolen? I quickly searched through my pockets and then put down my bag and unzipped it. I only had a few items inside and there was no sign of the passport. I looked in the zipped compartments, but it wasn't there. I couldn't believe this. Andrew had spent £600 on flights and I wasn't going to be able to board the plane because I had lost my passport. I had no money, no medication and I was exhausted.

A female security guard saw me frantically searching through the bag and came over. I tried to explain, but could barely get the words out because I'd started crying. The last couple of days had all become too much. The woman kneeled down beside me and looked through the case.

'What's that?' she asked, pointing at the nine-in-a-row shirt. Before I responded she picked it up and unfolded it, and my passport came tumbling out. I had hidden it in the strip for safekeeping while I was in the hostel and had forgotten. I've never felt such relief. I thanked her and finally made my way through security and on board. I collapsed in the chair, exhausted. I asked the man sitting next to me on the plane to take a picture so that I could send it to my nephew and let him know I was on my way home, all thanks to him.

I had a few hours to wait in Oslo and then it was on to London. From London, I took a flight to Edinburgh, where my saviour, Andy, had driven through to pick me up. I finally arrived home in Glasgow shortly after midnight.

What a couple of days. I can just about talk about it now without breaking into a cold sweat, but, apart from my first trip to Ukraine, this was the worst of my travels. Although it didn't feel like it at the time, it was all worth it. The hostel, the cancelled flights, the expense, the extra night's stay, the panic, stress and upset, every minute of it, because it hadn't just led to me meeting another of the players – it had also been my introduction to a really nice guy and his wife. In fact, I still keep in touch with Lee and his mum, Sheila, to this day. And that encapsulates the special breed of person that is the Gers' nine-in-a-row squad.

Nicky Walker and Davie Kirkwood

TRACKING DOWN a former player to a shortbread factory sounds like there would be a real story attached to it, but Nicky Walker was just about the easiest of the nine-in-a-row squad no longer involved in the game to locate. That's because Nicky is part of the famous Walkers Shortbread family who have been producing the sweet treats from their home town of Aberlour since 1898. I called the factory and was put through to Nicky, and we arranged a date when I would drive up and meet him. With my German Shepherd, Tilly, keeping me company on the long journey, I jumped in the car early one morning and made the long trek north.

Joseph Nicol Walker was born in 1962, the great-grandson of the founder of the family business, also named Joseph. He played with his local team, Aberlour Villa, and then made the switch to Elgin in the Highland League as a youth, where he was spotted by the legendary Jock Wallace. Big Jock took Nicky to Leicester in 1981, and he made his debut against Chelsea at Stamford Bridge. He made six league appearances before he followed Jock to Motherwell, making 30 league starts in the 1982/83 season. When Rangers called on Wallace to return to Ibrox and attempt to revive the club's fortunes during the stagnant early eighties, Nicky once again followed his boss and signed on at Ibrox.

He wasn't an automatic starter at first, but had established himself as number one by the time of the arrival of Graeme Souness, who promptly signed Chris Woods. Therefore Nicky had to settle for being back-up, although he did play in the famous League Cup Final penalty shoot-out victory over Aberdeen in 1987. He made 12 league appearances in the nine-in-a-row years, all coming in the first season. He played in the 3–1 home win to Hamilton Accies on 16 November and then featured in the following 11 league games, including the famous New Year's game versus Celtic when we won 4–1 at Ibrox on 3 January 1989, with goals from Gough and Butcher and a Walters double doing the damage.

Following a couple of brief loan spells, Walker left Rangers in 1990 and signed for Hearts, where he tussled with Henry Smith for the number one jersey. It was during his time at Tynecastle that he won his first Scotland cap, playing against Germany in March 1993 at, appropriately, Ibrox. He spent four years in Edinburgh, including a loan spell with Burnley, and then moved to Partick Thistle, where he had a good spell, picking up his second cap with a substitute appearance against the USA. He moved to Aberdeen for a season, but turned down an extended contract in order to go part-time with Ross County and begin to learn the family business from his dad. He spent four years with the Dingwall team, had a brief spell back with Aberlour Villa and then moved on to Inverness Caledonian Thistle for a year, retiring shortly before his 40th birthday to concentrate fully on the family business.

I spent an hour with Nicky and he was a lovely guy. We had a chat about football and he told me how he now spends much of his time travelling to countries like America and Canada promoting the company's products. We were sitting outside the office on a wall when I realised we had disturbed a wasps' nest in a nearby bush and I saw a swarm of them coming towards us. I pulled Nicky away and told him to watch his back. If we hadn't moved when we did we would have been treating a few stings. Luckily we escaped unharmed and, before I carried on further north, where I had another meeting arranged, Nicky made sure I wouldn't be doing the next part of the journey without some snacks and presented me with a bag packed full of goodies from his factory.

Nicky could have gone straight into the family business, but instead he followed his passion and lived a life so many of us can only dream of – pulling on the colours of the famous Rangers.

Tilly and I got back in the car and continued northwards on another three-hour-plus drive as we made our way to Wick. Awaiting us was former midfielder Davie Kirkwood, who was now manager of Wick Academy.

Davie was signed from East Fife by Graeme Souness when he was 19, having made his debut – and scored – for the Methil club when he was just 16 and still at school. Rangers had previously tried to sign him just before his first match, but it couldn't happen because he was on an S form at East Fife. Davie learned his deal to Rangers was agreed when he was in class at Fife College, studying electronic engineering, and journalists turned up asking him what he thought about signing. What a way to find out! On his way through to Glasgow he had to stop in Kirkcaldy to buy a suit and have a haircut to fit in with Rangers' strict rules.

He made his debut in the final game of the 1986/87 season against St Mirren, but found it tough to make the breakthrough in Glasgow as there were so many talented midfielders ahead of him. He only featured twice in the nine-in-a-row campaign, at the end of the first season, with starts against Dundee United in a 2–0 home win on 2 May and a 2–1 victory at Dundee four days later. He also came on as a sub in the famous European Cup games against Dynamo Kiev, but, after a short loan spell back at East Fife, his time at Ibrox was coming to an end.

He moved to Hearts in a £100,000 transfer, where he spent a season, and then played with Airdrie for four years. He turned out for the Lanarkshire team against Rangers in the Scottish Cup Final in 1992 and then moved to Raith Rovers for the final six years of his career. He featured in the Kirkcaldy club's famous European match against Bayern Munich, but by that point he was being bothered by a knee injury, which cut his playing days short.

The Scotland under-21 cap returned to Rangers as part of the youth coaching department in the 2002/03 season and enjoyed greater success in this role than he had done in his playing days at Ibrox. Under his watch, future first-team players Allan McGregor, Alan Hutton, Chris Burke, Ross McCormack and Stevie Smith all made their breakthrough. He later took charge of the Ross County youths and then became manager of Wick, where he spent a season before moving on to Brora Rangers, spending three years there before quitting in order to devote more time to the taxi company he had bought into in the Black Isle.

I had called Wick Academy and spoken to the chairman, who told me it would be fine to come up on a matchday and meet Davie. I arranged to meet him outside the ground, where he signed my top and I took a photograph. We had a quick chat, but he had to go in and prepare for the game.

Since I had Tilly with me, I didn't bother waiting for the match. Instead I went for something to eat and began the long drive south. We stopped partway, pulling off to a side road out in the country, the middle of nowhere, and settled down for the night in pitch-black surroundings. Anything could have been out there and I wouldn't have had a clue. At least I had Tilly with me. Not that she helped me get much sleep – she snores and was particularly loud that night! Bleary-eyed, I gathered myself together at dawn, had a quick bite to eat, and continued on back to Glasgow, powered by the sugar rush of Walkers Shortbread.

Neale Cooper

NEALE COOPER made his Rangers debut on one of the darkest days of the nine-in-a-row years.

It was 8 October 1988, just two months into the first season of the nine, and Rangers were playing Aberdeen at Pittodrie. The rivalry between the two teams was already fierce, but this match took it to a new level and in some ways it's now worse than the Old Firm matches. This was the day of Neil Simpson's sickening challenge on Ian Durrant, which left the hugely gifted young midfielder's knee and career hanging by a thread. It was a vicious challenge by Simpson, the worst incident in 90 minutes of thuggery from the Aberdeen team that went unpunished by referee Louis Thow. Cooper had actually just won the ball in a sliding tackle on the edge of the Rangers box, but was barged off it, and the loose ball was picked up by Durrant. When Simpson charged at him, Durrant's leg buckled under the strain of the assault and he was carried off in agony.

Later in the first half, Cooper was booked after reacting badly to yet another shocking challenge from Stewart McKimmie on Mark Walters, who was replaced at half-time by Davie Cooper due to the way he was being treated. Five minutes before half-time, however, Cooper opened the scoring, hitting a terrific right-foot shot from outside the box after a knockdown from a corner. He celebrated the goal with some gusto, no doubt due to the abuse he'd been taking from the home support.

You see, Cooper was an Aberdeen legend who had been part of Alex Ferguson's dominant side of the early eighties. He won two titles, four Scottish Cups, a League Cup, a European Cup Winners' Cup and a European Super Cup during his career in the north-east. Born in Darjeeling, India in 1963, he moved to Aberdeen at an early age and came through the ranks with his home-town team, even working as a ballboy when he was a kid. He made his debut as a 16-year-old defender in 1980, replacing the injured Willie Miller, but there was no way he was going to split up the Miller–McLeish backline, so Ferguson reinvented him as a defensive midfielder and it was here he became an integral part of the successful team.

He moved south in 1986 to Aston Villa and spent two seasons there, but the move didn't work out, and when Graeme Souness came calling he returned to Scotland. He still hasn't been forgiven by many Aberdeen fans for moving to Rangers, but he never hid during those matches against his old team, and he played his part in that first title success in the nine-in-a-row years. After that Aberdeen game, which we lost 2–1, Neale played in eight of the next nine league matches, including a 3–1 away loss to Celtic and, on 26 November, a 1–0 home win against Aberdeen, which must have been sweet. He also came on as a sub in the New Year game against Celtic, which we romped 4–1, and came off the bench at Pittodrie as we won 2–1. The following season wasn't so prolific for Neale. He made two starts – an away defeat to Motherwell on 3 October and the home win against Dundee United 11 days later – and a sub's shift in the final game of the season away to Hearts on 5 May 1990, which finished 1–1.

He made 17 appearances for Rangers before moving on, returning to Aberdeen but failing to feature due to injury. He spent a brief spell at Reading and then moved to Dunfermline, where he spent five productive years, and then the 13-times under-21 cap played two seasons at Ross County, where he was also manager. He left the Highlands in 2002 and then took up the reins at Hartlepool for two years. He was Gillingham manager in 2005 and then Peterhead boss from 2008 to 2011, before returning to Hartlepool midway through the 2011/12 season.

And that's where I met him. I called the club, spoke to his PA and told her why I wanted to meet Neale. She spoke to him and called me back later to say he would be happy for me to come down. I had a look at the fixtures and saw the team had an away match at Bradford coming up, so I called back and asked when they would likely be leaving to head south. I was told it would be 7.30am, so I said I would be at the stadium before then.

I drove to the north-east coastal town on the Friday evening and stayed in a bed and breakfast just 500 yards or so from the football ground. The next morning I woke at the crack of dawn and made my way along to the stadium. I was there in plenty of time, before the players or the bus.

When I saw Cooper coming out of the ground a half hour or so later, I walked over to him and introduced myself. He greeted me like his long-lost brother and gave me a big squeeze, like a bear hug. He was the most down-to-earth person I've met and he asked me all about my mission. He told me, in a nice way, that he thought I was mad. He wasn't the first and wouldn't be the last to say that!

He signed the shirt, I took a picture, and then it was time for him to get on the bus.

I also had to be on my way, because, as I explained to Neale, this was just the start of my day. I had another player to meet and autograph to collect, and I only had a small window of opportunity to make it happen. There was no time to spare, so it was back in the car for the next leg of my journey.

Chris Woods

I WAS on a cross-country drive to Liverpool to meet Chris Woods at Everton's Goodison Park ground, where he was the long-term goalkeeping coach.

When I saw they were playing at home on the same day I was going to be at Hartlepool, I aimed to strike off two in one trip. The helpful lady I talked to at Everton a couple of weeks earlier checked and confirmed it was fine to visit that day, but added that I should be aware that the manager, David Moyes, had a cut-off point before games when the door was closed and no one was able to come or go. I was advised that if I arrived after that time, I wouldn't be able to have the shirt signed. I estimated that it gave me a half-hour window before the door was slammed shut.

What a goalkeeper Chris Woods was. He arrived at Ibrox as part of the original English Invasion soon after Graeme Souness took over in 1986 and helped return the league title to Rangers after too many years away. He also set a new British shut-out record between November and January of that season, when he went 1,196 competitive minutes without conceding a goal. He moved to Glasgow in a £600,000 transfer from Norwich, where he had enjoyed five years, but his career began ten years before he came to Scotland. He was 16 when he joined Nottingham Forest, and within a year he was the understudy to the newly signed Peter Shilton. It was a position with which he was to become all too familiar on international duty. Although he never played a league game for Forest, he did pick up a League Cup medal in the 1977/78 season, keeping a clean sheet in the final and replay. He also has a European Cup medal thanks to being on the bench.

At 19, he moved to Queens Park Rangers in a £250,000 move – a hefty sum in 1979 – and was installed as first-choice number one. From there he went to Norwich and then Rangers. He was an instant favourite at Ibrox and was part of a solid line of defence that also included world-class players like Terry Butcher and Richard Gough. If a team engineered a chance that beat those two, then more often than not Woods would be there to clear the danger. He was a great all-round keeper and had no real weaknesses.

Woods didn't play as often as he would have liked in the first of the nine-in-a-row seasons, as he came down with labyrinthitis, an infection that affects balance, and he missed 12 games in the middle of the campaign. The following season he played 32 of 36 games, and in three-in-a-row he was an ever-present. So that made it all the more surprising when he was sold in the summer by new manager Walter Smith, who had taken over just a few games before the end of the season. As mentioned earlier, Andy Goram, a Scottish international, was brought in from Hibs due to UEFA's three-foreigner rule for European competition. Rangers had lots of English players and Walter had to reduce the number. Clearly he thought it was better to keep outfield players, but it was a real loss and Goram took a while to fill Woods' gloves.

He moved on to Sheffield Wednesday, where he spent five years, including a loan at Reading, and then spent a season at Colorado Rapids in America. He had a loan at Southampton and a brief spell at Sunderland, before ending his playing career in the 1997/98 season at Burnley. Woods also had a strong international career and could have had much more than the 43 caps he achieved between 1985 and 1993 had it not been for Peter Shilton, who was regarded as the country's number one even in his later years. He was behind Shilton in the pecking order at the World Cups in 1986 and 1990 and also the Euros in 1988, although he did play one game in that tournament. He was number one by the time Euro '92 happened and kept two clean sheets in the opening two games, but England were knocked out at the group stage.

He became goalkeeper coach at Everton, working under old gaffer Walter Smith at first. He spent many years there, only moving on when he followed David Moyes to Manchester United. In 2015 he was named West Ham's goalie coach.

Back to Everton, and I turned up at Goodison in plenty of time and made my way to the players' entrance. I explained why I was there and was allowed in, but then had to wait in the foyer for someone to come for me. I watched lots of club legends arrive, including former manager, the late Howard Kendall, the man who guided the team to its greatest success in the eighties. A woman approached me and said she would take the shirt and have it signed. I asked if it would be possible for me to come as well and meet Chris. She said no, so I explained I needed a picture of him with the strip after he signed it. There was some toing and froing and eventually she said she would take a picture for me, but it wouldn't be possible for me to meet him.

A few minutes later, I was asked to follow her and another member of staff and we made our way under the stand to the dressing room. I thought maybe they had relented and I was going to meet him after all. When we reached the dressing room door, the woman took the shirt and camera from me and asked me to wait while she went inside. A minute later, she reappeared and returned them to me. I don't blame Chris for what happened – he likely knew nothing about it until he was handed the shirt to sign and probably had no clue I was standing on the other side of the door – but it was a disappointing conclusion having travelled all that way, especially when it was organised in advance.

With my shirt and camera tucked safely back in my plastic bag, I left the stadium and returned to my car. It had been a long and exhausting day – not to mention an expensive one due to the fuel bill – so I made my way to my daughter's house in Leeds and spent the night there, before concluding the epic trip the following morning.

Ally McCoist

WHAT MORE can be said about Ally McCoist the footballer?

Rangers' greatest-ever goalscorer, one of the most famous players in our history and a hero to hundreds of thousands of fans around the world.

He scored 355 goals for the club, won two European Golden Boots – the first player to win the accolade in back-to-back seasons – and developed a lethal striking partnership with Mark Hateley that went a long way towards nine-in-a-row.

And he did it all with a smile on his face and an infectious sense of humour.

The striker from East Kilbride, Lanarkshire, was born in September 1962 and played for Fir Park Boys' Club before signing with St Johnstone in 1979. His form saw him attract the interest of a number of clubs by 1981, including Rangers, but he signed with Sunderland for £400,000 while still a teenager. The move seemed to come too soon for him, however, and his scoring record was poor. In 1983, John Greig brought him back north for £185,000. It might have been the best money a Rangers manager ever spent.

Ally scored on his opening day debut versus St Mirren, but took time to settle and went through a tough period where the fans were on his back, so much so that it looked like his long-term future might not be at Rangers. But he knuckled down, scored a hat-trick in the Old Firm League Cup Final win and ended the 1983/84 season with 20 goals. The next campaign he scored 18, he fired 27 in 1985/86 and he was an ever-present in all competitions in Graeme Souness's first season as boss, scoring 38 goals. In 1987/88 he scored 31 league goals and 42 in all competitions.

His nine-in-a-row record stands at 184 starts, 47 substitute appearances and 137 goals. If injury hadn't hit hard, there is no doubt those figures would have been much higher.

In the 1988/89 campaign he made 18 starts and one appearance from the bench, and scored ten goals, including two in the famous demolition of Celtic in the 5–1 game on 27 August and another in the 2–1 away victory in April. He also scored the only goal away to Hibs on 12 October and at home to Motherwell on 8 April. He missed just two games during two-in-a-row: a match at Dundee on 3 March that finished 2–2, and the goalless draw against St Mirren two weeks later. He also came on as a sub twice and scored 14 goals that campaign. It was during three-in-a-row that McCoist found himself on the periphery of the team. His relationship with Souness seemed to sour as the manager chose a front two of Hateley and Johnston. He even publicly reprimanded the striker for going to the Cheltenham races in March of 1991. Ally gained the nickname of The Judge that season due to the amount of time he spent on the bench, but still managed to put a smile on the frustrating situation, coming down the tunnel one afternoon with a teapot to keep himself warm on the sidelines. He started 15 games and appeared in a further 11 as a substitute, scoring 11 goals. He scored a memorable double against Aberdeen at Ibrox on 22 December, including a stunning volley from the edge of the box, in a game that finished 2–2. He was injured towards the end of the season and missed six games in the nerve-shredding run-in, but did come on as a sub in the final match against Aberdeen.

With Walter Smith in place as boss, Super Ally was reinstated as the number nine alongside Mark Hateley for four-in-a-row. He only made two starts and a sub appearance in the first nine games due to injury, but then played every game from the 4–0 away drubbing of Airdrie on 5 October until the end of the season. In the 44-game campaign he scored 34 goals in 37 starts. He scored a double in that Airdrie match, one of three consecutive braces, with the others coming against Hibs and St Johnstone. In total, he scored eight doubles in the league, including in the final-day 2–0 win at Pittodrie on 2 May, and fired a hat-trick in the 4–1 victory over Falkirk at home on 7 April. His overall total of 39 goals saw him win the Golden Boot, outscoring the rest of Europe's strikers, and he won both the Players' Player of the Year and Sportswriters' Player of the Year awards.

If that was a good season, five-in-a-row was outstanding – at least until April. Again, it was a 44-game season and he started 32 and appeared twice as a sub. He was sitting on 39 league goals and 49 overall when he broke his leg while playing for Scotland in Portugal with seven games of the season left. There is little doubt he would have smashed through the 50-goal mark, but he still won his second Golden Boot despite the horrific end to the campaign. Before the injury he was unstoppable. He scored a double in the shock 4–3 defeat to Dundee at Dens Park on 15 August 1992, which was the last time we would lose in 44 games. He was proud to be made captain for the day in Richard Gough's absence against Dundee United on 26 September, and scored. He was given the armband the following weekend against Falkirk and scored all the goals in the 4–0 win. Those were part of a run of 12 goals in six matches, which he joked was his best scoring run since he struck 11 in seven with the Boys' Brigade. Between September and November he bagged 15 in nine. Who can forget his goals in both legs of the Battle of Britain, especially the counter-attack in the second leg at Elland Road that ended with a diving header and effectively killed the tie against Leeds? For his season to end in such cruel fashion was a real blow, and, truth be told, it carried over into the next two campaigns as a series of niggling injuries kicked in as he tried to return to full fitness.

He made 16 starts and five substitute appearances in six-in-a-row, striking seven goals. His first appearance was on 2 October, away to Raith Rovers. He scored in the 2–1 defeat against Celtic on 30 October at Ibrox and struck a double at home to Dundee in a 3–1 win on 10 November, but his most important goal that season – and one of the most memorable of his career – came not in the league but in the League Cup Final against Hibs, the week before he scored in the Old Firm game. He was sent on by Walter with the score locked at 1–1 and struck a magnificent overhead kick to win the cup. Unfortunately he picked up another injury after the Dundee match and was out until an appearance from the bench against Hibs in a 2–0 home win on 12 February. He scored in 2–1 away wins over Hearts and Partick on 26 and 29 March, against Raith Rovers in a 4–0 win at Ibrox on 16 April and finally in the 2–1 loss away to Motherwell on 26 April.

Seven-in-a-row was almost a non-starter due to injuries. He made just nine appearances, including only four starts, and scored a solitary goal, in the 1–0 home win on 25 November against Aberdeen. Between his start away to Dundee United on 4 December and the end of the season, he made just one substitute appearance, again versus Dundee United, in a 1–1 stalemate on 4 February. A month into eight-in-a-row, Ally turned 33. Coupled with his injuries over the previous two campaigns, it would have been understandable if he had slowly petered out. Instead, he had a return to form that saw him score 16 league goals in 18 starts and seven appearances from the bench. He struck doubles in victories over Raith Rovers and twice against Falkirk, and scored a hat-trick in an exciting 4–2 match away to Raith on 30 March, when we came from behind. He also scored in the 3–3 classic Old Firm game at Ibrox on 19 November.

After signing a new two-year contract, he played his part in the historic ninth season, making 13 starts and 19 substitute appearances and scoring ten goals, including a hat-trick against Dunfermline in the 5–2 away victory on 17 August and a double in the 4–3 home win over Hibs on 7 December. His last goal of nine-in-a-row came in the 6–0 away drubbing of Raith Rovers on 15 April. Ally did all he could to help drag the team over the line to the tenth title, but it wasn't to be, and his last Rangers game was in the Scottish Cup Final, when he scored and was denied a stonewall penalty that could very well have led to the cup coming back to Ibrox.

He signed with Kilmarnock in the summer of 1998 alongside Ian Durrant and played three seasons in Ayrshire. He struck a hat-trick against Hearts and his final goal for Killie was, appropriately, against Celtic on 20 May 2001. Super Ally retired at the end of that season, a few months shy of his 39th birthday. As he was winding down his playing career, he had already found another vocation where he was a natural – television. His cheeky-chappie persona was perfect for light entertainment such as *A Question of Sport*, where he was a team captain, and chat show *McCoist and MacAulay*. He also starred in a movie with Robert Duvall, called *A Shot at Glory*, and became a respected football pundit.

It came as a surprise when new Scotland boss Walter Smith asked Ally to become his assistant in 2004. Ally had been a loyal servant to his country as a player – first appearing for the under-19s and under-21s, then accumulating 61 caps and 19 goals for the full side – but few had regarded him as management material. Again, he was a natural in the position and helped Walter bring a level of pride back to the national team. Ally turned down the Inverness Caledonian Thistle job in 2006, but couldn't knock back club management when he joined the returning Walter at Ibrox in January 2007. The management team, including Kenny McDowall, despite severe financial restraints, achieved incredible success, including three title wins in a row, a clutch of cups and an incredible 19-game European run that culminated in the UEFA Cup Final.

Walter stepped down in June 2011 and anointed Ally as his successor. At first, it seemed to be going well. The team were 15 points clear at the top of the league early in the campaign and, although they dropped four points behind in the New Year, a title challenge was still a real possibility. Then the unthinkable happened and new owner Craig Whyte plunged the team into administration, leading to the club being docked ten points.

What happened next is well known. With the club demoted to the Third Division, Ally had only five players on the books days before the first game of the season and no licence from the SFA to actually play the game. A lot has been written about Ally's tactical choices, his management style, the players he bought and some of the decisions he made before and after he stepped down as manager in December 2014 (although he remained contracted to the club until the following September). But it shouldn't be forgotten the way he galvanised the supporters in those dark days, with his famous 'we don't do walking away' speech and in ensuring the club wasn't stripped of trophies when the SFA embarked on its witch-hunt.

I had Ally sign the shirt outside the main door after a match during that tough time, and, as always, he couldn't have been nicer, greeting me with a smile and being full of praise for what I was doing. Regardless of what happened during his management reign, Ally is one of the legendary players of Rangers and that will never be forgotten.

His goals shot us to nine-in-a-row.

Barry Ferguson

THE FINAL match of the nine-in-a-row era was insignificant apart from one aspect.

A 3–1 defeat at Tynecastle on 10 May 1997 was the hangover from the historic events of a few nights earlier when the iconic title was finally won. But a glance at the starting line-up shows one new name – a teenager called Barry Ferguson. There had been a buzz growing around the talented young midfielder, more so because he was the younger brother of Derek, who had turned out in the same central position a decade earlier. Stories of how Barry had been in and around Ibrox from a young age thanks to his sibling, growing up in the company of players like Durrant and McCoist, were great copy for the newspapers.

Barry played the full game that day, where all four goals came in the last 12 minutes, and was praised for his display. The *Sunday Mirror*'s report the following morning said 'it was the elegant Ferguson, who showed all the smart touches of his elder brother, who impressed most'.

In Walter's final season in charge, Barry played 12 times. It's very likely he would have played more if he hadn't picked up a pelvic injury in March while playing for Scotland under-21s, which ruled him out for the rest of the season. By that point he had already been named in the *Sunday Times*' 'New Faces' feature as one to watch, and in April the tabloids were reporting that Newcastle, Sunderland and Arsenal were ready to bid more than £1m to take him south. The Gunners seemed particularly keen, sending their chief scout to watch him three times. At the end of that disappointing season, he said he wasn't going to sign the new five-year deal on the table until he determined whether new boss Dick Advocaat was going to give him a chance. He certainly did, and the contract was signed by the start of July.

Barry Ferguson, as everyone knows, quickly became a sensational player under the Dutch manager and flourished in a midfield overflowing with international talent. Without doubt the greatest Scottish player of his generation, and perhaps the generations before and after, he was made club captain in 2000 when he was just 22 years old. He lifted the Player of the Year award at the season's end and signed an extended six-year deal. His performances in Europe against quality teams like Bayer Leverkusen were magnificent, and who can forget that stunning free kick he scored in the classic Scottish Cup Final win over Celtic in 2002? He captained the team to a treble the following year and won two more Player of the Year awards.

So it seemed baffling when he decided to move south in August 2003 in a £7.5m deal, especially when it was to Blackburn. He should have been aiming much higher than the Lancashire side if he felt the need to leave. His new boss, Graeme Souness, made him captain the following summer, but he was out of the team for a long period after suffering a fractured kneecap. He seemed to realise he had made a mistake and wanted to come back to Rangers. He handed in a transfer request and got his move in January 2005, playing his part in the dramatic run-in that led to Helicopter Sunday and yet another title triumph. He played through the pain the following season, taking injections to allow him to take to the pitch despite having snapped ligaments.

But he fell out with new manager Paul Le Guen, and was dramatically stripped of the captaincy and dropped in December 2006. It was the French manager who wouldn't survive the fallout, leaving the following month. Although not the same player he had been in his first spell, Fergie still played his part and led the team well as Walter returned to the dugout and took us all the way to the UEFA Cup Final in Manchester in 2008. That match was Barry's 400th game for the Gers, and he came closer than anyone to scoring when he clipped the outside of the post in the second half. It might have been a different outcome had that one crept in. He made 82 appearances in Europe for Rangers and could have had more. That impressive total gave him the distinction of making the most European appearances both by anyone playing for a Scottish club and by any Scot playing in Europe, beating Dave Narey and Kenny Dalglish respectively.

The infamous late-night drinking session on Scotland duty and subsequent rude gestures to press cameras saw him and fellow Ger Allan McGregor dropped by both club and country. While he would never play for the national team again, Walter did eventually grant him a few fleeting appearances in the run-in to another title success. The writing was on the wall though, and after 431 games and 60 goals, Ferguson's Rangers career was finally over. He signed for Birmingham in the summer, reuniting with Alex McLeish, and won the League Cup with the Midlands side, defeating Arsenal in the final despite playing for an hour with a broken rib.

He moved on to Blackpool and spent three roller-coaster years with the Seasiders, which included being sent out on loan to neighbours Fleetwood Town and then taking over as boss back at Bloomfield Road, guiding them away from relegation by two points, despite winning only three of his 20 games as boss.

It was while he was in the Vegas of the North that he signed my shirt. Ian Holloway, the eccentric boss who took Blackpool into the Premier League, was still in charge at the time. It was my mate who noticed Blackpool were playing in a cup tie on a Sunday afternoon, and he suggested we drive down to hopefully meet Ferguson. We left early and made great time going down the road. Too great, because we arrived hours sharp. We nipped into the town centre and bought breakfast at one of the greasy spoons before heading back round to the tidy wee stadium.

We checked where the players would arrive, and then we parked up and waited. It was absolutely freezing, which made the time go even slower. Two hours passed before we saw Ferguson arriving. We jumped out of our car, and as we approached him I wondered how he would be. Years before I had seen him outside Ibrox on a couple of occasions and noticed he could be quite a frosty character. On this occasion, thankfully, he couldn't have been nicer. Perhaps it was because we told him we'd driven down especially, or maybe we had just caught him in a good mood. We had a chat about Rangers and football in general, talking about how great Blackpool had done against the odds in the past couple of years. Just then a tiny pink Smart car passed by. Barry pointed it out and said it was the manager's. I couldn't imagine Walter or Souness driving a car like that!

We thanked him and returned to the car to begin the three-hour drive home. If I had waited a couple of years I would have had far less distance to travel, because soon after keeping Blackpool in the Championship he parted company with the Lancashire club and landed the manager's job at Clyde, based at Broadwood in Cumbernauld, Lanarkshire.

He might only have been a footnote in nine-in-a-row, but Ferguson created his own memorable legacy in the decade that followed.

Derek Ferguson

WHILE I was chatting with Barry, he told me his brother, Derek, was doing some community football work at St Mirren's training ground, the Ralston Training Complex in Paisley, and I would be able to catch up with him there.

Derek and Barry Ferguson were the only brothers to have appeared for Rangers during nine-in-a-row. While Barry made a cameo at the very end, Derek was there from the beginning, and if things had worked out he might have been there for the duration and perhaps even played alongside his wee brother in the centre of the park. Unfortunately that wasn't to be, and it was very much a case of what might have been.

Indeed, Derek and Ian Durrant looked to be the two outstanding Scottish talents in the mid-eighties, and they could have dictated the play for years to come for both Rangers and Scotland had life worked out differently. Injury curtailed Durrant's progress, while a series of run-ins with Graeme Souness and question marks over his behaviour caused Derek's downturn in fortunes.

The Lanarkshire midfielder was signed by Rangers when he was just 12, with Celtic, Dundee United and Manchester United also keeping tabs on him. Being a Rangers fan, there was no doubting which team he would choose. He played in Tam Forsyth's testimonial when he was only 15, and his competitive debut came at 16 in the League Cup victory over Hearts in October 1983, John Greig's final game as manager.

Despite his youthfulness, Derek became one of the few bright spots in a team bereft of them, and when Souness took over in 1986 and brought in a better calibre of player, it seemed it could only enhance Derek's career. Yet by the time the nine-in-a-row years began in 1988, Ferguson was in and out of the team and having issues with the boss. Overall, he made just 16 starts and five substitute appearances, scoring two goals, during the nine era. It wasn't always a case of fleeting appearances. Soon after Souness became boss, Ferguson was named man of the match in the League Cup Final victory against Celtic. But manager and player would develop a difficult working relationship that would boil over into conflict. Injuries didn't help – two separate shoulder injuries in 1989 caused him to miss many games. His only Scotland caps came a year earlier, against Malta and Colombia, but once again it really should have been more.

During the first campaign, 1988/89, Derek made 12 starts and four substitute appearances. He was a sub and a starter in the first two games, missed the next ten, was a substitute and then a starter again, missed another six and was a substitute once more on Hogmanay away to Hamilton. He struck a sweet left-foot shot from outside the box when he came on, and it proved to be the only goal of the game. He then started the next eight games and showed his undoubted ability with a good goal away to Aberdeen on 14 January in a 2–1 win. He made a great run through the middle that was spotted by Ian Ferguson, who fed him the ball with a cushioned pass over the defence, and Derek finished well. He might also have had the first goal, too. His header from six yards was goal-bound, but it hit Munro on the way in and the full-back was given the credit.

The following season he made just three starts and came off the bench twice. He was a sub in the opener against St Mirren on 12 August, when we lost 1–0, and missed the next three before starting in the 2–2 and 1–1 draws against Dundee and Dunfermline on 16 and 23 September. His next appearance didn't come until 14 April, coming on in the 2–1 home win over Motherwell, and he started the following week in the 1–0 win at Dundee United.

The writing was on the wall when he was sent to Dundee on loan that season, and sure enough he was sold to Hearts in 1990 for a Tynecastle record fee of £750,000. He played well enough in Edinburgh in his three seasons to secure a move to England in 1993, his former teammate Terry Butcher signing him for Sunderland. He remained in the north-east for two years and then came back over the border, where for the next 11 years he played for a long list of clubs. He was with Falkirk for three years and then spent a season at Dunfermline. By the time 1999 came around and he was 32, he played a handful of games for Portadown in the Irish League, then Partick Thistle, a brief spell in Australia with Adelaide Force and back home for a short spell with

Ross County. Clydebank was next, where he played a couple of seasons, followed by Alloa Athletic and two seasons with his home-town team, Hamilton Accies. He finally called it a day with Raith Rovers in the 2005/06 campaign.

Derek had a taste of management while at Clydebank in 2001/02 and later had spells as coach at Albion Rovers and assistant manager, then manager, at Stranraer. In 2009 he became boss at junior side Glenafton Athletic and had a spell as assistant at Dumbarton.

He is also a pundit for BBC Radio Scotland's football coverage, and I'd previously met him at the broadcaster's HQ while I was collecting signatures from various sportspeople and celebrities for other shirts, which I auctioned off to pay for my travels. I didn't have the nine-in-a-row shirt with me on that occasion. When Barry told me where I could meet his big brother, I decided to go along to Paisley rather than gambling on seeing him again at the BBC.

It was a cold winter's night when I made my way to the Ralston Training Complex. As I approached the pitches, I saw there was a game going on and spotted Derek refereeing. I stood on the touchline, clutching my bag containing the shirt, and waited for the match to come to an end so I could approach him. Once again Derek proved what a nice guy he is. More than happy to sign the shirt and have a picture taken, he chatted away while he did so and was really down to earth. I told him I had been down at Blackpool recently to see Barry and we discussed how well the Seasiders had been doing.

As it turned out, I saw Derek a few more times after that evening, over at the BBC. And every time he would remember who I was and ask how my challenge was coming along and how many signatures I still had to collect. He always made time to talk and seemed a really approachable and supportive guy. It's a shame we didn't see him at Ibrox for many more years and watch him team up with his wee brother. But he still played his part in nine-in-a-row and gave us some great moments of skill during those seven years when he lived his dream of turning out for the famous red, white and blue.

Andy Gray

PEOPLE HAVE told me more times than I can count over the years that what I'm doing is crazy. So it seems fitting that I met the next player on the list thanks to a Rangers supporter who did something equally mad.

Satty Singh runs the famous Mr Singh's Indian restaurant just off of Charing Cross in Glasgow city centre. He's a passionate bluenose, so much so that he named his two sons after players from the nine-in-a-row era. Mark Walters Singh came along first, but his wee brother's name is a little more unlikely.

The story goes that during a dominant Old Firm performance at Parkhead in the New Year's game of 1994, in which Rangers were 3–0 up within the first half hour, Satty said he would name his newborn son after the next Rangers player to score. The chances of it being the perennially injured Ukrainian Oleg Kuznetsov, who came off the bench in the second half, seemed slim. But Satty's a man of his word, and the new addition to the family was officially named Oleg Kuznetsov Singh.

Perhaps Satty felt he had found a kindred spirit when he read a newspaper article about my search for the nine-in-a-row legends. He called the publication and told the reporter he might be able to help me connect with some of the names on the list I'd yet to meet, as Rangers players and staff past and present often frequented his restaurant. My number was passed to him and Satty was as good as his word.

He had already helped me meet one of my idols in his eatery (more on that one later) when he called to tell me Andy Gray and a few other ex-players had made a booking for later in the week.

Andy had been invited up to Ibrox to MC the 140th anniversary celebrations, where a number of legends from throughout the decades were brought on to the pitch in front of a sell-out crowd. He looked like he was enjoying himself that night as he introduced some of our greatest-ever servants, stalwarts like John Greig and Derek Johnstone. But then that's no surprise – Andy is a massive bluenose just like every one of us in the stands. Yet it looked like the chance to turn out for his boyhood heroes had passed him by after a stellar career played out mostly in England.

He made his breakthrough at Dundee United as a 17-year-old striker and scored 46 goals in 62 league games, prompting Aston Villa to sign him when he was 19. He won the Golden Boot in England in 1976/77, and in 1978/79 he was voted both the PFA Young Player of the Year and the PFA Players' Player of the Year. After four years he moved on to Wolves, where he spent another four years. But it was his time at Everton, 1983 to 1985, when he had the greatest success, winning the league, the League Cup and the Cup Winners' Cup – scoring the first goal. The 20-times-capped forward moved back to Villa in 1985, but his second spell wasn't so productive and, after a loan spell at Notts County, he signed for West Bromwich Albion as he wound his career down.

In September 1988, manager Ron Atkinson called Andy into the office and said he'd taken a call from Graeme Souness. 'He wants you to go to Rangers,' Big Ron told him. Andy's jaw dropped. 'You've got to be joking,' was about all he could muster for a response. Rangers were facing a striker crisis after Kevin Drinkell joined Ally McCoist on the treatment table following a league win over Hearts. We were to play the Tynecastle side again four days later in a Skol Cup semi-final and our options were looking limited – and that's when Souness got on the phone to West Brom. It was a dream come true for Andy.

He started the semi-final on the bench, with winger Mark Walters playing through the middle and scoring the opening goal. Scott Nisbet struck the second, and then Andy came on to set up Walters for the third. Gray made 14 appearances – three starts and 11 as a substitute – in the league in the 1988/89 season as the club began the long road to nine. His league debut was as a sub in the 2–1 home win over St Mirren on 24 September, and his first goal was against the same opposition, again from the subs' bench, at Love Street on 29 October in a 1–1 draw. His second came just a few days later, once more coming off the bench, at home to Hearts in a 3–0 win on 1 November. His third goal was his first while wearing the number nine jersey, in a 3–1 win over Hamilton Accies at Ibrox on 16 November. Andy finished off his scoring with a double away to Dundee on 6 May in a 2–1 victory. His unexpected Rangers career was over at the end of the season, but he'd done enough to earn a league winner's medal and complete a long-held ambition.

Soon after he left Rangers he took a call from Sky TV, which at that time was just starting out, asking him if he was interested in becoming involved in its new football coverage. It was going to take a few more months to launch, so Andy played for non-league Cheltenham until the broadcasters were ready for him. As the satellite channel went from being watched by miniscule audiences to becoming the most dominant force in English football, Andy was with them all the way thanks to his popular commentaries and match analysis. He ceased working for Sky in 2011 due to inappropriate comments, but continued to work in the game, covering football with Richard Keys for beIN Sports, a Middle Eastern TV network.

Satty advised me of the best time to turn up and, sure enough, Andy was sitting round a table with Derek Johnstone and Gordon Smith having a catch-up when I arrived. I also spotted Michael Mols eating at another table. A waiter took me over and I nervously introduced myself to the lads – three players who definitely knew how to find the back of the net. I must have sat with them for half an hour as we had a laugh and a joke and reminisced about years gone by at the club.

Andy was a genuinely nice bloke and showed an interest in my project. He told me I was doing a great job and once I was getting close to the end he would get me on to his radio show on Talksport to publicise it, but sadly he was gone from there by the time I was down to the last few names. He put his arm around my shoulder for the picture and proudly signed the shirt as DJ and Smudger looked on. Andy told me playing for Rangers was a very special time for him and his family, and scoring some important goals was also special. To look back knowing he played a part in the historic nine-in-a-row, being a fan – well, it doesn't get much better than that. Realising a childhood dream is something not many people achieve, so for that alone it's worth quoting Andy's catchphrase: take a bow son, because you deserve it.

Brian Reid

DEFENDER BRIAN Reid has the distinction of being Graeme Souness's final signing for Rangers before the gaffer moved on to Liverpool.

The Paisley teenager had been turning out for Morton since the age of 18 and really came to prominence in two great displays in the cup against Motherwell, with Morton eventually losing on penalties in the replay early in 1991. Despite him being on the losing side, other clubs took notice of Reid's performances, and Nottingham Forest's Brian Clough came to watch him. He made a bid, as did Rangers, but Clough's offer was £50,000 higher. Morton left the decision up to the player and there was only ever one choice for the childhood Rangers fan.

Misfortune was to strike just a few weeks after he signed during three-in-a-row. Reid was playing St Mirren in Campbell Money's testimonial when he was caught with a bad tackle. His cruciate ligament was gone. He wasn't the first Rangers player to suffer a serious knee injury, and unfortunately he wouldn't be the last. He made three consecutive starts in the league prior to that sad incident, helping to keep clean sheets against Dunfermline, Hibs and St Johnstone in 1–0, 0–0 and 3–0 results on 30 March, 6 April and 13 April. He would next feature in the league two years later, at the tail end of the five-in-a-row campaign, in a 1–0 loss at Aberdeen on 12 May and a final-day 2–1 win at Falkirk 72 hours later.

After a loan spell at Newcastle in 1994, where he failed to play, Brian moved on from Ibrox in 1996 with just those five league appearances to his name, returning to Morton in a £200,000 move – just £100,000 less than what we had paid for him. He put his career back on track at Cappielow and earned a move to Burnley. After a season there he headed to Dunfermline, had a loan spell at Blackpool which became permanent, came back to Scotland to join Falkirk, enjoyed a few seasons at Queen of the South and finished his playing career at Ayr United in 2007. Having already coached the kids at Ibrox, he was appointed manager at Somerset Park and was twice promoted and twice relegated during his five-year stint in charge. He later managed Global FC in the Philippines and the country's under-23 squad, had a five-month spell in charge of Nuneaton Town and was appointed Stranraer boss in 2015, but it was during his time in Ayrshire that I met with him.

I called the club and spoke to someone in the administration team. It turned out Brian was in the office at that moment, so they passed him the phone and I explained what I was doing. Brian said I should come down any training day and he would sign the shirt. I turned up a few days later and caught Brian just before he went on to the training field to take that day's session. As it transpired, our meeting was just two days before he was sacked, and when I saw he had moved to the Philippines I was glad I hadn't put off taking a drive to the seaside.

Mo Johnston

THERE IS no doubting the most controversial signing of nine-in-a-row – Mo Johnston.

The former Celtic player, who had been photographed with Parkhead boss Billy McNeill in May 1989 stating that he was returning to his former club and intended to spend the rest of his career there, signed for Rangers in July and caused headlines and hysteria. Most of the news stories focused on Johnston being a 'high-profile Catholic', whatever that actually means, in a time when Rangers predominantly signed Protestants. Graeme Souness wanted to destroy that notion and he did it in the most remarkable way, nicking the prodigal son from the other side of Glasgow and devastating both the Parkhead hierarchy and its fanbase so indelibly that many still haven't got over it.

The Sun broke the story on the morning of 10 July – but, living down south, I hadn't seen the Scottish version of the tabloid, so it came as a complete shock to me when I heard the news. I was a lorry driver at the time, and I was driving along the motorway coming back from Blackpool when it came over the radio. I was in absolute shock and genuinely upset by it. I just couldn't understand why we would make such a signing. I had seen Johnston play against Rangers, and watched him being sent off against us and riling the fans up. He appeared to hate us and, for many, the feeling was mutual. It took me a while to accept it, but with the benefit of hindsight I realise now that I was just being daft by being against it at first.

I wasn't alone in questioning the signing, though. Television reports and newspaper articles interviewed fans on the streets and in pubs, and a number of them expressed misgivings at the decision to bring him to Ibrox. Now I realise just how much guts it must have taken for the wee man to make the move. He had been a hero to the Celtic support in his time there between 1984 and 1987, winning the title with them. He'd ended up at Parkhead after an impressive two seasons with Partick Thistle when he was still a teenager and a prolific season at Watford. He moved to France with Nantes for two seasons, but when it became known that he was looking to move on, his old club came calling and that's what led to the famous photo call and interview with Billy McNeill.

But the deal was nowhere near the finishing line, and lots of clubs were sniffing around. The only phone call Mo agreed to take via his agent, Bill McMurdo, was from Graeme Souness. Rangers were the biggest and probably richest club in British football at the time, and the hugely talented striker deserved to be playing for a team of our calibre. There was also the aspect of creating a little piece of history, and clearly that enticed Mo rather than put him off, because he was soon paraded at Ibrox in a £1.5m transfer under the prideful watch of Graeme Souness. It was a life-changing decision, one that would mean he could never live in Glasgow again and would require the constant presence of bodyguards. But it was worth it, for all concerned. Well, maybe not Celtic, but that's OK.

The furore in the media had led to expectations that thousands would stop attending Ibrox as some sort of protest. Instead, 5,000 were locked out of the big pre-season friendly against Tottenham Hotspur, whose line-up featured a young Gazza. The fans applauded Mo's every touch in a show of support, just as they had done in the three friendlies prior to this one. The support from his teammates was just as solid, once he got past the ribbing. Upon arriving at the pre-season training camp in Il Ciocco, Italy, he found a separate table had been set for him in the dining room with just bread and water on the menu. And kitman Jimmy Bell wouldn't put his gear out for him in those first few days. But it was all banter, and soon the hard work would begin in convincing everyone that he could live up to the hype.

He was an ever-present in the league in his first season, the two-in-a-row campaign, starting all 36 matches. But the team made a poor start, losing the first two games against St Mirren and Hibs, meaning the pressure was on when they headed to Parkhead in the next match. Johnston was booed mercilessly throughout the contest but stayed strong, as did Rangers, who churned out a 1–1 draw. By the fourth match, and the seventh of the season including cup games, Mo had yet to score. The pressure was building. A hard-fought match against

Aberdeen at Ibrox on 9 September ended with a 1–0 victory, and it was Johnston who claimed the goal with a well-taken header.

He was off the mark and would score the only goal in another tight home match, this time against Hearts on 30 September. There was one team he really had to score against to convert any fans who had lingering doubts about him doing the business for Rangers. That moment came on 4 November and in the 88th minute, against his old team. Gary Stevens crossed the ball in, Chris Morris failed to clear it properly and Mo controlled it on the edge of the box and swept it low past Pat Bonner and into the corner. The players went wild, the fans went wild and Mo went wild. He ran to the corner of the Copland Stand and Main Stand, and on to the track, to celebrate in front of the supporters. He said later it was the moment that made him feel accepted as a Rangers player, and from there he never looked back. Graeme Souness, on the other hand, was looking back – and to the front, sides and all around. He was fearful for his star man's safety and when he asked Mo what he planned to do that night, he was horrified when the striker told him he was going to a fancy dress party in nearby Kirkintilloch. Security was immediately doubled up, just in case.

That goal came in the midst of a five-game scoring run, and the number ten ended the season as Rangers' top scorer in the league with 15 goals, including another against Celtic in the second match at Ibrox, on 1 April, when the Teddy Bears won 3–0, with Ally and Walters also scoring. In three-in-a-row he started 29 games and scored 11 goals, teaming up with new strike partner Mark Hateley. He scored on the opening day of the campaign against Dunfermline in a 3–1 win and capitalised on a defensive mistake to put away a calmly taken lob to open the scoring against Celtic at Parkhead on 25 November in a 2–1 victory.

By the time the four-in-a-row campaign was underway, Souness had left and Walter Smith was now in charge. Walter was of the opinion that Ally McCoist was a better foil for Mark Hateley than Mo, and so, when Everton came in for the striker in November 1991, he allowed Mo to leave. He did make ten starts in the league prior to moving, scoring five goals. In his last start he scored in a 1–1 home draw against Falkirk on 26 October, and his final appearance came from the bench, the only time he was a sub in a Rangers league match, in a 3–2 defeat away to Dundee United on 29 October.

The 38-times-capped Mo spent a couple of seasons at Everton before coming back north to Hearts, where he played for a year. His agent, Bill McMurdo, revealed in a tabloid interview years later that Walter considered bringing him back to Ibrox as he prepared to leave Tynecastle – but that never transpired, and instead Mo went to Falkirk for two seasons. He then moved to America, signing with Kansas City Wizards, where he spent the final five years of his career before retiring in 2001. He later managed New York Red Bulls and Toronto FC and lives in the States to this day, far away from the city where half the population still cannot accept the decision he made in the summer of 1989.

So when I turned on my telly to watch a live Rangers cup match and saw Mo in the stadium's studio as a pundit, my eyes went as wide as saucers. At this time I lived in Middleton Street, just a five-minute walk from the stadium's front door. I didn't even wait for the final whistle as I was afraid he would leave early, so I pulled on my jacket and shoes, grabbed the shirt and walked round to the ground. I stood at the security barricades placed around the main entrance and caught the attention of the doorman, who I knew well by now due to all of the hours I'd spent waiting for players. I asked if Mo was still inside, and he told me he was and that he would definitely be leaving by this exit as a taxi was booked for him. It paid to know these guys on the door, as they would often give me a nod and a wink.

The game finished and thousands of fans streamed out to make their way home. A few waited around the front beside me, hoping to catch a player or two as they left. I waited and waited and waited. I was standing there for what felt like an age. Most of the fans had left by the time Mo finally emerged. I don't think those who were still milling around even recognised him at first. He was wrapped up with a big jacket and scarf, but I clocked him immediately and approached him as he walked across the mosaic and down the steps. I explained to him that I was collecting the signatures of every nine-in-a-row player, and asked whether he would mind signing the shirt and having his picture taken. He said, 'Of course not,' and found a spot to sign. He seemed a nice guy and had a big smile on his face as he posed with the shirt. It was at that point the other fans who were still hanging around recognised him, and a little group gathered round him as he and his friend tried to make their way to the waiting taxi. I thanked him for his time and made my way back round the corner to my house.

I thought of how I had felt that day in the lorry when I heard the news of his signing and how it worked out, with all those crucial goals he scored and the many others he set up. He proved me wrong, and he clearly still has a lot of time for the club all these years on, proving the old adage really is true – once a Ranger, always a Ranger.

Derek McInnes

DEREK MCINNES has the honour of scoring the final goal in Rangers' nine-in-a-row years.

He scored the 674th goal of the glory run on 10 May 1997, in a 3–1 defeat at Hearts just three days after the ninth title was won at Tannadice, and the celebrations were no doubt still in full flow. The strike assured a place in the history books for the Paisley-born midfielder who lived the dream of playing for his boyhood heroes during one of the club's greatest eras.

McInnes came through the ranks at nearby Greenock Morton and played there for seven years, until he was snapped up by Walter in 1995 in a £250,000 transfer. He made 27 appearances during nine-in-a-row, including 12 from the bench. His debut came in the eighth campaign, starting in the 1–0 win against Partick Thistle at Ibrox on 9 December 1995. He made four more starts that season, against Motherwell, Falkirk, Raith and Kilmarnock, and also came on as a sub versus Killie.

He was more involved in the ninth season, making ten starts and a further 11 substitute appearances. He played in the opening game, a narrow 1–0 victory over Raith on 10 August, and also featured twice against Celtic – once from the bench when we won 2–0 at Ibrox on 28 September, and as the number nine in a 1–0 away triumph on 14 November.

Derek was one of the few from the old guard to remain after Dick Advocaat took over as manager in 1998. He went to Stockport on loan that season, but did feature sporadically for the Little General, most notably in Europe, where he was used effectively in a sitting midfield role, but he moved on for regular first-team action in 2000.

Following a brief spell at Toulouse, he joined West Bromwich Albion and enjoyed three good years in England, leading to a Scotland call-up at the age of 30. He won two caps, against Denmark and Portugal, and then returned north in 2003 to sign with Dundee United. He moved to Millwall for the 2006/07 season and then finished his playing career with St Johnstone, where he was also appointed manager.

He guided the Perth team back to the Premier League in 2009, and his leadership skills triggered interest from Bristol City, where he was persuaded to take over in 2011. Although he kept them in the Championship in his first season, the move didn't work out and he was sacked in January 2013. He became Aberdeen manager later that year, winning the League Cup in 2013/14 and also picking up the Manager of the Year award.

It was during his time out of the game between the Bristol City and Aberdeen jobs that I met him.

I was listening to *Sportsound* on Radio Scotland one Saturday afternoon when I heard he was the studio guest, so I made the short walk along to the BBC headquarters from my house in Ibrox and waited in the foyer for him to come off the air. The guy at reception gave me a little nod when Derek was on his way downstairs, so I took the shirt and pen out of the bag in readiness. A few seconds later, I had the autograph of the final scorer from nine-in-a-row added to the top and a picture to go with it.

A lot of people think McInnes will one day return to Rangers as manager. Whether or not that ever happens, he's already secured a place in history as part of our greatest-ever squad – one of the lucky few.

Kevin Drinkell

GRAEME SOUNESS once described Kevin Drinkell as the hardest-working striker he had ever seen.

He arrived at Ibrox in time for the start of the nine-in-a-row campaign in a £600,000 move from Norwich, where he had spent three seasons and won the Second Division's Golden Boot award for his goalscoring prowess. 'Drinks' had started his career at home-town team, Grimsby, in 1976, at 16 years old and remained there for eight years, helping the club secure two promotions. He turned down a move to Manchester United in 1987, and Spurs were in for him at the same time as Rangers, but he chose to come north. He started 32 of the 36 league games that first season and scored 11 goals. His first one was in the famous 5–1 thrashing of Celtic in the third game of the campaign, on 27 August 1988. Mark Walters crossed the ball into the box and Drinkell made perfect contact, his diving header sending the ball flying into the net.

He struck against Celtic later in the season too, another header that helped the Gers win 2–1 on 1 April, ending a nine-year period without winning at Parkhead. Kevin also scored in three different league games against Motherwell, struck the only goal away to Hibs on 25 March, fired in against Dundee, Hamilton and Dundee United, and scored twice in the title-winning victory over Hearts at Ibrox on 29 April.

The close season saw the incredible signing of Mo Johnston, and Drinkell wasn't ready to go into a rotation system, so he decided to leave the club. He had actually featured in all four league games before his £800,000 transfer to Coventry City, coming off the bench in the opening two games – defeats to St Mirren at home and Hibs away – and then started at Parkhead in a 1–1 draw on 26 August and a 1–0 win over Aberdeen at Ibrox on 9 September.

Drinkell's two years at Coventry included a loan spell at Birmingham. He then returned to Scotland to play two years at Falkirk, and finished his playing career at Stirling Albion in the 1994/95 season, when he was also installed as manager. He guided the club to the Second Division title in 1996 and was voted the division's manager of the year. He left Stirling in 1998 and became boss at Montrose for two years. When he left, he underwent hip replacement surgery, a hangover from the punishing style of play during his on-field career. Drinkell had a brief spell as East Fife's assistant in 2013 and has had various business interests.

I wasn't sure what had become of him until I read a newspaper article in 2014, which said he had taken on a job as a Mercedes-Benz car salesman for Arnold Clark in Grangemouth. I called the branch and asked if he was working there, and the receptionist passed the phone to him. He said I could come over and meet him, but asked for it to be 10am on Sunday morning, because he would rather do it before his bosses came in or customers started showing up. A few days later, I drove over and arrived before 10am. He brought me into the showroom, signed the shirt and let me take a picture, but he wasn't a particularly chatty guy, so it was only a brief encounter. It was another easy one scored off the list – and I was happy to Drinks to that!

Bonni Ginzburg

LOVED ONES voiced their concerns about me travelling to war-torn Israel to meet former goalkeeper Bonni Ginzburg after I had successfully tracked him down. I could understand their worries, because barely a day passed by without another bad news story about the conflict between Israel and Palestine. I've never let that sort of thing bother me, and I'm glad I listened to my instincts, because my short trip to Tel Aviv is probably my favourite of all the journeys I made during my quest.

My online research found that Bonni was now a football pundit on Israeli TV, so I looked up a number for the main sports channel in the country, Sport 5, and called them. I spoke to a really helpful guy there, I told him my story and he promised to pass my number on to Bonni. A few days later, Ginzburg called me, and told me I should let him know when I was coming over and he would meet me. That was one of the easier contacts I made!

I flew via a place that was becoming like a second home, Amsterdam Airport, and arrived in Tel Aviv to a security presence I've never seen before or since. The airport was jam-packed with officers patrolling the terminal. It wasn't just one security checkpoint I had to pass through, it was three. I was asked the purpose of my visit, and I explained I was there to meet Bonni Ginzburg, which seemed to be sufficient because they allowed me to pass through.

It was the early hours of the morning by the time I took a taxi to my accommodation. I wondered why there was such a heavy security presence outside, but then noticed the American flag flying on the building adjacent to mine and realised my neighbour for the next two nights was the American Embassy. That might make the stay a little more interesting, I thought. I realised quite quickly when I stepped inside the hotel that it wasn't actually a hotel, but rather a hostel. The concierge who checked me in was a chatty guy, and when he saw the Rangers top I was wearing he began talking about football and told me he followed Rangers. This was exactly why I always wore the colours on my trips – they so often sparked conversations. I told him I was here to meet Bonni, and he said he knew him. Maybe it was the Rangers connection or perhaps it was just good fortune, but I was given my own room with two single beds, and when I woke up the next morning I realised my window looked on to the beach, which was just yards away.

Bonni had commitments and wasn't able to meet me until the evening, so that gave me the day to explore the city. I walked two or three miles through the streets and found myself in the market area. It was like The Barras on steroids. There were hundreds of stalls as far as the eye could see, and the area was just a mass of people. Anyone with claustrophobia should avoid this market, because at times it's impossible to move in the sea of bodies. The best way I can describe it is like being on the underground after a game at Ibrox – anyone who's ever been on the train at that time will know exactly what I mean. It's Sardine City. It was quite scary from the aspect of too many people in a confined space, but I didn't feel afraid about anything bad happening as far as the conflict was concerned. In fact, I was surprised to see Arabs selling Islamic wares next to Israeli stallholders. Every so often there would be a security checkpoint within the vast market, which everyone had to pass through. Such a tightly packed area would be paradise for a suicide bomber, so the checks were completely understandable. I felt totally safe as I walked around, happy the security was so visible. I picked up a couple of little mementos to take home as gifts and then made my way out.

One of the things I liked about the city was the number of street performers dotted all around. I found a spot to sit down and watched a woman in her eighties singing her heart out as she busked. Her impassioned performance attracted hundreds of passers-by. I took my time to watch a few more performers on my walk back to the hostel. Bonni and I had kept in touch throughout the day and he said he would come to the hostel to meet me. He called as I was walking along the street where my digs were and said he could see me in my Rangers top. All of a sudden he started singing 'Follow Follow' down the phone, and a moment later he was before me, greeting me in a warm embrace. He asked me how my day had been and if I was enjoying the city. I loved it, I told him. We went to a bar just a couple of doors down from the hostel, on the other side of the Embassy, for dinner and a few drinks. It quickly became apparent that just about everyone knew him. He was a big celebrity in the country, like Ally McCoist in Scotland.

We spent a couple of hours chatting, talking about former Rangers and Israel player Avi Cohen, who had died following a motorbike accident a short time before my trip. Bonni told me Avi had been his best friend and he had been with him the day before the tragedy. We spoke about his time in Glasgow as well and his memories of playing for Rangers.

Bonni was brought to Ibrox by Graeme Souness as an emergency signing in August 1989 when first-choice keeper Chris Woods was injured. Back-up goalie Lindsay Hamilton, who had been with the club since 1986 but had yet to play a game, thought he was finally making his debut in a League Cup match against Arbroath, but instead Bonni was bought from Beitar Jerusalem for £300,000 and was rushed straight to the stadium from the airport.

Bonni made his league debut in the next match four days later, 19 August, a 2–0 defeat to Hibs at Easter Road. Rangers were later fined because he hadn't been registered properly for either of his first two games. He played again the following week in the Old Firm match at Parkhead, which finished 1–1. He was back in the team in September, featuring in a 0–0 draw in the European Cup at Bayern Munich and in a 1–0 home win versus Hearts. His fourth and final league appearance came on 3 October in a 1–0 defeat at Motherwell. Bonni remained as back-up the following season, the three-in-a-row campaign, before returning to Israel to sign for Maccabi Yavne, the fourth club he played for in his home country.

Born in Tel Aviv in December 1964, his first professional team was Maccabi Tel Aviv, where he spent three years from 1984 to 1987. He then had a season at Maccabi Haifa and a year at Beitar before coming to Scotland. After his year at Yavne, he played for a further six clubs until he retired in 2001, with 68 Israeli caps to his name. After retiring he moved into the media, presenting a football highlights programme, taking part in the Israeli version of *Strictly Come Dancing* and commentating on football for the TV company I contacted him through, Sport 5.

Bonni asked me to pass his number on to Ally McCoist, as he was keen to reconnect with his old pal, and insisted that the next time I was in Israel I would stay with him. I would love it if there could be a next time. Bonni was a gentleman and a really nice, down-to-earth guy. It was around midnight when I said goodbye, and I decided to take another walk round the city and visit a few bars. In every pub I entered, some of the patrons would see me in my Rangers top and come over to start chatting about the Teddy Bears.

The following morning I took advantage of the beach on my doorstep and relaxed on the sand for a couple of hours. Despite it being winter, it was a toasty 25 degrees. I also met with the concierge from the hostel. It was his day off, and we went for a drink. We're firm friends to this day and still keep in touch via Facebook. As night descended it was soon time to take a taxi to the airport and prepare to make my way back through that heavy security operation.

My flight was in the early hours, and I was tired by the time I went through security at around 2am. I handed my passport over at the desk, and the woman on the opposite side of the glass looked down at it and then her head shot straight up and she stared at me. I could feel the butterflies flapping in my stomach again. You know what it's like – even though you know you haven't done anything wrong, the situation makes you paranoid. Why is she looking at me like that?

'What age are you?' she asked.

'Sixty-two,' I replied.

'Why are you lying?'

What was she talking about? What was happening? Now I was really beginning to worry. I imagined being dragged off to a room somewhere by a couple of heavies to be questioned about my whereabouts over the past couple of days.

'It's your birthday,' she said, suddenly breaking into a smile. 'Happy birthday!'

With all of the rushing around I had forgotten, believe it or not! I was 63 as of a couple of hours earlier. She had been joking with me, but I had thought I was about to be locked up! I made my way on to the flight with no further dramas and returned home with not just another stamp in my passport but, more importantly, another signature on my shirt. I might have forgotten at first, but this was one birthday that would live long in the memory.

Ian Durrant

IAN DURRANT was the most gifted Scottish player of his generation and, from his attacking midfielder role, he should have been the man to lead us through the many triumphs of nine-in-a-row.

Instead, he spent the first three years of the title-winning run trying to save his career after a disgusting, violent tackle just two months into the first season of the nine. Plenty has been written about Neil Simpson's assault, his face contorted in rage, in that match at Pittodrie on 8 October 1988. Durrant's knee was left in pieces and it's only down to his perseverance – along with nine operations and 1,000 stitches – that he returned and continued to play at the top level. I would rather focus on the positives of his career rather than dwell on the negatives, because Durranty was with Rangers for the duration of the nine titles and played his part in most of them.

The Glaswegian joined Rangers as a teenager in 1984 and made his debut in April of the following year. He scored on his Old Firm debut and was a bright spot in a struggling team. He continued to improve when Graeme Souness arrived, and learned from being around better players than before. The manager said he was good enough to play in Italy, but thankfully he was at Ibrox and was proving to be a dynamic midfielder with an eye for a pass like no other.

Ian started the 1988/89 season in good form, scoring in the 2–0 win at Motherwell on 3 September and in the next game, a 2–1 win at Hearts. He also scored in Europe against Katowice. He played the first seven league games, missed the match against Dundee, and unfortunately was back for that Aberdeen contest. That was the end of his season, and he wouldn't feature at all in two-in-a-row. He did try to make a comeback 16 months after the injury, playing against

Hearts reserves in February 1990 and scoring a penalty, but he suffered a setback and was out for another lengthy period. His next return came in April 1991 in a reserve match against Hibs at Ibrox. Thousands of fans famously turned out to watch him, and although he played with a bandage round his knee he emerged from the match unscathed. He was reintroduced to the first team, playing from the start in the goalless draw at home to Hibs on 6 April. He played the following week, again at home, and scored against St Johnstone, making a neat turn and hitting a left-foot shot from the edge of the box. The strike proved he was finally back after missing the best part of three seasons. He played in the 1–0 win at St Mirren the next Saturday and came on as a sub in the title-winning match against Aberdeen on 11 May, winning 2–0, and was able to finally join in with the celebrations.

He made nine starts and appeared as a substitute four times during four-in-a-row. The first was against Dunfermline in the third game of the season, a 4–0 home win on 24 August. He played in a further three games in September and October but was out again until two sub run-outs at home to Aberdeen and Airdrie on 25 and 29 February. Durrant had a strong finish to the campaign, playing in the final seven games. Five-in-a-row saw him finding a level of consistency and turning in some great performances both domestically and in Europe. He made 19 starts and came on 11 times in the 44-game campaign. One of those appearances from the bench came against Celtic on 22 August at Ibrox, scoring in the 1–1 draw. He started the move in midfield and was teed up just inside the box, where he smashed the ball high into the roof of the net. The following week he scored again, this time with Aberdeen the visitors. Roy Aitken had scored first, but Durranty equalised on 53 minutes, a smart one-two with Mikhailichenko followed by the ball being placed in the bottom corner from the edge of the box. He then set up McCoist for the second with a superb defence-splitting through ball that showed his vision for a pass was still there. Miko rounded off the scoring. Durrant scored against Celtic in the next derby at Parkhead on 7 November, his tap-in from the edge of the six-yard box the only goal. He also scored in the League Cup Final victory over Hibs that year, and in the Champions League, not only against Club Brugge but also with that stunning volley away to Marseille when we almost reached the final.

He started 14 games and appeared in another nine during six-in-a-row. He featured regularly until 11 December, the 3–0 home defeat to Dundee United, but didn't play again until the return fixture at

Tannadice, a goalless draw on 5 April, and featured in another three matches before the season's end. The 1994/95 campaign saw him start 16 league games, make ten sub appearances and score four goals. Those came in the 4 December 3–0 trouncing of Dundee United, the 3–0 victory at home to Killie on 25 February, the 3–2 win over Aberdeen at Ibrox on 8 April and the 3–1 defeat of Hibs at home on 16 April. The goal against Aberdeen came from Charlie Miller winning the ball in his own half; he played a one-two with Laudrup, who had his shot blocked, only for Durrant to slide in for the rebound. Before those goals, however, it appeared he was on his way out of Ibrox. Walter Smith sent him and Duncan Ferguson on loan to Everton in October 1994. Durrant looked gutted to be at Goodison, but was back up the road after five matches and made an impact in the second half of the seven-in-a-row campaign.

In eight-in-a-row he made six starts and nine sub appearances, and during nine-in-a-row he started four and came on five times. He didn't play between the 2–2 draw away to Raith Rovers on 2 November 1996 and the red-hot Celtic match at Parkhead on 16 March. His influence on that derby was crucial – chipping the ball over the keeper for the only goal of the match. Laudrup was there to see it into the net, but it appeared the ball was already over the line before the Dane connected. It feels appropriate that a Rangers man who had been through so much with the club since 1984 fired us towards one of the most important titles in our history.

Durranty made 79 starts and 49 substitute appearances, scoring ten goals, during nine-in-a-row. He played on with Rangers for one more year, leaving along with the bulk of the squad when Walter stepped down in May 1998. He turned out for Rangers 347 times, lifting three titles, three Scottish Cups and four League Cups.

Alongside his close friend Ally McCoist, Durrant moved down the west coast to Kilmarnock. Playing week after week saw Ian return to a level of form that led to his reinstatement to the Scotland team after years out of international football. The first of his 20 caps was against Hungary in September 1987 and the final one facing the Republic of Ireland in May 2000. He played more than 100 times for the Ayrshire club, but the legacy of his injuries was catching up with him and he had to come off at half-time of the League Cup Final against Celtic in 2001. He didn't play again until 13 months later, on 12 May 2002, when he made his swansong with an 88th-minute cameo against Dundee United in a 2–2 draw. The next stage of his career had already begun – he was youth coach before his official retirement, and afterwards he graduated to first-team duties.

In 2005 he rejoined Rangers, firstly to look after the under-19s and later the reserves. When Paul Le Guen walked out, Durrant was caretaker boss for one game – a loss at Dunfermline in the Scottish Cup – before being appointed first-team coach as part of Walter Smith's new management line-up. When Ally took over as boss, Durranty remained as first-team coach, but when McCoist left his post in December 2014, the under-fire board demoted Ian and put him back in charge of the under-20s. Having watched Rangers go through the worst and most turbulent years in our history, Durrant seemed to be on solid ground when the new board gained power and subsequently appointed Mark Warburton as manager. But after a season, the Englishman decided to make changes and Durrant was let go in June 2016.

I had Ian sign my shirt while I waited outside the gates of Auchenhowie one morning while he was still working for Rangers. I spent many hours hanging around the entrance of the training facility, asking current team players to sign various pieces of memorabilia which I would auction to fund my overseas trips. Durranty rolled down his car window as he drove out, signed the shirt and allowed me to take a photograph.

After a combined 25 years over his two spells at Rangers, it feels strange to think he won't still be going in and out of those crest-emblazoned gates every day, but with his wealth of knowledge he'll continue to work in the game. He experienced more than most at Rangers, good and bad, but he'll always be remembered as one of the greats. Never a truer word has been sung from the stands – he's blue, he's white and he really is dynamite.

Sandy Robertson

GRAEME SOUNESS once described Sandy Robertson as the best young player in Britain. High praise indeed for the young midfielder, especially coming from one of the greats of that position. Sandy was seen as a star of the future, but unfortunately he left Rangers having played just 30 times in a sad case of what might have been. Twenty-six of those appearances came in nine-in-a-row league games – 11 starts and 15 times from the bench.

His dad, Malky, had also been a professional footballer, and the young Edinburgh talent followed in his footsteps when he made his debut as a sub in the penultimate game of the first title-winning season on the march to nine, a 2–1 away win against Dundee. Sandy must have impressed the gaffer, because he started the following week in a 3–0 home loss to Aberdeen. He made just one appearance from the bench in two-in-a-row, a 3–1 win over Dundee United at Ibrox on 3 February.

Three-in-a-row, however, was undoubtedly his best season for the Gers. He made seven starts and eight sub appearances, giving him enough games for a winner's medal, and also featured in Europe and the cup. He started in the 2–1 away win against Celtic on 25 November and came off the bench in another two Old Firm games, but undoubtedly his biggest moment was on 20 April at St Mirren. The match was Walter Smith's first in charge after Souness had left for Liverpool and was a nervy affair. Aberdeen were breathing down our necks, and obviously the club was in a state of flux with what had happened in the previous few days. As the clock ticked towards 90, Robertson was sent on as Rangers searched for a goal. With five minutes left, Terry Hurlock played the ball out to Gary Stevens on the right, who crossed the ball into the box. Robertson, with his back to goal, took a touch which sent the ball up in the air; without hesitation he struck a left-foot volley over his shoulder and the ball flew into the net. It was enough to win the match and was an invaluable strike on the way to the title.

During four-in-a-row, the twice-capped under-21 star made three starts and three sub run-outs, while the following season he featured just twice off the bench – away to Dundee United in a 4–0 triumph on 26 September and in a 4–2 home win on Halloween against Motherwell. He was placed on the transfer list later that season, with four other players who weren't featuring. He moved to Coventry for £250,000 in 1994, but only played four league games. He came back north to Dundee United the following campaign, but his career went off the rails when he served six weeks of a three-month sentence in Saughton Prison for assaulting a nightclub bouncer. During that time it was revealed he had a previous conviction for another nightclub assault.

He was released from prison in October 1997, and Airdrie gave him a chance. He played a handful of games in Lanarkshire before signing for Inverness, appearing in 16 games and scoring one goal in the 1997/98 season. He played half a dozen games for Livingston and almost double that at Clydebank, and then decided to ply his trade in Australia. Sandy played for Morwell Falcons and Joondalup, but trouble was to strike again when he was glassed in a bar scuffle in May 2001. Sandy returned to Scotland and played a single game for Cowdenbeath, followed by eight for Berwick, and then signed for Raith Rovers in 2002 but didn't feature.

I wasn't quite sure how I was going to track him down, but it fell into my lap thanks to a newspaper article about my mission in early 2013. An Edinburgh restaurant owner read the story and got in touch with the newspaper and said he would be able to help me contact one of the players. The journalist passed my number on and the chap called and asked if I had met Sandy Robertson yet. I told him I hadn't and he said he knew him well and would organise a meeting.

A couple of weeks later he called again and said Sandy was going to be visiting the restaurant, and gave me a date and time to be there. Despite the stories I'd read, Sandy seemed a really nice guy, and we had a quick chat about his time at Rangers and that cracking goal at Love Street which gave Walter his historic first win for the club. No one could have imagined just how many more victories The Gaffer would enjoy across his two spells, but it might all have been very different were it not for wee Sandy's volley, which helped us to win the title on the final day of the season.

As we posed for a picture in front of the restaurant, I couldn't help but think of the historic period Sandy kicked off by scoring the first goal of Walter's regime. Things might not have worked out for Sandy's Rangers career, but that volley isn't a bad legacy to have.

Tom Cowan

TOM COWAN had what could be described as a fairy-tale start to his football career. The Motherwell-born youngster had only played a handful of games with Clyde before he attracted the interest of some big clubs. He was 17, playing part-time and serving an apprenticeship as an electrician at British Steel when Nottingham Forest came in for him. He travelled down to their training ground to meet manager Brian Clough, only to be told the legendary coach hadn't been in the mood to attend training that day. Tom was advised to go to his house to meet him instead. Clough tried to persuade the left-back to sign then and there, but Tom wanted to mull it over. When Graeme Souness made an approach soon after, there was only one place he wanted to go and that was Ibrox. After just 16 games for Clyde, he landed a dream move to the biggest club in the country.

He made his debut at home against Hamilton on 11 March 1989, in a game which the Bears won 3–0. He came on as a sub the following month in a 2–0 win at Ibrox over Hearts and made two further starts that season, 2–0 and 2–1 victories over Dundee United and Dundee in May. Tom was very much a squad player and opportunities were sporadic due to the form of Stuart Munro at left-back. The following season, two-in-a-row, he made just two substitute appearances – 1–0 and 2–0 wins at home against Hearts and Hibs in September and October – and one start, which came in a 0–0 draw away to Hibs on 30 December.

Three-in-a-row is the season he's best remembered for. After a sub appearance at Easter Road in a 2–0 win over Hibs on 19 January, Tom didn't feature again until the final three games of the season. Rangers were in a state of flux, struggling to deal with a series of injuries as well as the upset that had been caused by Graeme Souness's decision to move to Liverpool. A 1–0 win against Dundee United was followed by a crushing 3–0 defeat away to Motherwell, which left the title hanging in the balance as we prepared to face our rivals for the title, Aberdeen. Our backs were up against the wall that day at Ibrox and we really were the walking wounded. For Tom, that was literally the case. He broke his leg during the match and remarkably played on for several more minutes before going off. His efforts were worth it when Rangers won 2–0 to clinch victory and the league trophy.

With a broken leg to recover from and the summer signing of fellow left-back David Robertson from Aberdeen, Tom knew his time at the Gers was coming to an end. He was sold to Sheffield United for £350,000, where he spent three seasons, including two loan spells at Stoke and Huddersfield. The latter signed him on a permanent deal and it was the most settled period of his career. He was voted the club's Player of the Year in 1997, the same season he played most of a cup game in goals against QPR, who featured former Gers Mark Hateley and John Spencer in their ranks, after the keeper went off injured. Despite being just 5ft 7in, he put in a commendable performance, only losing an equaliser at the death to Hateley.

He also spent a year out injured after undergoing knee ligament surgery. Tom decided to put his time to good use. Thinking ahead to the end of his career, he embarked on a journalism course and wrote a book about his year on the sidelines and the recovery process. After five years at Huddersfield he moved to Burnley for a season and then transferred to Cambridge, for a spell which included a loan period at Peterborough. Up next was York City, during which time he also wrote a column for the local newspaper. When he was released he showed a commendable attitude by sending his CV to 70 clubs and telephoning every Second and Third Division club, a few in the First and a handful in Scotland.

His tenacity paid off, because he won a contract with Dundee and was suddenly thrown into European competition in the UEFA Cup. It was his first foray on to foreign soil since he had been deemed our man of the match away to Bayern Munich more than a decade earlier. But bad luck was to strike again when he was let go a few months later, as Dundee fell into administration.

He carried on, heading south to Carlisle and then falling down the ranks with short spells at Barrow, Workington, Hucknall Town and Stalybridge Celtic.

While I was trying to track him down, I came across a profile piece on him online which said he was now a fireman in Sheffield, his family home since moving from Ibrox in 1991. I know the area well, so had a fair idea from the description of his patch that he would work in one of three stations in the locality. He was based at the third station I called. He wasn't on shift at the time and they wouldn't give his number out, but the receptionist said she would pass a message on and, if he wanted to speak to me, she would be back in touch. A couple of days later she called me with his number and I arranged with Tom to go down and meet him during one of his shifts.

When I arrived a few days later I was invited into the station and introduced to him. He was a nice guy, very polite, but he was on the end of some good-natured abuse from his colleagues, who were taking the mickey because someone wanted his autograph. We posed with the strip in front of a fire truck – definitely one of the more unusual pictures from the journey – and had a quick chat about his time at Rangers. Sharing a dressing room with some of the huge characters and massive international names of the time was a great experience, he told me. He said he loved every minute of it, but knew after his leg break that his time at Ibrox was over and he would need to go elsewhere to carry on his career.

His dream to be a professional footballer and play for the mighty Rangers had come true. But as we chatted he revealed he had also had another childhood dream, and that was to be a fireman. Most of us aren't lucky enough to achieve one of our dreams, but Tom managed both – and it couldn't have happened to a nicer guy.

Gordon Durie

EVEN IN the early days of tracking down the players, before I started travelling overseas, I felt nerves in the build-up. Especially if they didn't know I was coming.

Would I turn up to the right place? Would they enter the stadium or venue by another entrance I didn't know about? Would I still recognise them? All of these questions raced through my mind while I waited for the player to arrive, frightened to look away for a second in case I missed him.

On this particular day I found myself in the car park of Cowdenbeath's ground, Central Park, one of the less glamorous stadiums in Scotland. I was awaiting Gordon Durie, manager of East Fife at the time, whose team were playing their local rivals that afternoon.

Durie was managing the club where he started his career, enjoying three years there in the early eighties. His form as a teenager saw him sign for Hibs in 1984, and after two seasons he moved to Chelsea. He played five seasons at Stamford Bridge, scoring 51 goals in 123 league games, and earned a move to capital rivals Tottenham Hotspur, in a joint club record signing of £2.2m. But the move to Spurs didn't work out, and he failed to see eye-to-eye with manager Ossie Ardiles.

Press reports stated both that Rangers were interested and that Durie wanted to come back north. Spurs turned down a £1.5m offer from Ibrox in January 1993, and it was 21 November before the move finally happened. With Durie now out of the first-team picture at White Hart Lane, he was sold for a cut-price £1.2m. Six days later, Jukebox made his Gers debut, the first of 87 league appearances during the nine-in-a-row years, away to Partick Thistle in a 1–1 draw.

He scored his first goals in his third game, a 2–0 away win against Motherwell on 4 December, and overall he scored 12 league goals that season, including hitting the net five games in a row between February and March. It was a great return from 24 appearances, and was much needed, with Ally McCoist scoring just seven goals that term due to persistent injury problems.

In the seven-in-a-row season he made 16 starts and four substitute appearances, scoring six goals. If that was somewhat disappointing, the following campaign gave him his best return at Rangers. From 27 appearances he scored 17 goals, including a hat-trick against Partick Thistle in a 4–0 away win on 14 October. He bettered that when he scored four goals in a 7–0 thrashing of Hibs at Ibrox on 30 December. Those goals were part of the ten he scored in a superb run between 25 November and 13 January. He topped off a great season by scoring a hat-trick in the Scottish Cup Final against Hearts, when we won 5–1. Despite his three goals, that game is known as the Laudrup Final, due to the amazing display the Dane put in, almost single-handedly destroying Hearts by scoring two and setting up Durie's three.

That final is perhaps indicative of Durie's Rangers career as a whole. A tireless worker and utility player who was full of selfless running and put the team before himself, but was often overlooked in favour of the big names when it came to judging his contribution. But his efforts shouldn't be forgotten. The ninth season saw his output curtailed once more because of injury, and he made just 16 appearances and scored five goals – one each against Hearts, Dunfermline and Kilmarnock, and two at Raith Rovers in a 6–0 victory on 15 April as we closed in on the big one.

Jukebox was one of the few to stay on after Walter Smith left at the end of the 1998 campaign. He was a fringe player during the Advocaat revolution and left at the end of the 1999/2000 season. He spent a year with Hearts, but an ongoing injury forced him into retirement at 35 years old. As well as his club success, Durie also earned 43 caps for Scotland and scored the goal against Latvia that clinched qualification for World Cup '98, to date the last competition the country has reached.

He took up a role coaching the under-13s at Rangers and became assistant manager at East Fife in 2010. He took over as boss in March 2012, but was forced to step down eight months later following a health scare. He became the under-20s coach at Rangers in July 2013 and, after Ally McCoist left as manager in December 2014, the board made him first-team coach. However, Mark Warburton brought his own men in with him when he was made manager in July 2015, and Jukebox left the same month.

Back to his days at East Fife, and I arrived early to ensure I didn't miss the team bus arriving. I had been waiting an hour or two when I saw a car coming round the corner towards the ground and it parked up not too far from where I was sitting. The driver and passenger doors opened, a young man stepped out of one side and an older bloke from the other. Straight away I recognised Jukebox.

I grabbed the shirt and jumped out of the car, giving him a shout as I caught up with him. The younger person was his son, Scott, who used to be on Rangers' books and was now playing for his dad's team. I explained briefly what I was doing and Gordon smiled, signed the shirt and posed for a photo. He had a game to prepare for, so it was nothing more than a brief encounter before he headed off inside the stadium.

It was only then, as I looked down at the fresh signature on the strip, that I was able to breathe a sigh of relief as another impromptu meeting went to plan.

Andy Dibble

THE CRAZINESS that nine-in-a-row brought out in everyone connected to Rangers as we tried to achieve the milestone can perhaps be summed up best in one player – Andy Dibble. Signed at a crucial juncture of the triumphant ninth season and playing just seven games for the Gers, albeit some of the most important in our history, he quickly fitted into the brotherhood of the squad and understood what winning nine-in-a-row meant for the club and the supporters. And maybe that's why he got a tattoo of the event to ensure he remembered his time at Ibrox forever.

He was in Toronto with some of the squad shortly after the end of that momentous 1996/97 season when Ally McCoist decided they should go to a tattoo parlour. Among the party were John Brown, Ian Durrant and Andy Dibble. Durrant had a Superman logo scribed on him and then Dibble was next in the chair. 'You need to get something to remember us by,' the players told him. Despite pleading that his wife would kill him, Andy relented and had 'Nine in a Row, 1997' tattooed on a shoulder. Then, as Dibble recalled in a newspaper interview, Ally decided it looked too sore and walked out before it was his turn!

Just two months earlier, when Andy was brought to Glasgow as an emergency signing for the injured Andy Goram and Theo Snelders, it seemed unlikely he would go on to be lauded by his teammates. In an interview years later, Brian Laudrup revealed that Dibble's first training session was a disaster and he failed to catch one ball. The players wondered if they would be better just putting an outfield player in goals for the next game, which just so happened to be against Celtic at Parkhead. This game was even more crucial than most Old Firm matches, because a Rangers victory would take us within touching distance of the sought-after ninth title.

In a white-hot atmosphere, Dibble handled himself well and did what he was called upon to do with ease. His debut in the Old Firm game made him the ninth Rangers keeper of nine-in-a-row, and he helped the team to a 1–0 victory. Despite goalscorer Laudrup's fear of losing a barrow-load of goals, Dibble had earned a clean sheet, which he would do another three times in the next six games, including that famous night at Tannadice when the team finally clinched the title.

The story goes that Walter Smith had gone to Manchester City inquiring about German keeper Eike Immel in his desperate search for a keeper. But he was unfit and instead manager Frank Clark suggested Dibble, who was third choice at Maine Road at the time. He was on the bench soon after signing to watch a 2–0 home defeat to Dundee United, but when Goram broke down injured again his moment against Celtic was quickly upon him.

Andy Dibble had a colourful career both before and after joining Rangers.

Born in Cwmbran, Wales in 1965, he made his debut for Cardiff on his 17th birthday in a 1–0 defeat to Crystal Palace. He won the League Cup with Luton Town in 1988, saving a penalty against Arsenal with ten minutes left, when they were trailing 2–1. The underdogs turned it round to win 3–2. He moved to Manchester City and was the number one keeper for his first two seasons there, before injury saw him relegated to back-up. During his nine-year tenure in Manchester he had five loan spells, but the most famous moment of his City career came when he lost a goal against Nottingham Forest, when opposition player Gary Crosby noticed Andy only had one hand on the ball as he prepared to kick it up the park. Crosby headed it out of Dibble's palm and stroked it into an empty net for a controversial goal.

In total he played for 21 clubs – including ten after leaving Rangers – in a long career that only ended in the 2005/06 season. It wasn't just that crazy tattoo that left a lasting mark on Andy's body. He broke a leg and also had a titanium plate inserted in his arm, but those injuries were nothing compared with the severe burns he suffered 18 months after leaving Rangers while playing for Barry Town in the Welsh league. His skin was ripped off when he slid on the pitch markings, and he spent two weeks in a burns unit and required a skin graft. The horrific injury was a result of the wrong chemical being used to mark the lines, and he received £20,000 in compensation.

After he finished playing he became a goalkeeping coach, first with Accrington Stanley then Coventry, Peterborough and, from 2010, Rotherham United. And that's where he was when I made him the next target on my list.

Now, I know this might seem strange to some people reading this, but I didn't contact Rotherham in advance of travelling down to try to meet Andy. One Saturday morning I decided to get up early, fill the car with petrol and drive to Rotherham in the hope I could catch up with him, because I knew he would be around on a matchday. They were playing away from home, but I was fairly certain the team and staff would meet at the ground to board the bus and I would be able to see him there. As I pulled into the car park at Rotherham's temporary ground in Sheffield, which they were using while their new stadium was being built, I saw a bus with blacked-out windows pulling away. I parked the car and walked over to a security guard and asked if Andy Dibble was around.

'He's just gone away on that bus,' he replied. I was two minutes too late. They were playing at Bradford, so I decided to jump back in the car and head north to Leeds, where my daughter lives. I would visit her and then make the short journey to Bradford's ground in time for the game finishing.

Once I arrived at Bradford's Valley Parade stadium, I walked round the perimeter until I found the players' entrance. While I was waiting a young guy came out of the door and we started chatting when he saw me in a Rangers top. It turned out he was one of the Rotherham players. I explained to him I had driven down from Glasgow that morning in the hope of meeting Andy Dibble and have him sign my jersey, which I clutched in a carrier bag. The bloke told me to follow him inside and the next thing I knew I was marching through the stand's corridors and being led into the dressing room, where the rest of the squad were tucking in to some post-match takeaway pizzas. I had a slice while I waited for Andy.

Someone came in and told me he could see me now, and as I went into the corridor I saw the ex-keeper coming out of an office, where he was having a post-match debrief with the management team. I introduced myself and we had a quick chat but he had to return to the meeting, so I quickly had him sign the jersey and then I took a picture. It was a fleeting conversation and an even quicker picture, hence the blurriness, but it was straight after the game so I couldn't expect anything else, especially since I had turned up unannounced.

I would imagine he was quite surprised to see a bloke from Glasgow showing up at an away ground wanting him to sign a Rangers jersey. I was happy I had met him and began the drive back home.

A couple of years later, I saw Rotherham were coming north to play Morton in a friendly. I thought it would be nice to catch up with Andy again since it was such a rushed meeting the first time, so I did some digging and found out the squad was staying at Mar Hall, just a short drive from Glasgow Airport. I went along and met up with him and we had a nice chat about his time at Rangers and how much he enjoyed it at Ibrox. He told me he still had some of his jerseys from his brief spell here, locked away safely at his mum's house. I couldn't leave him a second time without asking to see his famous tattoo, so he rolled up his sleeve to show the fading letters inscribed that night in Canada.

The tattoo might have been waning but his memories of being an unexpected part of Scottish football folklore remain strong. Andy Dibble stood up when the call was made and did Rangers proud – the ninth, and final, goalkeeper of nine-in-a-row.

Mark Hateley

THE IMAGE of Mark Hateley, arms outstretched, his mouth wide open in screaming delight, after he scored the opening goal in the do-or-die three-in-a-row finale against Aberdeen, is one of the most iconic of the nine era. That powerful header, where he outjumped Alex McLeish and left goalkeeper Michael Watt with no chance, announced his arrival as a true Rangers striker. He scored the second goal that day too, a second-half tap-in after Watt failed to hold Mo Johnston's shot. It was a dream finish to a first season at Ibrox that had at times been a nightmare for the long-haired frontman.

It started off well enough, scoring in the opening league game with a header against Dunfermline, but then he failed to score again for more than two months. When it became obvious that Graeme Souness regarded Hateley and Mo as his first-choice pairing and McCoist was relegated to the bench, the fans turned on the Englishman. He finally scored on 3 November, a double against Hibs at Ibrox, and also in successive games, scoring against Celtic in the 2–0 home win on 2 January and getting the only goal at Tynecastle three days later. In total he scored ten league goals in his first season, from 30 appearances and three substitute appearances.

It perhaps wasn't a surprise that it took him a while to get going. He had suffered a number of injuries and gone through operations, missing a lot of game time, in the years leading up to his Rangers move. The son of professional footballer Tony Hateley, Mark was born in Derby in November 1961 and started his career with Coventry City in 1978. He spent five years there, including a loan spell with Detroit Express in America as an 18-year-old, before moving down to Portsmouth. His 22 league goals in his first season were enough for AC Milan to make a £1m bid to the Second Division side. It was a tumultuous time for Milan and they had twice been relegated in recent years, but Hateley made a great start, scoring four times in the opening six matches. Then it came time for the derby, which Milan hadn't won since 1979. When he scored the winning goal with a trademark towering header, soaring above Collorati, he entered Milan folklore and was nicknamed Attila by the support. Unfortunately he went on to suffer a number of injuries and missed a lot of games.

After three years he was moving on and Rangers were one of several clubs, including six Italian sides, Bayern Munich and Monaco, which were interested in signing him in the summer of 1987. He chose the latter and won the French title in his first season, but injuries were to befall him again. In 1990, Souness finally got his man. With the problematic first season in the record books, Hateley started four-in-a-row with a bang, scoring a hat-trick in the opening-day match on 10 August 1991, with St Johnstone on the end of a 6–0 battering. He made 29 starts and one appearance from the bench, and scored 21 goals in that 44-game season. Other noteworthy goals came with a double in the 2–0 Parkhead triumph on 31 August, another brace at Aberdeen in the 3–2 victory in December, a goal against Celtic on New Year's Day in a 3–1 win and a hat-trick against Airdrie in the 5–0 match on 29 February. That was the season Walter Smith paired Mark with Ally and they quickly became one of the most effective and deadly striking duos that Rangers or Scottish football has ever seen.

He played in 37 of the 44 games in the all-conquering 1992/93 season, scoring 21 goals again and furthering his almost telepathic understanding with Ally as they proved unstoppable together. His performance at Elland Road in the Battle of Britain clash with Leeds was immense. His goal inside two minutes of the kick-off was a stunning strike from the corner of the box – eerily similar to a goal he scored against Motherwell in his first season – and his cross for McCoist's diving header in the second half was perfection. His form saw him recalled to the England squad against Czechoslovakia and he added one more cap, his first in four years, making it 32 in total.

With McCoist injured for most of six-in-a-row, Hateley had to stand tall and helped us to another title with 40 starts, two sub appearances and 22 goals, which included six doubles. Two of those came against Aberdeen in a 2–0 home win on 1 December and in the 4–2 Ne'erday Old Firm game at Parkhead. The seventh campaign started well for Mark, as he hit 11 goals in the first 15 games, including a double at Parkhead in the 3–1 win on 30 October, but then he suffered an injury and only scored a further two goals over the rest of the season, managing 23 starts overall.

He was suffering with injury at the beginning of eight-in-a-row and underwent cartilage and ankle operations that were to keep him sidelined for a month. Before he was back fit, however, the shock announcement was made on 24 September 1995 that he was leaving, joining up with former Milan teammate Ray Wilkins at Queens Park Rangers. Wilkins said Hateley needed a new challenge and offered £1m – big money for a player who was weeks away from his 34th birthday, so Hateley returned south. It was a terrible move for the big man. He struggled to score, the fans turned on him and he suffered more injuries. He realised he had left Rangers far too soon and wished he had never left.

On 15 March 1997, as we limped towards the nine-in-a-row finishing line, Walter pulled a rabbit out of his hat. With Gordon Durie, Seb Rozental and Erik Bo Andersen all injured and, having just lost at home to Dundee United, The Gaffer had a dearth of available strikers. Up next was Celtic at Parkhead in one of the most pivotal derbies in memory. So Walter turned to the past and gave QPR £300,000 to allow Mark to head back north in time for the match. The news might have upset Celtic's preparations, and Hateley certainly upset them on the park, too. His nuisance value helped the ball make its way through to Durrant, who lobbed the ball over the keeper, with Laudrup on the line to make sure it hit the net for the only goal of the game. Perhaps Mark was too wound up, because he was sent off on 66 minutes after a bust-up with goalkeeper Stewart Kerr, but he had played his part and victory was ours.

After he returned from his suspension, he scored one more goal and quite appropriately it was against Dunfermline at Ibrox – his last goal for Rangers mirroring his first in his debut seven years before. It seemed only right that Hateley was back for the nine-in-a-row celebrations after all he had contributed, making 162 starts, seven substitute appearances and scoring 88 goals during those years.

The following season he moved on to Hull City, where he was also manager, and his career came to an end in 1999 in Dingwall of all places. He was brought in to Ross County by his friend Neale Cooper, but was let go after just two games after the manager decided his presence was having a positive impact on the opposition.

Hateley remains connected to Rangers to the present day although he was embroiled in controversy when accused of becoming too close to some of the unsavoury incumbents of the club during our dark days, but he continues on in an ambassadorial role and can be found in the stand at most games. It was when he was coming out of Ibrox after a match one night that I had him sign the shirt. I had watched him on other occasions in the shadow of the Main Stand when I didn't have the top with me and noticed he would only sign a few autographs before moving on. I knew I would have to be quick, because when he became mobbed it was his cue to move on. As he came out of the front door, I stopped him before anyone else reacted, and he signed the shirt and posed for a photo before other fans swarmed round.

Hateley was one of only two players to be signed twice during nine-in-a-row, once by Graeme, once by Walter, and on both occasions he proved to not only be one of the greatest number tens but also one of the best headers of the ball we've ever had the privilege of cheering on.

Theo Snelders, Pieter Huistra and Peter Van Vossen

THE DUTCH Revolution at Rangers might have taken place in the months after the break-up of the nine-in-a-row squad, when new manager Dick Advocaat signed many of his countrymen for roles both on and off the park. But three Dutchmen also played their part during nine-in-a-row, to varying levels of success.

Winger Pieter Huistra was the first player from the Netherlands to sign for the Gers, arriving in 1990. Goalkeeper Theo Snelders came in as back-up to Andy Goram, and striker Peter Van Vossen arrived with the expectation he would fire the club to glory. Each of the trio was capped for his country.

It made sense that I would meet all three of them on one trip, from both a financial and practical viewpoint. First I had to track them down and make arrangements.

I started with Snelders. I read online he was the goalkeeping coach with FC Twente, the team where he started his playing career. I called the club and, somewhat surprisingly for Holland, the receptionist couldn't speak English. Thankfully she passed the phone to a colleague who could and I explained my story. He called me back shortly after with Theo's number. It was all very straightforward – he told me to let him know once I had a date confirmed, and he would meet me at FC Twente's stadium.

Next I phoned Groningen to connect with Pieter Huistra, but I didn't realise he'd moved on by that point to become assistant manager at Vitesse Arnhem. The officials at his old club were still helpful though, and passed on a number for him. Finally I called Amera City, where Van Vossen was assistant manager, and was given details for him.

Getting in touch with these guys was much easier than it had been with many of the ex-players, and that's because they were all still involved in the game. If only some of the others had been as easy to track down! Each of them said they would be available on the date I was planning on travelling, so I booked the flights and the B&B and began navigating the rail network that I would rely upon to take me to the three men. If this was going to work, I would need to be hopping on and off a lot of trains with little time to spare.

I'd been in Amsterdam Airport a number of times, due to it being a frequent stopover destination, but this time I had the chance to go into the city. I arrived on a late-night flight in February 2013 and made my way straight to the B&B to rest up before the big day. Next morning, I was out of my room and on the way to the train station at 6am, taking the train south from Amsterdam to Hilversum. I got off there and changed to Dronten, which took me east, then switched again and alighted at Meppel. I caught another train to a stop I've now forgotten as I headed south-east, and from there I caught the train to Almelo, then Hengelo, jumped off there and rushed to another platform for the short journey to Enschede, near the German border.

Theo had told me it was around a two-mile walk to FC Twente's ground from the station. What I didn't realise was that it was out in the middle of nowhere. At first I walked through a housing estate but the farther I walked, the more desolate it became, until there was only a house every 200 yards or so. Of course, I couldn't read the street signs and I was getting worried I was going the wrong way. Any time I passed someone I asked if I was going the correct way for the stadium. Those who understood told me to keep going in the same direction and eventually I would see the ground in the distance. If I thought catching the seven trains to bring me here was stressful, the walk was just as bad. I called Theo as I approached the ground and he came out to greet me, giving me a firm handshake and saying how good it was to see me.

Theo joined Rangers in March 1996 on a three-year deal from Aberdeen, where he had spent eight years and been a huge success. With current reserve goalie Colin Scott, who had come up through the youth ranks, on month-to-month contracts, Walter was keen on bringing in steady cover for Andy Goram, which would allow Scott to find first-team football elsewhere. The 32-year-old Snelders admitted he had been happy at Aberdeen but couldn't turn the move down.

Born in 1963, he made his debut for FC Twente in 1980 and played for his home team for eight years, until Sir Alex Ferguson recommended him to his old club. He made an immediate impression at Pittodrie and was voted the Players' Player of the Year in his first season in Scotland. He also picked up his solitary Dutch cap at that time. Some said he was never the same after a collision with Ally McCoist when Aberdeen took on Rangers in 1990. In treacherous conditions, Ally slid and the resultant damage was a fractured cheekbone for Snelders that required four metal plates to be inserted. He went to the World Cup in 1994 with the Dutch squad but didn't feature, and when Rangers came calling two years later he made the move to Glasgow.

He made his debut just a few days after signing, in a 4–2 away win over Raith Rovers. His only other outing in that eight-in-a-row season was away to Kilmarnock on 4 May, winning 3–0. He played four league games in the historic season that followed, between the sticks for three games in a fortnight in October and November – Aberdeen at home in a 2–2 draw, a 5–0 win at Ibrox against Motherwell and another 2–2 draw, this time away to Raith Rovers. His final league match of the campaign was on 4 January in a 2–1 win at Easter Road.

Snelders might have played more games for Rangers had circumstances been different. There had been debate over his state of mind ever since he had pulled out of a World Cup qualifier against West Germany in 1989 due to nerves, and there were persistent rumours it happened at Rangers too. He played a handful more games in the following season and then fell further out of favour when his countryman Dick Advocaat, the coach who had taken him to the World Cup, arrived as the new manager. Theo fell down the pecking order, eventually coming after Klos, Charbonnier, Niemi, Mark Brown and even a 16-year-old Allan McGregor in the queue for the goalie gloves. He left in 1999, returning to Holland to play for MVV before retiring in 2001 and becoming a coach.

Theo took me inside the stadium and asked me about my journey and how Rangers were doing. He took me on a tour of the stadium, showing me the trophy room, the dressing rooms and up into the stands. He compared the capacity and atmosphere to Ibrox and talked about the passion for football in Glasgow. I even met former England manager Steve McLaren, who was the gaffer there at the time, as we passed each other in the corridor. Theo signed my shirt and posed for a photo and then took me to the club shop, where he gave me a bag of goodies.

He was a really nice guy and I could have chatted to him all day, but I was becoming increasingly aware of the time and my need to be back at the train station. I felt rude but I had no other choice but to tell him I needed to go. My train left in 20 minutes and I had that walk back – I was probably pushing it as it was. 'Don't worry about it,' he told me. 'I'll take you to the station.' He drove me in his beautiful 4x4 and I arrived at the station in plenty of time. He maybe didn't play too often for us, but he definitely showed he has Rangers class.

I waved goodbye and went down to the platform, where I caught the train for Arnhem. It had already been a long day and I struggled to stay awake. An announcement over the tannoy woke me and I realised we had come to a stop. The carriage was emptying and as I looked out of the window I saw what appeared to be the majority of the train's passengers standing on the platform.

'What's going on?' I muttered, looking around. There was no one left in my carriage. I stood up, confused, and then thought I'd best grab my bag and disembark until I knew what was happening. I hadn't understood the message over the speakers, obviously, but I guessed there had been a mechanical fault. Now that I was on the platform, I saw the front carriages were being taken off. I asked a fellow passenger what was going on and he explained the front half of the train was going on to Arnhem, but the rear carriages, where I had been sitting, were being hooked up to another train and would be going to Dusseldorf. If I had been in a deep sleep then there's every chance I would have woken up in Germany.

We were soon back on board and moving again, and when we arrived in Arnhem I changed trains once more to take me to Doetinchem. This is where I was to meet Pieter Huistra.

I loved watching Huistra play for Rangers. He played the game with a smile on his face, and I'll never forget his look of sheer joy when he scored the equaliser away to Club Brugge during that amazing Champions League run in the 1992/93 season. Pieter looked like he genuinely enjoyed playing the game, and that made watching his skills a pleasure.

The winger with the sweet left foot signed for Rangers for a bargain £250,000 from FC Twente, where he had spent the previous three seasons. He also played for Groningen and Veendam on his way up the ladder.

He took a little while to adjust to the Scottish game, making more substitute appearances than starts (17 to ten) in the league in his debut season, the three-in-a-row campaign, but he soon found his stride. He made 25 starts and seven run-outs from the bench the following season, and 27 starts and three appearances from the bench during five-in-a-row. He also picked up three of his eight national caps while in Glasgow. His appearances were fleeting in comparison the next year (ten starts and 11 subs), but he was back in the starting line-up more often during seven-in-a-row, which turned out to be his final season. His first league game of the campaign came in October, a home win against Dundee United, and he started the next 14 matches. But he decided to leave in January to move to Sanfrecce Hiroshima in the Japanese league, where Dutch coach and future Celtic manager Wim Jansen was the boss. Pieter said he wanted to work with him.

His final game was away to Falkirk on 14 January 1995, and he signed off in style. He opened the scoring with a penalty and then fired Rangers level after Falkirk had gone 2–1 up. Stuart McCall then scored the winner in injury time. Likeable Pieter left the pitch shaking hands with the Rangers fans as he went up the tunnel in Scotland for the last time, with 87 starts, 39 substitute appearances and 22 goals his nine-in-a-row record. After a year in Japan he moved back to where it all began for him, Groningen, and then spent three years at Lierse in Belgium. After retiring he moved into coaching, picking up experience as assistant trainer for Holland's under-17s and assistant for Hong Kong's team. He spent four years as reserve team coach at Groningen and then became assistant manager at Vitesse Arnhem. From there he was assistant at Ajax and also their reserve team manager. He became manager of Groningen, then De Graafschap, and more recently he was technical director and briefly head coach with Indonesia's national team, then head coach of league side Persipasi Bandung Raya, before returning to Japan to become head coach at Iwaki FC.

Thankfully he was in Holland rather than the Far East when I made contact. I advised him when I was due to arrive and he agreed to meet me at the train station. Unfortunately I wasn't going to have much time with him, so I really appreciated him coming to the station to help me keep on schedule. I rang him when I was nearing his stop. The train's final destination was Doetinchem and then it would turn back to Arnhem, so I had to make sure I was on it. As we pulled in I spotted Pieter. He hadn't changed much from his Rangers days and looked like he could still do us a turn. I rushed off the train as the doors opened and hurried over. We had spoken on the phone a few times but I still felt very ignorant just spending a few seconds with him. There was only enough time for him to sign the shirt and pose for a picture. I apologised and told him I would hopefully see him again sometime, and with that I hopped back on the carriage. He gave me a wave as the train pulled away, probably wondering what had just happened.

I stepped off at Arnhem and changed for Utrecht. At the Utrecht station I was waiting for my final train to Amsterdam when a man approached me. He pointed to the Rangers shirt I was wearing and said they were his British team from watching us in Europe regularly over the years. We got chatting. His name was Michael Schuttler, and he told me he was the station manager. He went off and bought me a coffee and a biscuit, which I hugely appreciated because all I'd eaten since the morning was a Frankfurter sausage during one of my switchovers. We exchanged Facebook details and still keep in touch. He jokingly calls me Sir John due to all the well-known people I've met, but it was becoming obvious as I stepped on to my last train of the day that one famous person I wouldn't be meeting on this trip was Peter Van Vossen. I had kept my options open with the ex-striker because I couldn't be certain what time I would make it back to Amsterdam. He was aware of the tight schedule, and, while I hoped I might be back at base earlier, it was obvious I had been far too ambitious. Peter lived in Almere, an island-like city to the east of Amsterdam, which would require more travel to reach. I was up early for my flight home the following morning and it would be very late by the time I reached Peter. I called and he told me not to worry and we would rearrange our meeting for the next time I was over.

It was almost a year later before I gathered enough money for another flight to Amsterdam. This one was really on a budget – no B&B this time. I went out on a morning flight and went straight to the train station, destination Almere. I called Peter to confirm I was on schedule and he said he would meet me at the station.

Van Vossen is one of the more infamous nine-in-a-row era players, and that's for one reason – not something he did, but rather something he failed to do. During the pivotal final season of the campaign, Rangers were playing a crucial away game to Celtic on 14 November. It had been a tight game. Rangers were leading 1–0 but had missed a penalty. Peter came on with 12 minutes remaining and made an interception in his own half. He and Jorg Albertz then beat the offside trap and were through on goal with just goalkeeper Stewart Kerr to beat. Albertz unselfishly passed it to Van Vossen, which took out the keeper. The striker had an empty net to tap the ball into from seven yards, but somehow he managed to lift it over the bar with his right foot. Albertz put his hands on his head and Walter Smith turned his back in disbelief. The Rangers end gasped while the rest of the stadium let out a sigh of relief. It was one of the worst misses in Old Firm history. Truth be told, it was one of the worst misses in professional football. Celtic had a penalty saved afterwards and Rangers escaped with the narrow victory, but Van Vossen admitted the next day he had barely slept due to replaying the miss again and again in his mind. No one else would forget it either, and even today a particularly easy miss is known as a Van Vossen.

Unfortunately the miss defined his Rangers career. He had been signed ten months earlier, in January 1996, in a swap deal for Oleg Salenko with Turkish side Istanbulspor, where he had spent an unhappy period. He had previously played for VC Vlissingen, Beveren, Anderlecht and Ajax before his Turkey misadventure, and he must have thought his career could only go from strength to strength at Ibrox. He made his league debut as a substitute on 20 January during eight-in-a-row, on the day Hearts came to Ibrox and won 3–0. Not the best beginning, and he only made three league starts and three more substitute appearances over the remainder of the season, failing to score. During the nine-in-a-row campaign he made six starts and came off the bench seven times, including that ill-fated run-out at Parkhead, and scored five goals, all away from home. He scored a double at Dunfermline in August, followed by another double the following month at Kilmarnock, and fired one in during a 2–2 draw at Raith Rovers in November. Like the man he swapped clubs with, he found that life wasn't working out at Ibrox as either he or Walter Smith had envisioned. He played only once the following season, being more or less consigned to the reserves (where he scored 13 goals), but he was hopeful his career in Glasgow was about to be revitalised when Dick Advocaat, his former manager with the national team, took over from Walter in the summer. It didn't work out like that, though, and instead he was used as a makeweight in the deal to bring midfielder Giovanni Van Bronckhorst from Feyenoord.

He spoke out against the club after he left, drawing the ire of Advocaat and the Dutch players who had moved to Ibrox, but he seemed a really nice guy when I met him at the station. In the intervening years he had also played for De Graafschap, VV Bennekom and Vitesse Arnhem after leaving Feyenoord, before embarking on a coaching career. He was assistant manager at Almere City when I went over, his third assistant's job (after AGOVV Apeldoorn and RBC Roosendaal) and more recently he became gaffer at Fortuna Sittard.

My meeting with him was similar to the one I had had with Huistra, although not quite so rushed. I saw him getting out of a 4x4 with what looked like his wife and two kids waiting in the car. We had a quick chat about his time at Rangers, and he told me he had been happy at Ibrox. I couldn't fail to mention that miss, the Van Vossen as I called it, when I brought the incident up, and he said he finds it funny now but not so much at the time.

He asked me if I needed a place to stay for the night and offered me a bed at his house. It was a lovely offer and completely unexpected. I thanked him but declined, explaining I had a flight early in the morning. He insisted the next time I was in Holland that I stay with him and his family. What a gentleman. He signed the top and posed for a picture, and then it was time to let him be on his way as I returned to the platform.

I went straight to the airport once I was back in Amsterdam. My flight was at 6.45am, so I decided it was easier just to wait in the terminal for the rest of the night. Anyone who hasn't been in Amsterdam Airport will fail to comprehend just how big it is. There are signs up all around, with estimated walking times underneath just to get to other points within the airport, so from one end to the other it will say 45 minutes or maybe 28 minutes from one terminal to the next. It's a massive place. It can be quite daunting at first, but I'd passed through it so many times by this point that I was beginning to know my way around.

My second Dutch trip ended rather unexpectedly. I was standing outside the terminal having a cigarette and was just about to go back indoors when I saw a guy rushing towards the entrance, ready to throw away a cigarette he'd just lit. 'Here mate, don't throw that away,' I said. He passed it to me as he hurried by, clearly late for a flight. A couple of draws in and I realised this wasn't a normal roll-up, this was an Amsterdam special. Ah well, when in Holland, I thought, and I finished the rest of it off.

The flight home was one of the most relaxing I've ever had.

Joachim Bjorklund

WALTER SMITH did his business early in the summer preceding the nine-in-a-row season. He made just two signings, clearly not wishing to upset the balance of his squad as he went into what was one of the most crucial campaigns in the club's history. One of those acquisitions was Swedish centre-back Joachim Bjorklund. He was bought from Italian side Vicenza, where he had just moved the season before. Rangers had been interested then too, so when he became available again so soon the club made its move.

Jocky, as he quickly became known in Scotland, was 25 when he came to Ibrox, having started his career with junior team Oster before making his name at Brann. Gothenburg came calling, and then there was his brief foray into Serie A before he arrived in Glasgow in a £2.7m transfer. He made 29 league starts in the nine-in-a-row campaign and was fairly solid if not spectacular, with the occasional mistake ensuring he wasn't the replacement required for Richard Gough, who was edging ever closer towards the end of his Rangers career. Perhaps one of his most memorable – and important – moments in a Rangers jersey came in the final Old Firm match of the ninth season, when a victory would all but assure we would clinch the title. Gough wasn't fit enough to last the full 90 minutes, and, after he was subbed, Celtic looked to be through on goal. But a last-ditch sliding tackle from Bjorklund cleared the danger and made sure the slender 1–0 victory belonged to the boys in blue.

He featured regularly the following season too, but didn't last long under new manager Dick Advocaat. He was part of the new-look squad's pre-season in Norway but was sold soon after to Valencia, ending his two-year spell at Ibrox. He spent three seasons in Spain before returning to Italy, this time with Venezia. He then came back to the UK, signing with Sunderland, and finished his career at Wolves, where he made five league appearances before retiring through injury. He was prolific for his national side throughout his career, earning 79 caps and featuring in Euro '92, World Cup '94 and Euro 2000.

Jocky was another of the nine-in-a-row squad that the Scottish-based players I knew hadn't kept in touch with. Nobody I spoke to was aware of his whereabouts, so I turned to the internet to track him down. I discovered he was a scout for Valencia and also did some football punditry for Swedish television, so I sent some emails and called a couple of numbers at the station that I thought might get me in touch, but, as had happened many times before, the language barrier proved a hindrance.

I turned to Facebook, typed 'Bjorklund' into the search engine and diligently went through the profiles one by one, looking at pictures in the hope I was staring at one of Jocky's relations and I might spot him in a photo. It wasn't the quickest way to track him down – in fact it proved very time consuming. But I stuck with it and I'm glad I did, because I eventually came across a woman's profile that had pictures of her with Jocky. This must be his wife, I thought. From what I could determine, she ran a modelling agency and they seemed to live in Spain.

I sent her a message, hoping she could read English, and explained who I was. A short time later she replied, giving me Jocky's number and telling me to give him a ring. Result! He was a helpful, friendly guy and said that rather than me travel over to Europe, he would soon be coming to London to visit his parents, so suggested I meet him at Gatwick Airport. That would save me the worry of trying to find enough money for flights abroad, so we made the arrangements.

I flew down south and only had a short wait before his flight touched down. I met him as he came through arrivals. We had a little chat and he told me it was his parents' anniversary, so he'd decided to surprise them. We took some pictures in the terminal and I walked him round the corner, where he suddenly stopped in his tracks. A big smile and a look of shock crossed his face as he rushed towards an older couple. It was his parents. They had got wind he was coming over to surprise them, so they thought they would turn up at the airport and beat him to it! They seemed very nice and when the family learned I was also taking the train further into London, they invited me to join them.

We made our way to the platform and were chatting away as we took our seats in the carriage. But we weren't long into our journey when I realised I had got on the wrong train for where I needed to be next. It was typical of me. I abruptly said goodbye and thanked Jocky for meeting me and then I disembarked at the next station. He seemed a really nice bloke and I would have liked to have spent more time chatting, but I had another appointment and it was with a player I had been trying to trace for years.

Nigel Spackman

IT'S AN honour to captain Rangers, even more so when you get to lift a championship trophy as skipper.

Nigel Spackman was captain the day the Gers won three-in-a-row, undoubtedly the most nerve-wracking and closest-run of the historic campaign. Rangers went into that must-win match against Aberdeen as the walking wounded, with big names like captain Richard Gough missing out and others in the squad despite not being fit. Spackman wore the armband as Rangers put in a defiant performance, despite losing John Brown to a snapped tendon and Tom Cowan to a broken leg during the match, winning 2–0 thanks to a memorable double from Mark Hateley.

Spackman had come to Glasgow nearly 18 months earlier, debuting at Tynecastle on 2 December 1989 in a 2–1 win over Hearts. He would be an ever-present in the team for the remainder of the league season and quickly proved worthy of the £500,000 the club had spent on signing him.

Midfielder Nigel started his career at non-league Andover and made his name at Bournemouth. From there he moved to Chelsea and then spent two years at Liverpool. He left Anfield for more first-team action, but spent only a few months at Queens Park Rangers, a fall-out with the manager leading to a demotion to the reserves. He was rescued by a phone call from Souness and was soon on his way to Glasgow. The manager was quick off the mark to replace Ray Wilkins, who left the club on 25 November. Within days Spackman filled the void and, despite having massive shoes to fill, he wasted no time in proving his worth.

Scoring a goal against Celtic will help endear a newcomer to the fans, and just a month after making his debut, Spackman did just that. He struck the only goal in the New Year derby on 2 January at Parkhead. He won the ball in his own half and quickly passed to Mo Johnston, who ran down the touchline and fed McCoist. He prodded the ball into the path of the on-running Spackman in the penalty box, who slipped it away.

In the aforementioned three-in-a-row campaign he missed just one league game, against Aberdeen at home on 22 December in a match that finished 2–2, and during four-in-a-row he missed only two league matches, a home win against Dunfermline on 28 December and the last game away to Aberdeen on 2 May, which finished in a 2–0 win.

Such consistency ensured Spackman was one of the first names on the team sheet. Yet early into five-in-a-row he was sold, returning south to former club Chelsea. He made just two appearances for Rangers that season, a 3–1 home win against Aberdeen and a 4–1 away victory at Motherwell. Andy Goram tells a story about him and Spackman having words about the goal they conceded in the Aberdeen game, which resulted in a fight between the two in the dressing room at half-time. That's unlikely to have had an impact on Spackman leaving. It was more likely to be due to the three-foreigner rule UEFA introduced for European competition, which deemed English players who played for Scottish clubs as foreign.

Yet it all could have been so different for Spackman, who was actually picked in 1991 by then-Scotland boss Andy Roxburgh for the squad to face the Soviet Union at Ibrox. Nigel qualified through his grandfather from Prestonpans, but was removed from the squad shortly before the game due to protests from England. At the time, the home nations had an agreement in place that two grandparents needed to be from the country in question in order for the player to be eligible (if he or a parent hadn't been born there). If Spackman had earned the Scotland cap and become 'Scottish', who knows how long he might have stayed at Ibrox?

Following his second spell at Chelsea, Nigel moved on to Sheffield United, where he would eventually become player-manager. In the same season Rangers were clinching nine-in-a-row, Spackman was dealing with Sheffield United's chief executive Charles Green, who the manager accused of selling players behind his back. Spackman eventually quit due to the toxic relationship with his boss, but little did we know how familiar Rangers fans would unfortunately become with Green. Spackman constantly spoke out about the Yorkshireman after he ghosted into power at Rangers in 2012, but it would be quite some time before the majority of the support paid heed to the former midfielder's warnings, by which point it was unfortunately far too late.

Spackman also had brief spells as manager of Barnsley in 2001 and Millwall in 2006, but by the time I made my move to meet him he was working as a pundit covering the English Premier League for a variety of TV channels, including Al Jazeera and a station in Singapore. I logged on to his LinkedIn page, which is basically an online CV, and contacted the broadcasters he was currently working with. Through a combination of the language barrier and unhelpful people I was unable to make any headway.

After months of trying to find him, another of the ex-players I was in touch with managed to secure a mobile number for him. I rang it again and again and left messages, but never received a reply. I assumed it was the wrong number, but the person who gave me it said to try texting instead. Sure enough, Nigel replied and invited me to London. Maybe he didn't take calls from unknown numbers.

After meeting Bjorklund, I located the correct train and eventually made it to Stamford Bridge, Chelsea's ground, where Nigel said I should meet him outside the stadium bar. It was a midweek and there was a legends reunion taking place, so there were quite a few other autograph hunters around.

I made my way to the bar at the arranged time and Nigel was there with a couple of other ex-players I didn't recognise. During our chat I mentioned I was hunting for his former room-mate at Ibrox, Basile Boli, who at the time had seemingly vanished off the face of the earth. He didn't know where the Frenchman was but told me a couple of funny stories about his old pal's exploits when rooming that I'd best not repeat! We made our way round to the turnstile named after him, where he signed my strip and posed for some pictures. He was a nice guy and I enjoyed chatting with him, but unfortunately I couldn't wait around as I had to catch a train home to Glasgow, but I was pleased my day trip to London had resulted in another two names being scored off the ever-shortening list.

Alan McLaren

WHAT A defender Alan McLaren was. And what a shame he had to quit the game before he reached his prime.

Born in Edinburgh, the centre-half came through the ranks at Hearts and grew into one of the country's best young defenders. He picked up his first Scotland cap in 1992, aged just 21, and one of his better-remembered matches came at Ibrox in a World Cup qualifier against Italy, when he carried out a masterful man-marking job on the prolific Roberto Baggio.

His form for club and country didn't go unnoticed and, with Hearts needing money and McLaren being their key asset, he wouldn't be at Tynecastle much longer. Rangers came in for him and he moved in a part-exchange deal, with Dave McPherson and £2m heading along the M8 to Gorgie.

Alan started 78 league games during nine-in-a-row, scoring five goals and appearing once as a substitute. He had quite the debut, starting against Celtic at Parkhead on 30 October 1994, during the seventh campaign. McLaren was unflinching and helped his new team to a 3–1 win. He played a further 23 league games that season, only missing two matches – a 1–1 draw at home to Dundee United and a 2–0 defeat at Pittodrie on 4 and 12 February – in an impressive maiden year when he made the number five shirt his own. He scored his first goal away to Kilmarnock in a 2–1 win on 10 December and another in the April Fools' Day contest at Dundee United, which the Gers won 2–0.

He was ever present in eight-in-a-row and struck three goals. The first was away to Kilmarnock again in a 2–0 win on 8 November, the next was against Motherwell at Ibrox on 10 February in a 3–2 victory and, most memorably, the third was at home to Celtic on 17 March in a 1–1 draw. Gazza played a free kick into the box and McLaren met the ball on the penalty spot with a glancing header that flew into the keeper's bottom left-hand corner.

He missed the first half of nine-in-a-row due to a knee injury, his season only beginning in the 4–2 win over Kilmarnock at Ibrox on 17 December. He missed just two more games from then on – a 2–1 win at Easter Road on 4 January and the final game of the season at Hearts on 10 May. Perhaps his greatest moment in a Rangers jersey came three days before that Tynecastle match, however, when he was captain in Richard Gough's absence on the night we secured nine-in-a-row at Tannadice.

Little did any of the supporters know it would be one of the final times he would wear the famous light blue. The knee injury was serious, and two operations failed to repair the damage. He had a 25-minute run-out in Ian Durrant's testimonial in April 1998, but the end was near. Doctors warned him he could end up in a wheelchair if he didn't stop playing and so, at just 27, Alan was forced to retire. At the press conference announcing the end of his career, an ashen-faced Walter Smith commented, 'He would have been captain of Rangers, without a doubt, and the obvious progression would have been to do the same with Scotland. Alan missed half of last season and when he came back he had more problems but soldiered on and helped us win that ninth championship.'

That wasn't about to be forgotten, and it was good to see how well Rangers treated him. Although his contract ran out in May 1998, the club gave him another year's wage and paid for him to go to college on a business degree course. They also organised a benefit match for him against Middlesbrough, which took place at a sold-out Ibrox on 2 March 1999. His good friend Paul Gascoigne was chairman of the testimonial committee and featured for both sides in the game. Ray Wilkins, Robbie Fowler and Stuart Pearce also turned out for Rangers and John Barnes, Chris Waddle, Kenny Dalglish and Bryan Robson featured for Middlesbrough. The game finished 4–4 and Alan came on in the 72nd minute to score a penalty.

The club also gave him a role in the hospitality lounges at Ibrox on matchdays and, almost 20 years on, Alan is still a popular fixture in the suites every other Saturday. During my countless vigils outside the main door I saw him numerous times. He can appear to be a grumpy guy but that's just his persona. He's actually a nice bloke. I was in no rush to get Alan's signature because I knew he was at every match and

I didn't always have my nine-in-a-row shirt with me while I waited at the ground. Sometimes I was there to have the current players sign memorabilia that I could sell to fund my foreign trips. But on this particular day I did have the shirt with me and, as I saw him walking round from the Copland Road end towards the main door, I stopped him and asked him to sign it.

It was such a shame that his career was cut short, but it's good to see he is still part of the Rangers family. And it's well deserved, because he has his own special place in our history for being the captain on that glorious night in Dundee when we finally made it nine.

Gordan Petric

SOMETIMES I had to take a gamble in my search for the players. If I wasn't phoning a series of hopeful-sounding names from the phone book, I was messaging guys who I thought might be nine-in-a-row alumni on Facebook or standing outside Ibrox in the hope of spotting one of the 86. When I saw Scotland were playing Serbia at Hampden in a World Cup qualifier one Saturday afternoon in September 2012, I decided it was worth heading along to the national stadium and searching for a needle in a haystack. That was nothing new, but the problem was the needle might not even be in the haystack.

Gordan Petric was an imposing, stern-looking defender, a massive unit who looked capable of causing a fair deal of damage if the situation warranted it, so it was no surprise he made a decent career in the game as a central defender. Born in Belgrade in 1969, he began his career at OFK Belgrade before moving on to Partizan Belgrade. In his first season there he worked under Ivan Golac, and when the eccentric manager took over the reins at Dundee United, he brought Petric to Scotland with him. The big man had an impressive couple of seasons at Tannadice and did enough to interest the Old Firm. When Celtic made inquiries about a possible deal, Walter left a three-day tour of Denmark with the squad to come home and complete a £1.5m transfer for the Yugoslavian international.

Petric played his part in the final couple of seasons of the nine. He made 56 league starts and four substitute appearances, scoring three goals, in the nine-in-a-row years. During eight-in-a-row he played in the first 32 games and appeared from the bench in the title-clincher against Aberdeen. He scored away to Raith in a 2–2 draw on 28 October 1995. The following season, he started 24 games and made three substitute appearances. He scored in back-to-back wins, against Dunfermline in a 4–0 drubbing at Ibrox on 5 April and in the 6–0 demolition at Raith Rovers on 15 April. He was in the squad for the ill-fated tenth season and played under Dick Advocaat in the new manager's opening games against Shelbourne in the UEFA Cup, but with Lorenzo Amoruso, Craig Moore and Colin Hendry ahead of him for the defensive positions, he moved on to Crystal Palace and then had a short spell at AEK Athens in Greece. One season after leaving Ibrox he was back in Scotland, signing for Hearts. In 2001 he returned to Partizan Belgrade, but after failing to play a league game and following a short loan deal with Sichuan Dahe, he retired.

He moved into business affairs, but in 2007 he became general secretary of Partizan Belgrade and the next year he was made vice-president. In 2012, the five-times-capped Petric took on his first managerial role at Bezanija and was named Serbia assistant boss in 2014. He had two brief stints as coach at Sindelic Belgrade and Zemun in 2015, and in 2016 he was named gaffer at Serbian top-flight club Cukaricki.

Before all of those managerial appointments, however, his country was playing the nation where he had spent half of his career, so I had a sneaking suspicion he might turn up at the match. It was nothing more than a hunch. That's not to say I didn't try to find out in advance. I contacted the SFA and asked if they could tell me if he was coming to the match as a guest, but they wouldn't give me any information. Not that I was surprised – any time I approached the body and asked for help I never received anything in return. I thought that was poor form, considering I had loaned my shirt to the Scottish Football Museum at Hampden for them to put on display.

I arrived at the stadium early and took up a position at the top of the stairs in front of the main entrance. If Petric was coming to the game, surely he would go in through the front door. It also gave me a bird's eye view of the crowds of supporters approaching the front of the ground. I waited and waited, but as the clock ticked quickly towards kick-off, I began to think he wasn't coming after all. Plenty of familiar faces walked by me as I became increasingly anxious that I had perhaps missed him arriving.

Former Old Firm foes Tam Forsyth and Bertie Auld came up the stairs and I had a quick chat with them. They're both lovely guys who would happily talk for hours. I took a picture of them and thought it was likely to be my only photo that day.

There were only 15 minutes to kick-off when through the mass of fans I spotted this tall, well-dressed figure making his way towards the Main Stand. As he came closer I thought it had to be Petric and, as he reached the top of the stairs, there was no mistaking this distinctive giant of a man. He was with a younger male, who I guessed was his son. I approached Gordan with the shirt in my hand, told him I was trying to meet every player who played during nine-in-a-row, and asked whether he would mind signing it. His English seemed to have slipped since he left the UK but he agreed to autograph it and posed for a picture too, before disappearing inside.

As I walked away I could hear the screams from the supporters as the teams took to the park. That was nothing compared with the roaring relief I felt inside as I not only scored yet another name off my list, but avoided forking out on a costly foreign trip too.

Brian Laudrup

IT'S EASY to look back on the nine-in-a-row years and realise how good we had it as Rangers fans, but one thing we don't overlook is how lucky we were to have Brian Laudrup wear the colours for four years in the 1990s. He's quite possibly the greatest player Scottish football has ever seen, and it says a lot for the unique nature of playing for Rangers that he stayed here so long when he could have moved to just about any top club in Europe.

In an interview with the BBC website in 2015, Brian revealed he knocked back an offer from Barcelona early on in his Rangers career. 'So you'd prefer to play at Falkirk on a Tuesday night?' Walter asked him. 'Yeah, I love it,' the winger replied. He had finally found the stability he'd searched for years for, so was in no hurry to give it up. Born in Vienna in February 1969, where his footballer father, Finn, played, the Dane was a youth player at Brondby before graduating to their full team in 1986. He moved to Bayer Uerdingen for £650,000 in 1989 and impressed enough for Bayern Munich to pay £2m for him after just one season. He was there two years before moving to Fiorentina in another £2m transfer in the summer of 1992, when he also helped Denmark to a shock European Championship victory and was named by FIFA as the fifth best player in the world. After the Florence club had been relegated in 1993, he went on loan to rival Italian side AC Milan and played his part in their Champions League triumph.

He was on the move again in the summer of 1994, and this time it was to Ibrox. In the BBC interview, he said Walter told him he'd been watching him for years and offered him a free role on the pitch, which was music to Brian's ears. It became immediately apparent we were watching a phenomenal talent when he ran the show on the opening day of the seven-in-a-row season against Motherwell on 13 August. He supplied a perfect cross for Hateley to score, and then collected a clearance from a Motherwell corner on the edge of our box and made a diagonal run to the opposition's penalty area, leaving players floundering in his wake, and set up Duncan Ferguson to strike home.

His close control was stunning, almost as if the ball was attached to his foot, and he had a turn of pace that would take him away from defenders on the occasions his wizardry didn't. His skills befitted the number 11 jersey he wore, and he could score goals too. Overall he made 151 appearances for Rangers and scored 45 goals. Those figures included 89 starts and 28 goals during nine-in-a-row. In that first season he started 33 games, missing the away games on 7 and 14 January, the 1–1 finish against Partick and the 3–2 win over Falkirk, and also the 4 March away game when we drew 1–1 with Hibs. He scored ten goals in the league, his first coming away to Falkirk in a 2–0 win on 17 September, and scored at Parkhead in a 3–1 victory on 30 October. It wouldn't be his last against Celtic. He won the SPFA Player of the Year and the Football Writers' Player of the Year at the end of his first season.

Unfortunately he missed a large part of eight-in-a-row due to injury. He only played two games before spending time on the treatment table, returning and scoring in the classic 3–3 Old Firm game on 19 November. He also scored away to Hibs on 3 March in a 2–0 win. He was back to his best in the pivotal ninth season, starting 33 games and scoring a phenomenal 16 goals. Among the notable strikes were his 25-yard thunderbolt away to Celtic on 14 November, the only goal of the game, and the solitary goal of the second away game at Parkhead on 16 March, which he was credited with nudging in after Durrant had chipped the keeper. It wasn't just in the league he excelled, of course, scoring a stunning goal in the semi-final of the Scottish Cup against Celtic and putting in a performance in the showpiece game in May that earned the match the title of the Laudrup Final, scoring two goals and setting up the other three in the 5–1 thumping of Hearts.

But the most famous of all his goals at Rangers was that crucial flying header from Charlie Miller's cross at Tannadice on 7 May 1997, which finally clinched the hallowed ninth title. He would never score a more significant goal. He said later that in terms of importance, the match was up there with the final of Euro '92.

Just weeks later there were reports that AC Milan were to bid £3m for Laudrup, who was entering the final year of his contract. Then Ajax came in with a £4m offer and it looked like the maestro, who picked up the Football Writers' Player of the Year award for the 1996/97 season, would be exiting Ibrox so that we wouldn't lose him for nothing at the end of his contract. However, David Murray was willing to let that happen and persuaded him to stay. He was appointed captain at the beginning of the next campaign, but gave it up when Richard Gough answered Walter's SOS call and returned to the club. Laudrup's form in his final season was disappointing, and in February he announced he would be moving to Chelsea in the summer, as he wanted to play in the Premier League. Unfortunately his Rangers career didn't end the way we would have hoped.

Tabloid reports stated he was the highest-paid player in England, yet he only played seven league games before quitting and returning to Denmark with Copenhagen. He finally moved to Ajax at the end of the season, but retired when he was just 31, citing an Achilles tendon problem which made it too painful to train and play. It was a crying shame that such a talent was forced to retire at least five years before his time.

The 82-times-capped Laudrup revealed he had come close to rejoining Rangers just a year after he had left, but decided it wouldn't be wise to return. He stated in an interview in 1999 that he realised he'd had everything he wanted in Glasgow, and when he looks back 'I know Rangers were the best club in my life ... it was the best decision of my career.' He became a television pundit in Denmark after hanging up his boots, and won the battle with his scariest and most important opponent in 2010 by successfully fighting lymphoma.

He still returns to Scotland occasionally to watch Rangers, and it was on one of those trips that I was lucky enough to meet him. It was organised by Satty Singh, who I previously mentioned as the Rangers supporter who runs the famous Mister Singh's Indian restaurant in the city. As stated earlier, I also met Andy Gray in the establishment, but Laudrup came first. Satty had read about me in a newspaper article and asked for my number in order to help. He called and said Brian would be there on Saturday night for dinner, and told me when to come along.

A few nights later I arrived and introduced myself to Satty, who nodded towards a table where I could see Brian sitting with a group of men I didn't recognise. They were still eating, so Satty asked me to sit in the waiting area and said he would bring Brian over when he was finished. A short time passed and I saw Satty go over to the table and speak to Brian and look towards me. The Great Dane came over and shook my hand as I introduced myself and told him about my project.

Satty allowed us to go into a side room, where Brian signed the shirt and posed with me for a photograph. I thanked him for what he contributed to the cause during nine-in-a-row and for showcasing his amazing skills for Rangers over the years. He seemed a humble guy, soft spoken, and said how much he'd enjoyed it. I managed not to ask him why he was so good, but instead thanked him again for his time. As he made his way back to the table, I expressed my gratitude to Satty for setting the meeting up.

As I walked along Sauchiehall Street I couldn't help but break into a huge smile. I had just met one of the greatest talents to ever pull on a Rangers jersey, the one and only Brian Laudrup.

Ian McCall

IAN MCCALL made 21 league appearances between 1987 and 1989 and his nine-in-a-row statistics read four starts, five substitute appearances and one goal.

That solitary strike for the wide player came during his first appearance of the 1988/89 season, and what a shot it was. It came on 17 December against Hibs and was the only goal of the game. It was certainly a strike that deserved to claim victory. After winning a free kick out on the right side at the Copland Road end, McCall made his way to the corner of the penalty box. Wilkins took the short free kick, slipping the ball to McCall, who took a touch and then hit a lovely, curling left-foot effort into the top corner beyond Andy Goram. The goal earned him a starting place in the next game, at Hamilton, which we won 1–0, and he came on as a sub against Celtic in the New Year's game, which finished 4–1 to Rangers, and in the 2–1 defeat at Motherwell four days later on 7 January. He next appeared in the penultimate game of the season, a 2–1 win at Dundee, and in two-in-a-row he made twin sub appearances and two starts. His last game was against Hibs on 28 October 1989 at Ibrox, a 3–0 result for the Gers.

McCall started his career with Queen's Park in 1983 and earned a move to Dunfermline. After Rangers, he led a nomadic lifestyle, playing for Bradford, Dunfermline, Dundee, Falkirk, Hamilton, Happy Valley in Hong Kong, Partick and finally Clydebank. He became manager at the Bankies and then moved on to Morton, Airdrie, Falkirk, Dundee United, his childhood team Queen of the South and Partick. After four years out of the game he was appointed Ayr United boss in 2015, but when I met him it was around the time he had left Thistle in 2011.

It wasn't a planned meeting. Instead, it was one of those 'wait and see' encounters that came from hanging around the main entrance after a game at Ibrox. When I saw McCall exit, I realised he was one of the names on the list and rushed over to him. The problem with meeting players outside the stadium or at functions is the crowds of people gathering round before I've as much as said hello, which is why I always preferred meeting them elsewhere and having more time with the guys. I managed to get a picture after the autograph, but by this point he had lots of punters around him as he made his way back to the car, so I didn't even have the chance to explain what I was doing, which I found was often of interest to the player. Nevertheless, waiting around had proved to be worthwhile on this occasion and meant Ian McCall was another name I didn't have to track down later.

Richard Gough

FEW, IF any, players epitomise what it means to be a Ranger more than Richard Gough. A model professional, he was the captain for the majority of the nine-in-a-row campaign and led by example, displaying a fearless and winning attitude and mentality that made all those around him strive to reach his standards. It also provided him with 18 medals while at Ibrox – half of which were the nine-in-a-row league medals.

Lionheart was born in Stockholm in April 1962 to his Swedish mum and Scottish dad, Charlie, the ex-Charlton Athletic player. He grew up in South Africa but eventually gravitated to Scotland, signing with Dundee United, where Walter Smith was coach, but only after he failed a trial at Rangers. While we were in the doldrums, he arrived at Tannadice in time for the Tayside club's greatest period, winning the league and reaching the European Cup semi-finals. His performances at the heart of the United defence saw him win a move to London with Tottenham Hotspur, and he captained the side as they reached the 1987 FA Cup Final. Early in the following season, he was lured back north and in the process became the first Scottish player to be signed for more than £1m when Graeme Souness brought him to Ibrox. He quickly established himself as an intelligent and dominant centre-half and was named Footballer of the Year in 1988/89. When defensive partner Terry Butcher was jettisoned in 1990, Goughie was his obvious replacement as captain. His first match officially wearing the armband was the League Cup Final against Celtic, and he showcased his leadership qualities when he popped up at the back post to knock home the winner in extra time, the match finishing 2–1. Gough excelled in his 50-plus Old Firm matches. He famously scored a last-minute equaliser in his debut against Celtic, just a week after he joined, in the infamous game that saw Rangers reduced to nine men and forced to play the majority of the match with Graham Roberts in goals. Then there were his outstanding displays in the backs-to-the-wall performances at Parkhead as we edged ever closer to nine.

He made 263 starts and scored 19 goals during nine-in-a-row. In season one he missed just one match of the 36, a 3–1 victory over Dundee at home on 21 January 1989. His absence allowed Jimmy Nicholl to make his solitary nine-in-a-row appearance. He scored four goals, all at home. These came in a 3–0 win over Hearts on 1 November, a 1–0 defeat of Aberdeen on 26 November, the easy 4–1 Old Firm victory on 3 January and the 3–0 triumph against Hamilton on 11 March. In the second campaign he played 26 matches, missing important games: one against Celtic, and two each against Aberdeen and Hearts. It was a similar story during three-in-a-row, the season he became captain, playing 26 times again. He missed six games between 10 November and 8 December, and four of the last five games in the tight run-in.

In the 44-match four-in-a-row he played 33 games and scored two goals – away to Dunfermline on 9 November in a 5–0 thrashing and at Motherwell on 30 November in a 2–0 win. He missed 19 league games during five-in-a-row, again scoring two goals, these coming against Partick Thistle and St Johnstone. He was relatively injury-free for six-in-a-row, playing 37 of the 44 matches and scoring away to St Johnstone, Hibs and Partick. He played 35 of the 36 matches during seven, scoring against Hibs on Boxing Day in a 2–0 victory, and 29 times the following season, finding the net against Partick twice and Raith. Goughie turned out 27 times in the all-important ninth campaign. He played the first 19 but missed the 2 January Old Firm match at Ibrox, which we won 3–1 thanks to two late goals. He scored five times – against Motherwell, Dunfermline, Raith Rovers and Hibs, and in the 2–0 home victory over Celtic on 28 September. Richard played only two of the final eight games due to another injury. He was declared fit for the important game at Parkhead on 16 March that all but cemented the ninth title, however, and also played in the shock Motherwell defeat at home on 5 May.

He decided winning the ninth title meant it was his time to depart, going out on top. He moved to Major League Soccer (MLS) in America, signing for Kansas City Wizards, and the 17 league games he played for the team were enough to have him included in the MLS Best XI for the 1997 season. Gough made a dramatic return to Rangers just five months after leaving, reacting to a plea from Walter, who was in the midst of a defensive crisis.

While the title was lost, Gough showed he still had plenty about him. He went back to America, signing for San Jose Clash shortly after his 36th birthday. During the off season there, he signed for Nottingham Forest on loan, and his performances left Walter, by then manager at Everton, in no doubt that Gough could and should be playing at a higher level. And so the two were reunited once again. Walter commented that Gough was the most fanatical player he'd ever worked with when it came to training and diet. It paid off, because at 37 he was playing in the English Premier League. He remained with Everton until 2001 and then had a brief spell at Northern Spirit in Australia the same year, a year shy of his 40th birthday. His international career wasn't so long lived. He earned 61 caps between 1983 and 1993, but didn't play for the national side again after a fall-out with Andy Roxburgh. Successor Craig Brown refused to play Richard throughout his tenure as boss, which was a diabolical decision – but it might have prolonged his Rangers career, so perhaps we should be grateful.

Goughie had a spell as Livingston manager in the 2004/05 season, but for the most part he has remained in America since retiring. For a few years he used to come back to Scotland regularly, and while he was home he did some media work. He would appear on Radio Clyde's *Super Scoreboard* phone-in show and would always be on air the same night each week. On one of those evenings I drove over to the studio in Clydebank and waited in the car park for the programme to end. Around ten minutes later Richard came out the main door. I jumped out of my car as he approached his own, and explained who I was. He seemed a pleasant guy and was more than happy to sign the shirt and proudly hold it aloft in the evening sun as I took a picture. I wished him all the best and thanked him for everything he'd done at Rangers.

Although Richard doesn't spend so much time in Scotland these days, he still keeps a very keen eye on the club's affairs, and he threw his weight behind the movement to have Dave King installed as kingpin. In September 2015, with the new board in place, he was named Rangers' global ambassador. I can't think of a better man to represent our great club around the world than our most decorated captain of all time, King Richard.

Erik Bo Andersen

I DIALLED the number and, as it began ringing, I cleared my throat and took a deep breath.

A man answered, speaking in his own language.

'Hello,' I said. 'Is that the Erik Bo Andersen who used to play for Rangers?'

There was a slight pause and then he replied, 'The one and only!'

With some players you are able to continue following their careers after they leave Rangers; others just seem to disappear. The latter was the case with the Danish striker. By the time I turned my attention to tracking down Erik, I had built up a decent database of contacts, including many of the ex-players from the nine-in-a-row period. I asked all of them if they were still in contact with him or knew what he was doing now, but nobody had a clue.

An internet search showed he had branched out into different fields since injury had forced him into retirement in 2003 when he was 34. According to an interview in the *Herald* a few months after he had hung up his boots, he was the director of a sandwich franchise. Further digging online revealed that in 2004 he was said to have invested all of his football earnings into buying a field just outside his home town of Randers (it must have been fate that he joined Rangers!), which he then developed into a fully functioning residential area and later sold off in 65 building plots for houses. In 2005 he was elected as a member of the Danish Liberal Party to represent the Randers municipality council, completing a four-year stint in office.

There was no more up-to-date information, so I was at a loss as to how to contact him. Then I thought about how I had eventually tracked down Paul Gascoigne – by using the Newcastle region phonebook until I spoke to his sister – and wondered if I could do the same for Bo Andersen. I searched the Danish phone book online, and as luck would have it there was only one Erik Bo Andersen listed for that area. As he said when he answered, he was the one and only. I explained my quest to Erik, and he immediately agreed to meet. He invited me to visit him in Randers, so as soon as I had enough money gathered I booked my return flights to Copenhagen and informed him of when I would be arriving.

Walter Smith signed Erik from Aalborg for £1.5m in February 1996, halfway through the eight-in-a-row season. The 25-year-old was a gangly 6ft 2in and had scored an impressive 50 goals in 98 league appearances for the Danish side – one goal every other game being a decent return by anyone's standards. The Rangers support dared to dream that he would have the same quality and impact as fellow Dane Brian Laudrup, and while it didn't work out that way, Bo Andersen gave a far greater return at Ibrox than he is often credited with.

He made his league debut away to Hibs on 3 March in a 2–0 win and scored a double at home to Falkirk in a 3–2 triumph on 23 March. He then fired a hat-trick at home to Partick Thistle on 13 April when Rangers scored five without reply, and followed that up the next week at Fir Park when the Gers won 3–1. Despite that return, he didn't become a fans' favourite and his ungainly style saw him gain the nickname of Bambi in some sections of the stands.

In the historic following season, he made seven starts in the league and 11 substitute appearances, and scored nine goals. Three of those came with another hat-trick, this time against Kilmarnock, at Ibrox a week before Christmas in a 4–2 win. But it was his contribution two weeks later, in the Old Firm game at Ibrox on 2 January, for which he is best remembered.

All Old Firm games are important, but this one – the New Year clash, and with Celtic doing all they could to stop Rangers reaching nine-in-a-row – was even more fraught than usual. Rangers' preparations were thrown into chaos ahead of the match when a flu epidemic swept through the dressing room. Two of our biggest players – captain Richard Gough and wizard Brian Laudrup – were ruled out, while Gascoigne, McCoist, McLaren, Moore and Van Vossen made it into the squad but were nowhere near 100 per cent. Bo Andersen was also under the weather with the virus and feared he would be out of the running after he was sick 24 hours before the match. Due to lack of numbers, however, he was named on the subs' bench.

There were a number of famous incidents in this game that make it memorable. It featured one of the most stunning thunderbolt free kicks ever seen in an Old Firm game, when Jorg Albertz showed why he was called The Hammer with a monstrous strike to open the scoring, Celtic goalscorer Paolo Di Canio lost the plot when Andy Goram twice kicked the ball off his back during a stoppage, and Celtic striker Jorge Cadete had a goal disallowed in a questionable offside call as they chased an equaliser. But, from a Rangers point of view, nothing was sweeter than Erik Bo Andersen's late contribution.

Assistant boss Archie Knox told the striker at half-time that they would need him to come off the bench with a big contribution in the second half, and in the 75th minute he replaced an exhausted, flu-ridden McCoist. It didn't give Erik much time to make an impact, but it was enough.

In the 83rd minute, Albertz jumped on an error in the Celtic defence and played the ball to Bo Andersen in the middle, who slotted it past the keeper into the bottom corner. The decimated team were winning against the odds, but they remained under heavy pressure as Celtic tried to salvage something from the match. Two minutes after Cadete's shot was ruled offside, Rangers broke up the field. Again, Albertz fed the ball to Bo Andersen in the middle, and once more he passed it into the net. Walter Smith rushed up the touchline, pumping his fists towards the fans in the enclosure as Ibrox went wild and the stricken team took one step closer to their Holy Grail.

This was a prolific period for Erik. Two days later he scored in a 2–1 away win at Hibs, and the following week he fired a double in a 4–0 home victory against Aberdeen. He missed the next game, only to score in a 3–1 win away to Motherwell on 18 January. Unfortunately he suffered a fractured skull in a clash of heads with Celtic defender Alan Stubbs in a Scottish Cup quarter-final clash at Parkhead and was stretchered off on 38 minutes. He didn't feature for the club again that season. When Rangers signed Italian striker Marco Negri in the summer, the writing was on the wall for Erik, and he was sold to Odense in his homeland for a cut-price £800,000 in October 1997, just 20 months after he had arrived in Scotland. He scored 18 goals in 34 league appearances, keeping up his one-in-two record. He became something of a footballing nomad upon leaving Glasgow, moving on to MVV Duisburg in Germany, Vejle back in Denmark and Odd Grenland in Norway, and finally the six-times-capped forward ended his career back where it had begun, in Aalborg.

I flew into Copenhagen and then caught a train that would take me to Randers – a harbour city and former market town, and the sixth-most populated place in Denmark. The three-and-a-half-hour journey was approximately 140 miles north-west from the airport. I called Erik from the train and he was waiting to greet me at the station. He was very friendly and took me on a tour of the city centre. Everywhere we went, people seemed to know him, which I suppose is only to be expected when he was such a public figure in the city. He asked me if I was hungry – I was starving – so he took me to a bustling restaurant and, although it appeared at first to be full, we were shown to a table in a corner of the room. Erik insisted in treating me to a steak dinner and then followed that up with a whisky, and then another and another, as he chatted about his time in Glasgow. He said talking about Rangers still gave him goosebumps. He loved the rivalry with Celtic and admitted there was nothing like it in Denmark. All in all, he looked back on his time with the club fondly.

After our meal and once he had signed my shirt, Erik said he had a business meeting he must attend. There were still seven hours until my flight, so I took another walk round the city and stopped at a bar for another couple of halves – Erik had given me the taste for whisky! It was also the middle of winter and bitterly cold, so I needed some warming up.

I made my way back to the train station and boarded, settling down in a seat for the long journey back to Copenhagen. A couple of stops later, a group of teenage boys came on. They were maybe around 17 or 18 years old and were dressed like they were going for a night out. One of the boys saw me in my Rangers top and came over and started talking about the club. I explained what I was doing in Denmark, and some of the guys spoke in perfect English about times they had watched Rangers on the television. One of them brought out a cigarette and put it behind his ear, and I said I was desperate for a smoke. He told me the train would stop for around five minutes at the next station, enough time to disembark and have a cigarette.

When the train pulled up, a few of us got out and sparked up. We were chatting away when I heard a beeping sound coming from behind me – it was the noise indicating the doors were closing. The shirt was still on board! I jumped for the door and pushed enough of my body through to stop the doors fully closing. They slid open again and I pulled the rest of myself off the platform and back inside, the rest of the young guys following me on. My heart was pounding as I returned to my seat, where I picked up the bag containing the jersey and clutched at the handles. I would need another cigarette just to calm my nerves!

As I calmed down, I realised I was feeling a little bleary-eyed after the whiskies, not to mention the early start on my travels that morning, and before I knew it I had fallen asleep.

I woke with a start as a text message pinged on my phone. It took me a second to remember where I was, and then I pulled my mobile from my pocket and opened the message.

Oh, my God.

'Welcome to Sweden,' read the text, sent by my mobile provider. Not only had I missed my stop, I'd ended up in another country! While I was sleeping I had gone through Copenhagen, over the Oresund Bridge and into the neighbouring nation. I looked at my watch – thankfully I still had a few hours before my return flight was due to leave, but that only partially consoled me. My heart thumping, I got off at the next station, Malmo, and hurriedly located a member of staff. I was in a panic by now, but he eased my worries when he said I could use the same ticket to go back over the bridge and that the train was every 40 minutes. The airport was the first stop from here.

Trying to make the best of the situation and knowing I still had a little time to kill, I asked how to get to Malmo FC's football stadium and was told to jump on the number two bus (just like at home, the number two bus takes you everywhere!). It was during the winter break, so the Swedbank Stadion was deserted. It was the scene of one of Rangers' worst European results in recent years, when we were knocked out of the Champions League qualifier following a 1–1 draw and had two men sent off.

I took the bus back to the train station and finally made it to Copenhagen Airport with a little less time to wait than I originally anticipated. I flew back to Glasgow via Amsterdam, by which time the whisky fog had begun to lift and I was able to raise a smile at my Scandinavian shenanigans.

Jorg Albertz and Scott Nisbet

I HAD met nine-in-a-row legends in car dealerships, libraries, restaurants, hotels and even in my own home. Now I was hoping to meet more of the legends in a shopping mall.

I arrived at Braehead Shopping Centre, a few miles from Glasgow Airport, early in the morning in readiness for it opening. Rangers were competing in the Masters Football tournament, an indoor six-a-side competition featuring past players. I didn't know which ex-Gers were going to be involved, but I assumed there would be some from the nine-in-a-row era and it was worth making the short drive to check.

As usual, patience was required. I had never been to Braehead before, so I wasn't sure where I should wait for the players to arrive. The competition was taking place in Braehead Arena, an all-purpose venue situated on the ground floor of the sprawling two-storey mall. I asked around and was advised it would be best to wait near the main doors closest to the venue. Time passed and the place became busy, not just with shoppers but with the punters turning up for the football tournament. I was concerned I was going to miss the players. There were so many people milling around that I could easily lose them in the crowd or just not get close enough.

The past couple of years of spotting players arriving through crowds at Ibrox paid off when I saw a familiar face opening the mall door and coming inside. It was Jorg Albertz. There was another familiar face behind him. And another and another. They were arriving together. I quickly scanned the line-up and saw there were two nine-in-a-row players I had yet to meet among the group – the aforementioned Albertz and Scott Nisbet.

They were trying to make their way towards the escalator in the food court, so I positioned myself in front of McDonald's and waited. It was important I didn't miss either of them after waiting for hours. I reached Jorg first, who seemed a cracking big chap, and then made my way over to Nissy, who was just behind him. Unfortunately there was no time to explain what I was doing, but I wished the boys luck and watched as they disappeared inside the arena. They won the tournament, of course. Winning is a habit you don't easily forget when you pull on that famous blue jersey, and both Albertz and Nisbet were winners who would have run through a brick wall for the Gers. While Nisbet was born a bluenose, Albertz quickly realised what the club was all about when he arrived in the summer of 1996 and will be a bluenose until the day he dies.

Born in Monchengladbach in January 1971, the German midfielder began his career with Fortuna Dusseldorf in 1990 and spent three years there before moving on to Hamburg, where he would be made captain. After three seasons he signed for Rangers in a £4m deal, on the same day defender Joachim Bjorklund joined, as Walter made the final push towards the historic ninth title. We soon saw why he was nicknamed The Hammer. He had the most ferocious left-foot shot and was absolutely lethal from dead-ball situations. Although we perhaps didn't see him at his full powers in that pivotal nine-in-a-row season due to him being deployed at left-back at times, he became a fans' favourite.

It helps when you score a monumental goal against Celtic. It was 2 January 1997, and the pivotal Old Firm game at Ibrox was brought to life by one of the greatest free-kick goals ever seen in the contest. From 33 yards out, Jorg lined up the dead ball and struck it with such ferocity and pinpoint accuracy that Celtic's wall and goalkeeper were helpless. The ball bulged into the inside netting at 78mph and looked to be picking up speed. Albertz wasn't finished yet. With the game locked at 1–1 and 83 minutes on the clock, he picked up on a defensive mistake and fed in Bo Andersen on the edge of the box, who fired the ball home. Six minutes later Jorg did the same again and played a perfect through ball to the Dane, who finished the game off. It was a midfield masterclass and the start of a long love affair with putting Celtic in their place. The Hammer scored eight goals in Old Firm contests and set up several more.

He made 31 starts in the league that year and came off the bench twice, only missing the 4–3 home win against Hibs on 7 December, the 1–0 loss away to Dundee United three days later, and the goalless draw at home to Hearts on 1 February. He scored ten league goals in the ninth season, a great return, with his first coming in the 2–1 loss at Hibs on 12 October.

He scored in five games in succession, against Hearts, Raith, Celtic (as previously mentioned), Hibs and Aberdeen, between 21 December and 12 January. He also struck in a 3–1 win at Motherwell on 18 January, away to Dunfermline on 8 February in a 3–0 victory, in another 3–1 win at Hibs on 23 February and at home to Dunfermline in a 4–0 result on 5 April.

The Hammer continued to score vital goals, both at home and in Europe, when Dick Advocaat took over as manager. The Little General brought in some magnificent midfield talents, but Albertz was more than a match for them. Yet it always seemed Advocaat wasn't enamoured by Jorg, with it being rumoured that he felt his work rate wasn't what it could be. The Hammer might not have been a tough-tackling midfield enforcer, but there is no doubting his importance – 82 goals in five years demonstrates that. There was constant speculation he was on his way out of Ibrox, and it finally happened in 2001, just six months before Advocaat stepped down. There's a feeling that had Albertz outlasted Advocaat he would have spent the rest of his career in Glasgow.

Jorg returned to Hamburg, but the move didn't work out and there were tabloid reports he could return to Rangers in 2002, but it failed to materialise. He spent a season at Shanghai Shenhua and then returned to Germany with Greuther Furth in 2004. He spent two seasons with his first club, Fortuna Dusseldorf, and retired in 2007. When John Brown took over as boss of struggling Clyde, he put out an SOS and The Hammer pulled his boots on for one last run-out. He made his debut on 15 March 2008 and scored a trademark free kick. He did the same thing ten days later in a 2–1 win against St Johnstone and helped his teammates stay in the First Division.

Now a member of Rangers' Hall of Fame, Jorg turned out for Rangers in a testimonial for William Murphy versus Linfield in 2008, and showed he had lost none of his power or precision when he scored a thunderbolt from outside the box for Rangers Legends against Manchester United Legends at Ibrox in May 2013. In the same year there was tabloid chat about him potentially opening a tapas restaurant on the site of a former public toilet in Glasgow, and he also opened a football school in Monchengladbach.

Whatever he does or wherever he goes, Rangers will always remain a part of one of the greatest foreigners to play for the club. In a perfect world, Scott Nisbet would still have been at Ibrox when Jorg joined in 1996. Born in January 1968, he should have been in the prime of his career, no doubt slotting into whichever position Walter needed the utility player to fill. But Nissy was three years retired by the time the ninth season began, his livelihood cut short at just 25 and his final game coming only three days after the most famous moment of his career.

Brought up in the tough Muirhouse scheme in Edinburgh, Scott was playing football in the street with his pals one afternoon in 1982 when Rangers boss John Greig and Davie Provan pulled up in a car. Nissy had been turning heads at Salvesen Boys' Club, and the management team were there to speak to Scott and his mum about signing for the Teddy Bears. The youngster bottled it and ran away, leaving his mum to fill in all of the paperwork and sign her boy up to the Gers! He made his debut as a forward against Motherwell in a 1–0 win on 7 December 1985, but, after an impressive game as a centre-half for the reserves the following year, which was watched by Graeme Souness, the 6ft 1in player was converted into a full-time defender by the gaffer. He spent a short loan term at East Fife during Souness's first season in 1986/87 and slowly made his way into the first-team plans.

Nissy made 54 league starts and five substitute appearances during the nine-in-a-row years. In the 1988/89 season, he started five games and made two substitute appearances. It was in one of those shifts from the bench, which was also his first appearance of the campaign, that he scored his only goal of the season, in a tough game on 17 September away to Hearts that we won 2–1. He also made five appearances for Scotland under-21s in 1988 and 1989. The following season he had four starts and three sub appearances, but it was during three-in-a-row that he really put a marker down. He made 15 starts that campaign, including a 2–1 win at Parkhead on 25 November and in the do-or-die final match against Aberdeen. Mark Hateley told him to fire an early high ball into the box in that game so he could test rookie Aberdeen keeper Michael Watt, and Nisbet duly obliged. He rated it as his favourite game.

The following season, 1991/92, was even better for Scott. It was once said that every Scott Nisbet pass was an adventure, but he was an honest big lad who was desperate to play for Rangers and gave his all. He made 20 starts in the four-in-a-row campaign and scored five goals. These came against Falkirk in a 2–0 away win on 7 September, two weeks later at St Mirren in a narrow 2–1 result, a fortnight later at Airdrie in a 4–0 demolition and two weeks later yet again at St Johnstone in a 3–2 win on 12 October. The fifth goal came, like all the others, away from home in a 3–1 victory at Dunfermline on 14 March.

The 1992/93 season, five-in-a-row, was to be one of the greatest in the club's history, but sadly it was also Scott's last. He was featuring not only in domestic matches but in the historic European run, and it was a moment of incredible good fortune that will forever be synonymous with Nissy. In a close Champions League contest with Club Brugge of Belgium, locked at 1–1, ten-man Rangers were desperate for a goal to come from anywhere. When Scott went in full blooded for a loose ball down the right-hand side, the ball took a wicked ricochet off the defending Brugge player's toe and went high up in the air towards the box. It bounced near the penalty spot as goalkeeper Dany Verlinden approached it for what looked like an easy collect, but there was an incredible spin on the ball and it bounced over the goalie's head. Despite the keeper's last-gasp lunge, it landed over the line. Big Nissy could hardly believe it. Neither could anyone else. It proved to be the winning goal and our European adventure marched on.

Three days later, on 20 March, he lined up against Celtic for his tenth league start of the campaign. Within the first 20 seconds at Parkhead, he tackled John Collins and felt his hip go. He carried on for a while longer but was forced to come off. It turned out he had an arthritic hip and was forced to retire. He had six operations just to give him more mobility, and the club organised a testimonial, which was held on 1 May 1995 as the current Rangers team played past players, including ex-captain Terry Butcher, managed by Souness. Nissy came on three times, once to score a penalty equaliser, as the old-timers went down 3–2. Kevin Drinkell scored the other goal for the defeated side.

Nissy set up a hairdressing and beauty salon in Edinburgh and launched a soccer school in sun-kissed Lanzarote. Then, in 2002, he returned to the pitch to play junior football for Arniston Rangers, turning out for the side on and off over the next several years. John Brown tried to sign him for Clyde after he impressed for the Bully Wee in a friendly against Manchester United, but an unlikely return to professional football failed to come off. Scott Nisbet made 118 appearances for Rangers and scored nine goals, and, just like Jorg, his heart will always be at Ibrox no matter where he is in the world.

Both players' Rangers careers were cut short for different reasons, but there's no doubt they each made a contribution to nine-in-a-row and scored goals never to be forgotten.

Davie Dodds

MUCH LIKE Andy Gray, Davie Dodds was a striker and boyhood Gers fan who thought his chance to play for the club had long since passed, but Graeme Souness made his dream come true in another one of those unlikely signings the gaffer was fond of.

The Dundonian played for Celtic Boys' Club until Dundee United signed him at 14, and he made his way up the ranks at Tannadice. He was initially part-time after turning professional, serving an apprenticeship as a painter and decorator, but became an integral part of Jim McLean's side. After going on loan to Arbroath in the 1977/78 season, he played his way into United's first team and not only won a league medal but also scored in every round on the way to the European Cup semi-finals in 1983/84. He moved to Swiss side Neuchatel Xamax in 1986, but personal issues meant he needed to return to Scotland and he signed for Aberdeen later in the year.

By 1989, Dodds was spending less and less time in the first team and was coaching the youths and reserves. One day, Aberdeen manager Alex Smith called and said a team wanted to sign him: 'Get yourself down to Govan.' Who wants to sign me there, Dodds thought? The idea of it being Rangers seemed so far-fetched that it failed to even cross his mind. Once it was confirmed it was the Teddy Bears, he drove nervously down the road, signed, and then called his dad, who was also a lifelong Gers fan. 'I've just signed for Rangers,' he told his old man. There was stunned silence on the other end of the phone.

The 31-year-old made 17 league appearances for the Gers over the next two seasons, filling in wherever he was needed – defence, midfield or up front. He started four games, made ten sub appearances and scored four goals in the two-in-a-row season of 1989/90. He made his debut as a sub in a 1–0 Ibrox victory over Hearts on 30 September and started the game the following week when we went down 1–0 at Motherwell. He was a sub against United in a 2–1 win at Ibrox on 14 October and scored his first goal, the winner, as a sub against St Mirren on 23 December. Not a bad Christmas present for a Gers fan, scoring his first goal for the club in front of a packed Ibrox. He also scored as a sub against Dundee on 13 January in a 3–0 home win, on 28 April at Ibrox against Dunfermline and, wearing the number nine jersey, away to Dundee in a 2–2 draw on 3 March.

In the following season he made three starts, away matches against Motherwell, Dunfermline and Celtic, and then retired at the end of the season. His Rangers career was just beginning, however, and he was installed as a coach. The twice-capped Dodds remained at Ibrox until 1997. Once he exited Rangers he left football behind, and was said to have returned to painting and decorating and also ran a bar in Dundee in later years.

I met him briefly at a Rangers function at the Thistle Hotel in Glasgow city centre towards the end of 2012 thanks to a fellow fanatical fan called Angus Laudrup Morrison. He also collects autographs, and we had met during one of the many hang-arounds outside stadiums and functions as we waited for players to emerge. He called and tipped me off that Dodds was going to be attending this particular dinner. He knew I had yet to meet Davie since he'd gone off the radar after leaving Rangers.

These nights are always a bit harum-scarum when it comes to trying to pin anyone down. As I mentioned in the Gazza chapter, lots of autograph hunters always turn up at events at the Thistle, and there must have been seven or eight there this particular evening. Imagine that scrum, plus all of the guests, in a packed foyer when you are trying to look out for a certain player passing through. It's very easy to miss someone in the crowd, so I was thankful when I spotted Dodds and managed to make my way through the crowd to him before he disappeared into the hall. It wasn't the time or place for a chat, so I just asked him to sign the strip and manoeuvred enough space to take a photo, and then he slipped away into the mass of people.

Thanks to Angus, another name was scored off the list.

John Brown

THE IMAGE of John Brown standing on the steps of the Main Stand one June evening in 2012, imploring Rangers supporters not to trust chief executive Charles Green, will forever be synonymous with the man nicknamed Bomber. He left his job as chief scout in protest at the new regime and continued to warn the fans of what was happening at Ibrox, even standing up at a farcical annual general meeting and leaving the club's incumbents in no doubt about what he thought of them. He was proved right in the end, and Bomber is still welcome at Ibrox today, whereas those he criticised will never be allowed to set foot anywhere near the stadium again. John did what he did because he loves the club – and he had displayed that same passion on the pitch 20 years earlier for the Teddy Bears.

The utility man began his career with Hamilton Academical in 1979 and spent five years in Lanarkshire before moving to Dundee, where he scored a hat-trick against Rangers in 1985. He also scored the only goal in a Scottish Cup tie against us the previous year. Brown revealed in an interview with the Rangers website that he kicked Souness in frustration during a match at Ibrox where Dundee were beaten 4–0. The rest of the Rangers team gathered round Brown but Souness held them off. The next morning the manager called Brown, and ten days later he was a Rangers player. From that moment in January 1988 until he retired, Brown gave everything to the team he loved.

During the nine-in-a-row years he started 176 league games, made 21 substitute appearances and scored 12 goals. In season one he made 29 starts and scored one goal, against Motherwell at Ibrox on 5 November in a 2–1 win. Injury disrupted his two-in-a-row campaign, with 24 starts and three substitute appearances. His only goal was at home to

Motherwell again, this time in a 3–0 victory on 9 December. For three-in-a-row he played against Celtic and Aberdeen in August and then didn't feature until the 1–0 defeat of Celtic at Ibrox on 4 November. He thereafter played in every game until the end of the season. He made 25 starts and came off the bench twice, scoring his now customary solitary goal against Motherwell at home on 29 September in a 1–0 win. He took painkillers just to turn out for the injury-hit team on the final day of the season against Aberdeen, when we had to win to lift the title. During the second half, his tendons snapped and he collapsed like he had been shot. The fact he managed to play at all says everything about his commitment.

Following on from that, four-in-a-row was another injury-hit season, with 18 starts and seven substitute appearances. His first game wasn't until 28 September, the 2–0 home loss to Aberdeen, and then he didn't feature again until 30 November, coming off the bench three games on the spin. He scored as a sub against St Johnstone in the 3–1 home win on 7 December, missed the next game and featured as a sub for a further three games, one of which came at Parkhead on New Year's Day 1992. It was the scene of one of his most memorable goals. As he ran with the ball towards the Celtic box in injury time, the opposition defenders backing off, he let fly with a left-foot shot that went in off the post. He jumped the advertising hoardings and ran towards the fans as he celebrated the 3–1 victory. He only missed two games during the remainder of the season, scoring against Airdrie in a 5–0 home win on 29 February and against Dundee United away on 11 April, which we won 2–1.

Bomber was a machine in the famous 1992/93 season. He played 39 of the 44 league games and featured in every European game, Scottish Cup tie and League Cup contest, bringing his total to 59 for the campaign, more than any other player. He struck four league goals, against Airdrie in a 1–1 away draw and in three separate matches against Motherwell, making up for not scoring against them the previous season. The goals came in the 4–1 away win on 2 September, the 4–2 home triumph on Halloween and a 1–1 draw at Ibrox on 10 April.

Unfortunately the remainder of his time as a player was beset by injury. In six-in-a-row he played the first two games and then didn't feature again until 3 November. He had 24 starts that campaign. The following year, he played in the second match and was then out until he came off the bench against Celtic in the 1–1 home draw on 4 January.

He made ten starts and three appearances from the bench, scoring one goal. That came in the 2–2 Ibrox draw with Falkirk on 11 March. During eight-in-a-row, he enjoyed a run in the team from February, making eight starts and six sub appearances. His last game was in the 1996 Scottish Cup Final; although he was still on the playing books, he never featured in the ninth season.

By then he was working as a coach, first with the under-18s and then the reserves. He only left Ibrox in June 2006, when Paul Le Guen came in as manager. He was later offered the Dumbarton management post but turned it down. He did accept the Clyde position in January 2008, and utilised his contacts to bring in new players and keep the Bully Wee in the First Division, yet he was sacked in 2009. He rejoined Rangers as chief scout in 2011 when Ally McCoist became boss, but the aforementioned behind-the-scenes turmoil cut short his second stint. He was appointed interim boss at Dundee in February 2013, a position that became permanent, but left one year on despite the team sitting joint top of the Championship at the time.

John signed my shirt in 2011, shortly before he was given the scouting position. He was coming from the car park in the primary school grounds across from the stadium while I stood with long-time kitman, Jimmy Bell. I took a picture of Jimmy with the shirt, and John said that was a collector's photo because the usually dour-faced Jimmy was smiling. I'd met and chatted with Bomber outside Ibrox before when I hadn't had the shirt with me, so he was familiar with what I was doing. I asked him if he had contacts for any of the players I was struggling to reach at the time, but unfortunately he wasn't able to help.

These days he remains a regular face around Ibrox – and that's exactly the way it always should be.

Terry Hurlock

THE SIGHT of Terry Hurlock in a Rangers strip, his unruly long-haired perm resting on his shoulders and his face an almost permanent picture of intensity, is a memorable one. So it seems somewhat fitting that my encounter with the tough-tackling midfielder was equally memorable and certainly not one to be replicated in any of my other meetings with the nine-in-a-row squad.

Hurlock was a surprise signing at Ibrox, coming to Glasgow a month before his 32nd birthday. The midfield enforcer took no prisoners, and perhaps Graeme Souness thought that was a quality missing from his side since deciding to restrict his own prowling to the touchline rather than the centre circle. Then again, perhaps the transfer came from higher up, as David Murray said in a newspaper interview in 2004 that Terry Hurlock was the only signing he ever forced through on a manager.

The cockney had been let go as a youth from West Ham, and played non-league football before Brentford picked him up in 1980. He spent six years there before playing a season at Reading and then joined his boyhood team, Millwall. He was a true hard man, but there was more to Terry's game than simply stopping the opposition. In the summer of 1990 he thought he would be demonstrating that in an Everton shirt, as he believed they were in for him. Instead he headed further north and signed on in Govan on 23 August for a transfer fee of £375,000.

He was an integral part of the squad the following season, the closest-run of the nine-in-a-row years as Aberdeen pushed us all the way to the last game of the season. Hurlock played 29 of 36 league games, scoring two goals, and endeared himself to the support with his passionate play. One of those goals was in his Old Firm debut, striking the ball from outside the box towards the Copland Road end, a slight deflection taking it away from the helpless Pat Bonner. Hurlock wheeled away, looking stunned that he'd scored in one of the most famous derbies in the world. He said in a later interview that he thought he was going to pass out afterwards, but he held it together and the game on 15 September finished 1–1. He also played an important part in the next Old Firm game on 25 November, robbing Stevie Fulton of possession and playing an incisive pass to sub Ally McCoist, who rounded the keeper to score the winner and make it 2–1. Terry's other league goal came against Hearts in a 4–0 win at home on 1 December.

Tel's stay was brief. With a winner's medal in his pocket, he was promptly on his way back south the following season, having completed the job he'd been hired to do. He moved to Southampton on 9 September 1991 for £400,000, meaning Rangers made a slight profit on a player who was days away from turning 33. He played in the Premier League before moving back to Millwall on a free in February 1994, but was sent off just nine minutes into his return. It was one of seven red cards he accumulated in his career. He moved on to Fulham in the Third Division in July 1994 but was forced into retirement after suffering a double leg break in a pre-season friendly against Brentford ahead of the 1995/96 season. Terry had enjoyed a good career, even picking up three England B caps and scoring a goal for his country, but undoubtedly Glasgow was the journeyman's career high.

Hurlock was in the news again in 2012, hired by Bob Crow to work alongside him at The National Union of Rail, Maritime and Transport Workers (RMT). No one would dare to cross the picket line if Terry was around! Although snarling and aggressive on the pitch, he was often said to be a big softie off it and he showed his caring side when he became involved in the charity work of blind Rangers fan Scott Cunningham, who undertook a series of mammoth charity walks with his guide dogs to raise money for The Guide Dogs' charity. Terry became a big supporter of the Travis Trek and Milo's Miles, as the events were called, and came back to Scotland to participate in the West Highland Way alongside Scott.

One of the autograph hunters I occasionally chatted with outside Ibrox informed me that Hurlock was coming to Glasgow for a Rangers dinner in April 2012. I was told he didn't come north for club events all that often, so I should try to catch up with him while he was here. The event was at the Crowne Plaza, just beside the Clyde and next to the SECC. As far as I was aware, he was the only one from the nine-in-a-row squad attending the dinner who I had still to meet, so all of my attention was focused on looking for Hurlock that evening.

While I waited outside the hotel, my phone rang. It was one of my mates to tell me he was currently in The Grapes, one of the Rangers pubs near the stadium, and had just seen Andy Goram and Terry Hurlock leave the bar and get into a taxi. I wouldn't have long to wait now.

Ten minutes or so later, a cab pulled up outside the hotel entrance. The door opened and I waited for a head to emerge from the car. Instead, I watched as someone stumbled and fell out from the back seat on to the pavement. The person was clutching a blue carrier bag, which he impressively managed to hold on to despite falling out of the taxi. As he scrambled to his feet I could see it was Hurlock, with Goram climbing out of the other side of the car, laughing.

I approached Terry and asked him to sign the top, but unfortunately there wasn't much opportunity to chat with him. As the taxi pulled away, the commissionaire of the hotel invited the pair inside. Before they did so, Terry posed for a picture with the strip, the blue bag still in his hand.

It was one of the briefest meetings of all my encounters – but also one that I, at least, am unlikely to forget.

Neil Caldwell

NEIL CALDWELL is another member of the nine-strong single-appearance club.

The full-back came through the Rangers youth ranks and made his only appearance in the league in the final game of seven-in-a-row (the season we finished with the biggest points gap – 15 over second-placed Motherwell). The 20-year-old started the 1–1 draw at home to Partick Thistle, just after he had been told he was being freed.

He moved on to Dundee United in 1995 and played five games at the beginning of the season, scoring his only senior goal against Cowdenbeath on 19 August. He spent a season at Tannadice but didn't feature after September, and he decided to slip down into the juniors, playing for clubs like Petershill, Blantyre Vics and Rutherglen Glencairn.

Tracking down Neil in 2012 was another time-consuming phone book effort. I'd been given a steer as to which area of Glasgow he might be living in, and I started working my way through the Caldwells in the relevant postcodes. After several days of calling, I eventually stumbled across his mother. She said she would talk with Neil and ask if he was willing to speak with me. I left my number with her and hoped for the best.

A short time later, Neil called my mobile and said he was happy to meet and asked where I lived. He explained he was a plumber and bought his supplies from a wholesaler in Shawlands, which wasn't too far from my home in Ibrox, and the next time he was there he would drop in to sign my shirt. A couple of weeks later he called to say he was around the corner, and the next thing I knew I had another nine-in-a-row player standing in my living room. He didn't have much time to chat because he was on his way to another job, but I appreciated him taking time out of his working day.

John McGregor

I HAD travelled the length and breadth of the British Isles meeting my heroes, but still there was one man left who I believed was in the UK that I just couldn't track down, and that was John McGregor. For years I hadn't been able to find any up-to-date information, despite asking some of his ex-teammates like Ally McCoist, but no one knew of his whereabouts.

I contacted broadcaster Tam Cowan through his BBC Radio Scotland football show, *Off the Ball*, and he put out an appeal for John, but no one responded. Perhaps John had gone overseas after all, but right now it felt like the big defender had just disappeared.

Originally from Airdrie, John made his name at Queen's Park, his form there across three seasons winning him a move to Liverpool in 1982, at which time they were a true football force. He was never able to make the breakthrough at Anfield over the course of five years, and, following loan spells at St Mirren and Leeds, the call came from former Liverpool teammate Graeme Souness to join him at Ibrox.

McGregor played frequently in his first season back in Glasgow and also featured in the 1988 League Cup Final win over Aberdeen. But injuries were to wreck his career, and he is another of the small group to have made just one league appearance in nine-in-a-row, playing from the start in a 3–2 win away to St Johnstone on 12 October 1991 during the four-in-a-row season.

After he was forced to stop playing, McGregor was retained by the Gers as coach of the reserve team, which later became the under-21 squad. The man nicknamed Mad Dog during his time as a player definitely hadn't mellowed now he was on the pitchside – in fact, for large chunks of his coaching career he was barred from the touchline, running afoul of both referees and the SFA and receiving a succession of bans as a result.

It came as a shock to McGregor and the majority of onlookers when he was suddenly let go by the club in 2003, bringing to an end his 16 years at Ibrox. In press interviews he gave in subsequent years, he appeared to remain angry about the way he had been released.

At a loss as to how else I could track him down, I went to the *Sunday Post* and did a story with them where I asked anyone with information on John's whereabouts to come forward. I couldn't believe it when, the day after publication, I received a call from the journalist who had written the article, telling me John's mother-in-law had been on the phone. John was working as a car salesman for Arnold Clark just a short drive away in Lanarkshire and would be happy to meet me. I called the Arnold Clark branch, spoke to John's boss and made arrangements to come out when John was next working. A few days later, I made the short drive from my home.

John said his workmates had been calling him The Scarlet Pimpernel since the article had appeared. We had a laugh about that and a chat about my mission. I told him about my trip to America to meet David Robertson, Ally Maxwell and Paul Rideout, and the great coaching set-ups out there. It seemed to me that John remained keen to be involved in football. He was a nice guy, and after he had signed my top and posed for a picture, I let him get on with his job.

Here I was, travelling all over the world, and the one man I had no information on was just a few miles away all along. It was a wee bonus and gave me an easy one to score off the list.

Jimmy Nicholl and Billy Thomson

AN UNLIKELY member of the single-game club is Jimmy Nicholl, a true blue from Northern Ireland who enjoyed two spells at Ibrox during a successful career but just one match during the nine-in-a-row campaign.

Born in Ontario, Canada, he moved to Ulster at an early age and was signed by Manchester United when he was 15. The right-back debuted two years later, in 1973, as a substitute against Southampton, and made his international debut at 18. He won the FA Cup in 1977 in a victory over Liverpool but moved on when Ron Atkinson joined as boss. He joined Sunderland on loan in 1982 and then signed for Toronto Blizzard.

During the North American off season he came back to the UK on loan, firstly with Sunderland in 1982/83 and with Rangers the following campaign. We weren't at our best at the time, but he did win the League Cup when we overcame Celtic 3–2 in the 1984 final. His final game of the loan period also came against Celtic, this time in the league, and he was sent off while wearing the captain's armband in the 1–0 win.

He moved on to West Bromwich Albion, where he spent two seasons, but when Souness arrived at Ibrox in 1986 he asked Nicholl to return north. By the time nine-in-a-row started, however, Jimmy was coaching the reserves and no longer featuring in the first team. He did step in for one match during the 1988/89 season, playing in a 3–1 win at home to Dundee on 21 January. Jimmy was only 32 and still had some games left in his legs, so he spent a season at Dunfermline and then became player-manager of Raith Rovers in 1990.

He delivered what are probably the two most memorable moments for fans of the Kirkcaldy club in 1994 and 1995. They won the League Cup in a final contested at Jimmy's spiritual home of Ibrox, overcoming Celtic on penalties after the match had ended 2–2. If that upset wasn't remarkable enough, he then guided them into Europe, where they met the mighty Bayern Munich in the second round. They were famously 1–0 up at half-time in the Olympic Stadium, before the fairy-tale finally came to an end.

A move to Millwall followed in 1996, but not before a final playing appearance for Bath, where he was sent off just before the hour mark, and a year later he was back at Raith. He next joined up with Jimmy Calderwood, becoming his assistant at Dunfermline, Aberdeen and Kilmarnock, and also had two spells as Cowdenbeath manager, a brief turn as Hibs' caretaker boss and a stint as Northern Ireland's assistant.

He was still with Kilmarnock when I turned my attention to meeting him. I thought I would be making a trip to Ayrshire, but after looking online I learned the team actually trained at the Garscube Sports Complex, part of the University of Glasgow's campus, in the north of Glasgow. As I read up on Killie, I realised I could actually tick two players from my list on the one visit, because Billy Thomson was the goalkeeping coach at Rugby Park.

Billy is another of the nine keepers who played during nine-in-a-row. He made his Rangers debut on 1 April 1995 – 20 years after joining his first club, Partick – in a 2–0 away win at Dundee United during the run-in to title number seven. He made history by becoming Rangers' oldest debutant at 37 years and 50 days, a record that stood until the beginning of the 2016/17 season, when defender Clint Hill played his first game in light blue at 37 years, eight months and 30 days.

Born in Linwood in 1958, Billy made just one league appearance for Thistle during his three years at Firhill before moving to St Mirren in 1978. He enjoyed six campaigns in Paisley and won seven Scotland caps during that period, and then moved to Dundee United. He was cover for Hamish McAlpine in his first season, but established himself as number one the following year and played in the UEFA Cup Final in Gothenburg in 1987.

Thomson had a loan spell with Clydebank and signed for Motherwell in 1992. He spent two years there until Rangers picked him up in a £25,000 deal as cover for Andy Goram and Ally Maxwell.

After that first clean sheet at Tannadice, Billy played in the 3–2 home win against Aberdeen on 8 April, a 3–1 Ibrox victory over Hibs on 16 April, a 2–0 defeat at home to Motherwell on 29 April and a 3–0 defeat at Parkhead on 7 May. The following season, he made just one league appearance, a 1–1 draw at home to Aberdeen on 11 November, although he did also play against Juventus in the Champions League, making his debut in the elite competition aged 38.

He moved to Dundee on a free in 1996, winding up his playing career at Dens Park the following year. He became goalkeeping coach there and returned to Rangers in the same capacity in May 2001. He was well regarded during his six years at Auchenhowie and developed young keepers like Graeme Smith, Lee Robinson, and future Rangers and Scotland number one Allan McGregor. It was after leaving Rangers that he joined Kilmarnock's coaching staff.

I arrived bright and early at Garscube Sports Complex one weekday morning in the hope I would spot the team training. I hadn't called ahead, so I went to the centre's reception and asked where I could find the Kilmarnock team. The bloke at the desk told me the team went swimming on this particular day each week, and advised that if I walked round to the side entrance I would see them coming out. I made my way over and waited for the squad to emerge.

I didn't have too long to wait, maybe half an hour, until the door opened to reveal a stream of what looked like footballers walking out. At the back of the queue were the coaches. Jimmy and Billy came out in quick succession, and I stopped them and asked if I could have a moment of their time. I brought out the shirt and explained what I was doing. Both men were brand new. They said 'well done' and told me they hoped I managed to finish my quest. Each of them signed the strip and posed for pictures, and Jimmy added that it was a brilliant group of players we had in that period.

There is no denying that fact, and both Jimmy and Billy played their parts in our success, on and off the pitch.

Scott Wilson

SCOTT WILSON is another member of the single-appearance club during nine-in-a-row, but it was far from the only time the defender turned out for Rangers. He went on to make 78 appearances in the back four and had his most prolific period under the guidance of Walter Smith's successor, Dick Advocaat, picking up league and cup medals while teaming up with multi-million-pound stars from across the world.

The Edinburgh-born player came through the ranks at Ibrox, signing in 1993 when he was 16. He made his debut in the Champions League as a 19-year-old rookie against Ajax in 1996, and his only nine-in-a-row appearance came in the ninth season, starting in the 4–3 home win over Hibs on 7 December 1996. He also picked up a handful of Scotland under-21 caps during his Rangers tenure.

He went on loan to Portsmouth in 2002 and left Ibrox the same year, by which point Alex McLeish was in charge, and signed for Dunfermline, where he spent the next seven years. He moved to Australia in 2009 to play for Ian Ferguson's North Queensland Fury, but managed just four games before suffering a serious cruciate and medial ligament injury, and had to call it quits. He went through his coaching badges in an effort to get back into the game, but when I tracked him down – thanks to a tip-off from Gary McSwegan – he was working for a heavy goods vehicle company in South Street, a ten-minute drive from Ibrox.

I spoke to him and arranged to come along to the firm's base during his lunch break, when he would be able to spare a few minutes. I went along with my friend, another autograph hunter, and we waited in the reception area for Scott to come down. As I waited, my mate brought item after item from a bag and laid them out on the table in front of us for Scott to sign. It was embarrassing. I hated it when people did that and Scott didn't look too enamoured when he came down the stairs on his break and saw all the memorabilia awaiting his autograph. He signed my shirt first and posed for a photo, but he wasn't too chatty and I felt he wanted to be back in the dining room having his lunch.

Once he had signed everything I thanked him and we went on our way. I vowed then to meet the rest of the players alone, rather than go with other autograph hunters.

Craig Moore

IT CAN be easy to forget just how long Craig Moore was at Rangers. He spent 11 years at Ibrox across two spells and, unusually, there is no doubt it was during his second run that we saw the best of him.

Born in New South Wales in December 1975 and raised there, Skippy started his youth career in his homeland with North Star and then the Australian Institute of Sport. It was there that Rangers' scouts picked him out, and he came to the other side of the world to sign for the Gers in 1993, when he was just 17.

He made 56 appearances during the nine-in-a-row run, and his first came in the sixth season, 1993/94, starting in the goalless draw away to Dundee United on 5 April.

Seven-in-a-row was the teenager's breakthrough campaign, as he made 19 starts, came off the bench twice and scored two goals. Those strikes came away to Aberdeen on 24 September in a match that ended 2–2, and at Partick Thistle on 13 May, when it finished 1–1. The Aberdeen game was a controversial one. Mark Hateley scored what appeared to be a late winner from a free kick after keeper Michael Watt had picked up a back-pass, but referee Les Mottram ordered a retake and immediately blew the full-time whistle. Gordon Durie was sent off after the game, and Hateley was assaulted in the car park afterwards.

Craig made nine starts and two sub appearances in eight-in-a-row, with his only goal coming off the subs' bench at Pittodrie when the Gers beat Aberdeen 1–0 on 7 October. He had more pitch time during the pivotal ninth campaign, making 23 starts and coming off the bench once. For the third straight season he scored away to Aberdeen, his solitary goal of the campaign coming in the 2–2 game on 1 March.

Moore wasn't always given an easy time of it by the fans, but this was due to the fact he was often played in the unfamiliar right-back role when he was actually a no-nonsense centre-half. When Dick Advocaat came in as boss, he played Moore in his preferred position and he looked good there. But, after rejecting a new three-year deal, he was sold to Crystal Palace for £800,000. Due to the London club's financial troubles and Moore realising he had made the biggest mistake of his life in leaving Rangers, he was back at Ibrox before the season was over, re-signing in April 1999. He was in his second spell at just 23. He scored on his return against St Johnstone and became an integral part of the side, although not before Advocaat subbed him early in the opening game of the 1999/2000 season against Kilmarnock. That kicked Skippy into action, and he became a stalwart for the Little General and his successor, Alex McLeish.

Moore was also very proud to play for his country, and this ultimately led to the demise of his Rangers career. Having played for Australia at under-17, under-20 and under-23 levels and winning 52 caps with the senior team, playing in three World Cups, he decided he wanted to represent his country at the Olympics in 2004. It would mean missing a vital Champions League qualifier for Rangers, and the dispute between Moore and McLeish effectively spelled the end of his time in Glasgow. He had a brief period with Borussia Monchengladbach in 2005, where Advocaat was boss, and then spent two years at Newcastle before going home to play with Brisbane Roar and Kavala. It was during his time at Roar that he was diagnosed with testicular cancer. Following an operation, he was thankfully given the all-clear and was back playing weeks later.

He retired after the 2010 World Cup but continues to be involved in the game. He became player mentor with the national team, operations manager at Brisbane Roar and manager of Gold Coast Premier League side Coomera Colts Soccer Club.

The Australia-based contingent of the nine-in-a-row squad concerned me, because I couldn't imagine being able to make that journey – or afford it – in order to track them down. So I was delighted when I heard a familiar Aussie accent on Radio Scotland's *Sportsound* programme one afternoon in 2011. It was Moore! I immediately grabbed the shirt, rushed round to the BBC building and waited for him to come off the air. When he came down the stairs, I approached him and we had a quick chat as he signed the shirt and posed for a picture. He told me he was back visiting (his wife, Heather, is Scottish) for a little while, and I quipped that he might just have saved me a very long flight.

Three days later, I was in a charity shop. I would often pop into these stores in the hope I could pick up a vintage football strip for pennies, have it autographed and then sell it on to help pay for my trips. On this occasion I spotted a shirt I didn't recognise. It was brand new, with the tags still on. I pulled it from the rack and examined the club badge. It was Northern Fury's top, the team Rangers had linked up with around ten years before. I paid £4 for it.

The following day there was a function at Hampden which I thought had potential for some decent names to appear, so I went along with a bag containing a few shirts, including the Fury top, and waited around outside. Soon after, I spotted Craig Moore approaching. Here was me thinking I would have to travel Down Under to meet him and now I had encountered him twice in a week! I asked if he would mind signing something else for me and pulled out the Northern Fury shirt. It must have been fate. He signed the top, and I later sold it for £55, giving me a profit of more than £50. That was a tank of petrol or a B&B for the night, so Craig ended up doing me two good turns – just like he did with Rangers.

Stephen Watson

WITH THE exception of Oleg Salenko, Stephen Watson was perhaps the hardest of the players to track down.

It took me years, on and off, and the trail was stone cold for a long time. I put a post on Facebook, my friend put out a plea on FollowFollow (the most popular of the Rangers fan forums), I called Everton FC – his home-town team and the one I'd read he supported – and even Liverpool, just on the off-chance he was living on Merseyside again.

Signed by Graeme Souness in August 1990 as a 17-year-old centre-half and full-back, Stephen spent seven years with youth side Maudsley, where he caught the eye of Rangers' scout in the area, Geoff Twentyman. Liverpool had shown an interest too, but when they hesitated, Rangers stepped in. Walter went down and watched him play and decided to offer him a deal. Stephen was also in the second year of a YTS scheme to be a cabinet maker, earning £29.50 per week, so it's safe to say his life was about to change. His parents moved north with him and the family settled in Kilwinning, Ayrshire.

Nicknamed Shmoo by his teammates, after the cartoon character, Stephen played in the youths and reserves for several years. He was preparing for a second-string match against Hearts on 14 April 1993 when coach Davie Dodds told him he would actually be starting for the first team that night. He played left-back in the hard-fought match at Tynecastle, making a crucial goal-line clearance in the 89th minute to ensure the game finished 3–2 to Rangers. He made his home debut three days later in a 3–1 win against Partick and started the reverse fixture at Firhill on 4 May, which finished 3–0 to the Jags. Stephen was also on the bench for the match in Marseille that could have seen Rangers reach the Champions League Final.

He moved to St Mirren in 1994, where he spent four years, and was developed into a midfielder. From there he played for two years in Honk Kong for Yee Hope, before coming home to Falkirk and having a brief run with Partick Thistle. He moved to the juniors and played for his adopted home-town team of Kilwinning Rangers.

I had been asking anyone and everyone with a Rangers connection if they knew Stephen's whereabouts, and eventually it paid off when I was told he was still living in Ayrshire. It was time for another tedious run through the phone book, calling a list of S. Watsons before I finally found him. He couldn't have been nicer when I called. We had a laugh about all the attempts I'd made to find him, and he invited me down to his home the following Sunday morning to sign the shirt. Stephen, his wife and their two kids invited me into their lovely semi-detached house with open arms and listened as I told them about my travels to meet the ex-players. One of Stephen's kids has a disability, and I think that inspired him when choosing an occupation after football. He told me about working with disabled kids in Merseyside through the week and then coming home at the weekend. It was a hell of a shift with the travel involved, but it was obviously something he was passionate about, and all power to him. We also chatted about Everton – his true football love – and his time at Rangers.

He signed the shirt, and I took a lovely picture of him with the strip alongside his family, including his niece, in the living room. We vowed to stay in touch and we have done. He's on Facebook now, and we message each other every week for a catch-up about football and life in general. Stephen is without doubt one of life's good guys and it was a pleasure to be invited into his home.

Duncan Ferguson

OF ALL the places around the world where I had met the players, no location was more surprising than where I saw Duncan Ferguson. The SFA's training centre in Largs.

I had read in the newspaper the previous day that he was coming to North Ayrshire to do his coaching badges. Ordinarily that would not have been news, because scores of the game's greats had earned their licences there over the years, but Duncan Ferguson had such a hostile relationship with the national body that it seemed inconceivable he would attend one of their courses.

The 6ft 4in striker saw his career interrupted by a jail term in Glasgow's notorious Barlinnie prison, a sentence brought down on him after he headbutted a player on the pitch at Ibrox while playing for Rangers. Big Dunc already had previous convictions, so this latest misdemeanour was pounced upon by the land's authorities and he was charged with assault. It seemed crazy that a typical act of on-field violence would result in a court case, but of course this wasn't the first time a Rangers player had appeared in the dock due to an on-the-pitch fracas.

It was 16 April 1994 and Raith Rovers were the opposition. The game was already notable for Duncan scoring his long-awaited first goal for Rangers since his transfer from Dundee United earlier in the season, but a second-half moment of madness sent the match into infamy. After a tangle with Jock McStay in the corner of the pitch at the Broomloan Road end, Ferguson turned and headbutted the full-back. There was no denying it, yet referee Kenny Clark – who had booked him earlier for his goal celebrations – took no action. The referee supervisor did, though, reporting the incident afterwards.

Jock McStay failed to turn up at the SFA hearing, but the association banned Ferguson for 12 matches on 12 May, despite Rangers asking for the tribunal to be postponed until after his court appearance. Dunc considered legal action on the basis that the decision could prejudice the upcoming court trial. He appealed the ban, allowing him to be available for the Scottish Cup Final. The SFA continued their crazy course of action by setting the appeal hearing for the start of September, even though the trial was set for 25 October. Finally sense was seen and the appeal was postponed until after the court proceedings. Subsequently the trial was moved to January and then adjourned until 9 May 1995. By this point, he had escaped Scottish football and moved to Everton. He was found guilty on 10 May and sentenced five days after Everton's FA Cup Final victory, when he came on as a substitute. He was given a three-month prison term due to it being his third conviction for assault, but he lodged an appeal.

His lawyer, and Rangers vice-chairman, Donald Findlay QC, argued at Edinburgh's Appeals Court in October that more than 120 Scots had been sent off for violent play in the 1993/94 season and not one of them had been charged with assault. But the argument fell on deaf ears, and Duncan became the first British professional footballer to be jailed for attacking an opponent on the pitch. He served half his jail term and was released on 24 November 1995. To make matters worse, in December an independent panel upheld the 12-match ban. Everton applied for a judicial review, so the suspension was frozen until the hearing. The decision was deferred on 19 January 1996 and he was finally cleared on 31 January, almost two years after the original sorry incident. He did play international football again, pulling on the dark blue 20 months after his last cap but it was fairly short lived and he retired from internationals in 1997 with just seven caps – and who can blame him after the way the SFA had acted throughout the court proceedings?

The prison sentence overshadowed Ferguson's playing career, but the truth is injuries caused more harm than the jail term. Yet his career started so promisingly. Born in Stirling in December 1971, he played with youth side Carse Thistle before Dundee United signed him on a professional contract in 1990. He made his debut that year in a 2–1 win over Rangers. He had a good touch and an eye for goal, and was strong. It wouldn't be long before Rangers showed an interest. We were fined £5,000 in May 1993 when it was deemed we had publicly tapped him up. Dundee United lined him up for a £3.25m move to Leeds, even though David Murray twice made a better offer, because United claimed they wouldn't sell him to a rival. According to newspaper reports at the time, the Tannadice side even wanted a clause put in his Leeds contract that the Yorkshire club wouldn't sell him to Rangers at a later date. It was petty, but in future years that would become par for the course with this club when it came to Rangers.

Eventually they couldn't turn our money down and the £3.7m deal (potentially rising to £4.1m dependent on Scotland caps) set a transfer record between two British clubs. His debut came in the third match of the six-in-a-row season, away to Celtic on 21 August. The game finished goalless. He played the next three games and came on as a sub in the fourth, but then he was out until an appearance off the bench on 29 March in a 2–1 win away to Partick. As previously mentioned, he scored his first goal in the Raith game, winning 4–0, and made one more start in a loss against Motherwell, along with a sub appearance in the 1–1 home draw with Celtic on 30 April.

The next season started well, as he came on as a sub on the opening day against Motherwell on 13 August and scored in the 2–1 win after great set-up play from debutant Brian Laudrup. He started the next game against Partick, and was a sub in the 2–0 loss at home to Celtic on 27 August and the 3–0 Ibrox win over Hearts on 11 September. That would be his final appearance, as he moved to Everton on loan alongside Ian Durrant. The midfielder returned after a month, but Dunc's move was made permanent and he finally found a home at Goodison. He loved it there and the fans adored him. So imagine their joint heartbreak and shock when he was sold to Newcastle behind not just his back but that of his new manager, Walter Smith. He spent two years in the north-east, but the move failed to work out and he returned to Merseyside in 2000, where he remained until he retired in 2006. He moved with his family to Spain, and when he came home five years later he volunteered to coach kids at Everton. He proved himself up to the task, was given a job and eventually worked his way up to first-team coach, firmly entrenched as a Toffees legend. It was his ascendancy in the coaching capacity that led to him coming to Largs.

I had never been to the coaching centre before and had no idea if Duncan would actually be there. For all I knew, it could just have been a newspaper rumour, but I felt it was worth taking the drive down just in case. I was taken aback by the size of the centre upon my arrival, and my heart sank. It was a sprawling, massive facility with more than one entrance, which was only going to make it more difficult to spot him. Of course, I didn't know when he would arrive, so I turned up at 8.30am, going on the assumption it would be a 9am start. It was a freezing cold day, and I ended up standing on an exposed corner, the cold wind rattling through my bones, so that I could see as much of the facility as possible.

The minutes move slowly when you're waiting around for an undetermined amount of time, but I was becoming accustomed to it. Paul Hartley was the first to arrive, and he seemed a pleasant bloke, saying 'good morning' as he passed by. I was growing more and more concerned as I waited, because I realised it was years since I'd seen him and I started to question whether I would still identify him among a steady flow of football men. I wondered whether he had actually walked by me already. The nerves were jangling and the doubts multiplying when I saw in the distance the imposing frame of big Dunc coming towards me. There was no doubting it was him, and I felt the pressure ease from my shoulders.

I walked towards him and explained what I was doing. 'That's some challenge,' he said with a smile. He signed the shirt, and I took his picture as he held it up. He wished me luck and said he hoped I would do it. I wished him all the best, and off he went to complete his coaching badges.

Duncan Ferguson might only have made eight starts and six substitute appearances, and scored two goals, in the nine-in-a-row years, but he deserves credit for putting his life and career back on track after the unprecedented actions and punishment handed down to him in Scotland when he was just 23 years old.

Steven Pressley

CENTRAL DEFENDER Steven Pressley has a unique claim to fame, although it isn't one I'd be shouting from the rooftops. He is the only nine-in-a-row player who went on to play with Celtic after leaving Rangers.

Born in Elgin in October 1973 but brought up in Fife, Pressley played for Inverkeithing Boys' Club before Rangers signed him in 1990. He made 27 starts and seven substitute appearances during the nine-in-a-row years, with his debut appearance coming from the bench in the run-in to the fourth title, featuring away to Motherwell in a 2–1 win on 23 April 1992. The following season he made eight starts, the first coming away to Airdrie in a 1–1 draw on 1 December, although he had come on as a half-time replacement for Richard Gough in the famous Champions League group match against Marseille at Ibrox on 25 November. He played in the next three games against Falkirk, St Johnstone and Dundee and also played in the matches against Hibs, Hearts, Partick and Falkirk, again, later in the season.

Six-in-a-row was Pressley's best season at Rangers. He made 17 starts and a further six substitute appearances. His one and only league goal came in a shock 2–1 home defeat to Kilmarnock on 28 August. He featured in all four league matches against Celtic that term: a goalless draw, a 2–1 defeat, a 4–2 win and a one-all stalemate. The following season he made two starts – again against Celtic, losing 2–0 at home on 27 August, and a 2–0 home win over Kilmarnock on 15 October. He was sold to Coventry City in a £600,000 deal before the end of the year, but after just 19 league games he was back over the border, signing with Dundee United. He remained there until 1998, when he moved to Hearts.

He enjoyed his prime years at Tynecastle, where he was made captain and also became a Scotland regular, racking up 32 caps to add to the 26 under-21 matches he played. He left eight years later when he led the players' revolt against controversial owner Vladimir Romanov. It was then that he moved to Celtic and, when he won the Scottish Cup with them, became the only player to have lifted the famous old trophy with three clubs. After leaving Celtic in 2008, he had a brief spell at Randers in Denmark and then finished his playing career at Falkirk in 2009, becoming assistant manager and then manager in February 2010. He was also part of George Burley's Scotland management team between 2008 and 2009, a strange move considering he was still playing at the time. He left Falkirk in 2013 to take over the reins at his troubled former club, Coventry, but was sacked in 2015 after his 100th game in charge.

In October of that year he became manager of Fleetwood Town, and it was at this point that I made contact with him at the Lancashire club. I had moved back south to a nice place in Pontefract, Yorkshire, by then and for a while I wondered if I would still be able to complete my shirt mission. My head had gone down for a while, but it was my nephew, Andy, who picked me up and convinced me I couldn't stop now. The geography of the Pressley location in relation to my new house demonstrated that my new address might sometimes have its advantages as I searched for the final group of players. I looked at Fleetwood's fixture list and saw they were due to play at Barnsley, just 20 miles down the road from me, later in the month.

I contacted the club and explained who I was, and was given Pressley's email address to contact him directly. I sent him a message, telling my story and asking if he would mind meeting me briefly outside Barnsley's ground before the game. I didn't receive a reply. Perhaps I had been given the wrong email address or had taken it down wrongly, and that was why he hadn't responded. The night before the match, I decided I was going to show up anyway and try to spot him arriving. I'd done it plenty of times in the past and it usually worked out. It was a bitterly cold day, and there was snow on the ground at Barnsley when I arrived. I knew from past experience that away teams would usually arrive at 1.30pm, so I made certain I wouldn't miss him by arriving at 11.30am.

The staff were great. I drove up to the security gates, which usually are only accessible to players, boardroom members, guests and some workers, but when I explained why I was there, the guard allowed me through to wait for the Fleetwood bus to arrive. There was a kids' match being played on an adjacent field, which I watched to pass time, but I made sure to keep an eye out for the bus. An hour or so later, one of the women working in security came over with a cup of coffee to warm me up. I was absolutely numb! It was a lovely gesture and she also told me the bus was on its way.

Eventually it arrived, and I stood and watched as the players stepped off one by one. The bus emptied and Pressley wasn't with them. But I had noticed a car driving in behind the bus moments earlier, and I looked over to see Pressley emerging from the driver's side. I approached him as he followed his players towards the entrance. I explained who I was and mentioned I had sent an email. I was taken aback when he confirmed he had received it. He never said 'sorry I didn't reply to you' or that it had slipped his mind, just that he'd received it. He stopped and signed the shirt and allowed me to take a picture, and then he went inside the stadium. That was it.

I returned to my car and thawed out on the way home. I was glad I hadn't driven all the way from Glasgow for that one.

The Other Signatures

AS WELL as the autographs of the 85 living players, I also had eight other men sign the shirt. Some of these names are no-brainers, others will prove controversial with a number of the Rangers support.

Walter Smith was a must-have. One of our greatest-ever managers and the man who delivered seven of the nine titles, and that's before we get to the miracles he performed in his second spell ten years later, there was no doubt he had to autograph the shirt. I asked him to sign it as he came out of Ibrox after a game one evening, but it was only when we met again as he was showing Sebastian Rozental around Auchenhowie years later that he grasped what I had been doing. Overall, he won an incredible 21 trophies as Rangers boss, together with a further seven as assistant, and led the club to a European final.

Archie Knox was Walter's assistant during The Gaffer's first reign between 1991 and 1998. A gruff, no-nonsense character on the touchline, he played with Walter at Dundee United in the seventies and had been Alex Ferguson's

Archie Knox

assistant at Aberdeen and Manchester United before Walter lured him away from Old Trafford. He had a 15-year career after Rangers, being assistant Scotland manager twice, also working at a host of clubs including Everton, Coventry, Motherwell and Aberdeen.

I met Archie while he was with the latter. They were down in the Central Belt to play St Mirren, so I drove to their stadium in Paisley bright and early and waited for the team bus to arrive. By the time it did, there were a fair few Aberdeen fans milling around. I approached Archie as he was stepping off the coach, and he was happy to sign the shirt and pose with me for a picture. I asked one of the fans hanging around to take the photo – he agreed, so I can only imagine he wasn't a Dons fan. When I turned round afterwards, there were a few guys wearing red and white scarves staring daggers at me. I think one or two shouted something, but I couldn't understand their accents, so I just smiled and walked away.

A couple of less obvious ones now. Jim White and Dougie Donnelly were the TV presenters who brought us the coverage of Rangers' triumphs throughout nine-in-a-row, Jim on STV and Dougie on the BBC. Quite often, watching video recordings of their shows was the only way I saw footage of the Gers while I lived in England during those glory years. Officially they're not Rangers men, but everyone thinks otherwise, and I had each sign the shirt as they were leaving Ibrox after games.

As stated elsewhere in the book, I would listen to BBC Radio Scotland's *Sportsound* coverage before the match every Saturday, and if they had a guest worth meeting, whether it was a nine-in-a-row player or someone from another era who might sign memorabilia I could sell to finance my travels, I would make the short journey from my home to the studio to await them. On this particular afternoon, they had former referee Kenny Clark on the show. I Googled him and saw that he was the referee who had failed to take any action against Duncan Ferguson for his headbutt against Raith Rovers. I decided this was an interesting part of the nine-in-a-row story, so on a whim I made my way across to the BBC's HQ. I took my usual seat in the waiting area until Clark came down from the studio, and asked him to sign the shirt, explaining why. He agreed, and as he was signing it he joked that he hoped no Celtic fans would pass by or there would be all sorts said about him.

Donald Findlay QC is not only Scotland's foremost criminal defence lawyer – he was also Rangers' vice-chairman for many years. He later became involved in football again, this time with his home-town club, Cowdenbeath, where he was chairman and, in 2016, became owner. I went along to Central Park, which also hosts stock car racing around the perimeter of the pitch (although not at the same time as the football, it should be pointed out!), and waited outside the stand for him to arrive. When I saw the top-of-the-range sports car pulling up, I had a fair idea it would be Donald. Out he came, looking as eccentric as ever, his pipe poking out from his distinctive facial hair. He seemed friendly and was happy to sign the shirt. I asked if he missed going to Ibrox, and he said he definitely did. Hopefully he can return the Blue Brazil back up the leagues after a poor few seasons.

Jimmy Bell is the club's long-time kitman, and man of many other trades, who is in with the bricks at Ibrox. Despite having a job most of us would dream of, he always looks miserable. I spotted him coming from the primary school car park across the road from the Main Stand, where the team and backroom staff used to park their cars, so I went over and asked him if he would sign it. He seemed delighted, and one of my favourite pictures from the project is of Jimmy proudly holding the

Jimmy Bell

shirt aloft with a huge grin on his face. John Brown passed by just at that moment and said I should keep the picture in a safe place, because a photo of Jimmy smiling was so rare it would be worth money!

Of all the meetings I had with non-players who signed the shirt, the most interesting was with Sir David Murray, the former owner and chairman who purchased the club for £6m in November 1988, just three months into the first season of the nine era, and presided over it until 2011, when he sold it to Craig Whyte for £1. I had called his office in Charlotte Square in Edinburgh in the first week of February 2012, explained to his secretary what I was doing, and asked whether David would mind adding his signature. She checked and told me to come and see him the following week, on Valentine's Day. Most Rangers fans have the date of 14 February 2012 seared into their memories, because that is the day Craig Whyte plunged the club into administration and set off a chain of events that almost killed us.

I was preparing to travel through to Edinburgh when I heard the unbelievable news. I imagined the arranged meeting would now be cancelled, but I called Murray's office to make sure. To my surprise, his secretary told me I should still come through. I arrived at his office a couple of hours later and was taken upstairs. As the door opened and I was led in, he put his hands up and the first thing he said to me was,

'I was duped.' Those were words he would infamously repeat in the hours and days since that day. 'Believe it or not but that's the truth,' he continued. He said Craig Whyte lied to him.

We sat down at his desk while two other suited men sat in the room and looked on. I don't know who they were. We had a quick chat and he signed the shirt and posed for a picture with it, then he called on his secretary and asked her to get me some goodies. She returned with a bag filled with a club tie, Rangers badges, a scarf and a few other bits and pieces, which I've since given away.

I know a lot of Rangers fans hold him to account for much of what happened, and for the controversy over some of the contracts that were offered to players after nine-in-a-row. I'm not too clued up on any of that, but all I can do is take a person at face value – and when he told me he had no idea about Craig Whyte's past, I believed him. I'm sure people will have their opinions about that, but it's how I felt. I thanked him for his time and made my way out, because as you can imagine his phone was ringing off the hook as the monumental news of what had happened at Ibrox took hold and people demanded answers.

It just seemed such strange timing that the day I arranged to meet the Rangers chairman and owner during the nine-in-a-row era, was the day the club was plunged into one of the biggest crises in its history. It's one encounter I will never, ever forget.

Oleg Kuznetsov

YEARS HAD passed, thousands more miles had been travelled, dozens of signatures had been added, but still that trip to Ukraine hung over me like a black cloud.

Coming home with one signature instead of three felt like a kick in the teeth, and the passing of time hadn't improved the feeling. I was down to the final handful of signatures, and wouldn't you just know that Mikhailichenko's two countrymen were still at large. I vowed I would never return to Ukraine, but how else was I going to meet the two Ukrainians?

As it stood, I had no idea where the Olegs, Kuznetsov and Salenko, were. I concentrated my efforts on Kuznetsov first and hoped he would lead me to Salenko. You might remember I had received a phone number on a scrap of paper from Miko on that nightmare evening in Kiev, which I called from the airport the next day. I spoke to someone I believed to be Kuznetsov, and we agreed I would meet him another time, hopefully closer to the UK while he was on national duty as coach with the Ukrainian youth team.

I dug out that number and called it again, hoping to make arrangements with Kuznetsov, but it didn't connect. I tried again a few more times over the next couple of weeks, but it didn't ring. My heart sank. He must have changed his number. There was no way I was going to call Mikhailichenko, so I went back to the BBC in Ukraine, which had helped out the last time. A journalist there got me a number, but this one was also dead. Next I contacted Dynamo Kiev, Oleg's former club, where he is regarded as a legend. I emailed and called and somehow managed to make myself understood, because they provided me with his details. Would you believe it, this number had expired as well.

I didn't know what else to do. As I sat at home one day, stressing about how I was going to find him, I tried each of the numbers again. My heart skipped a beat when the original number, the digits I'd received on the scrap of paper from Miko, began to ring. The foreign ring tone beeped and beeped – and then someone answered. He answered in a foreign language.

'Oleg?' I asked.

'Da.'

I could have jumped for joy. I explained again who I was and what I was doing, but I wasn't sure how much of it was being understood. He responded, but his English seemed very limited.

'Do you still coach the under-18s team?' I asked.

'Under-19s.' He then told me he was coming to Ireland at the end of the year with the squad.

'Will you sign the shirt if I come over?' He said yes, and that was the end of the conversation. When I hung up the first thing I did was look up the fixtures for the Northern Irish and Irish Republic youth teams, but I couldn't see any mention on their websites of a game against Ukraine. Bear in mind this was summer, so the games were potentially several months away and perhaps hadn't been officially announced.

I called the Northern Irish FA first, but they told me their under-19s weren't due to play Ukraine before the end of the year, so I called over the border and spoke to the Republic's association. I explained the full story, and the next thing I knew I was given the number for Paul Doolin, the Republic of Ireland's under-19 boss, and was told to call him directly and that he would give me the details. Once I'd explained the story yet again, this time to Paul, he said there were two scheduled matches between the countries, one in midweek and one on a Saturday, at Markets Field in Limerick.

I spoke to my nephew, Andy, and he said he would pay for both of us to go over. We booked the return boat ride to Belfast from Cairnryan and counted down the weeks until it was time for the next adventure.

Oleg Kuznetsov was born in East Germany in March 1963 and moved to the Soviet Union, where he played as a youth for FC Desna Chernihiv throughout his childhood from 1971 until turning professional with them ten years later. He was 20 years old when Dynamo Kiev spotted his defensive qualities and they signed him in 1983. Oleg played against Rangers in a hard-fought European Cup tie in 1987, and three years later Graeme Souness brought him to Scotland in a £1.2m transfer in October 1990.

His debut came in the 5–0 destruction of St Mirren at Ibrox on 13 October, two months into the three-in-a-row season, and he certainly looked the part, hitting the post in a strong personal display. The following week, in a game that finished goalless at St Johnstone, he limped off after 20 minutes. He was out for almost a year as the Rangers injury curse struck again. It was a familiar scenario that would only seem to grow worse as the years went on.

Oleg returned on 14 September 1991 in the 1–1 draw at home to Dundee United and played his part in the march to four-in-a-row. His next match was at Airdrie in a 4–0 win on 5 October, and he was a sub in the goalless Old Firm contest at Ibrox on 2 November. He then enjoyed an 11-game run from 16 November, a 4–0 home win over Airdrie, through to the corresponding away fixture in Lanarkshire on 4 January, which finished 0–0. Included in that run were a 3–2 win over Aberdeen and a 3–1 triumph over Celtic. He was next a sub in the 2–0 defeat to Celtic on 21 March and started in the 4–1 home win over Falkirk on 7 April. He also played in the 2–1 win at Motherwell and the home draw against Hearts, on 23 and 28 April.

During five-in-a-row, he clocked up eight starts and made one appearance from the bench; in six-in-a-row, he started four games and made two substitute appearances, one of which led to his solitary league goal for Rangers. He came on in the New Year's Day Old Firm match at Parkhead and scored the fourth goal in a 4–2 win. As I wrote earlier, this was the game where Satty Singh of Mr Singh's Indian restaurant, who helped me to meet Brian Laudrup and Andy Gray, declared that his newborn son would be named after the next Rangers player to score in the rout. And so, with a sweetly struck dipping volley from outside the box, Oleg Kuznetsov Singh was introduced to the world. Oleg's final appearance for Rangers was in the penultimate game of the season, the 1–0 loss away to Kilmarnock, on 7 May.

He never truly recovered from injury, and unfortunately we never had the opportunity to see Kuznetsov at his best. He was sold to Maccabi Haifa in July 1994, but only played a handful of games before signing for CSKA Borysfen Kiev in 1995, where he remained for two seasons but played few games before deciding to retire.

He moved into management and became assistant boss at CSKA Kiev in 1998, and then became their manager when they were renamed Arsenal Kiev in 2001. The following year, he returned to Dynamo Kiev as assistant for two years, and in the same period he became the Ukraine national team's assistant, a position he retained until 2007.

He was the assistant at FC Moscow in 2008 and then returned to the national side, where he won three caps during his playing career (he also earned 58 USSR caps and five for the CIS). He was under-18s/19s coach for three years, and was then in charge of the under-16s, the under-17s/18s and finally the under-19s, the position he held when I contacted him.

Andy had finished up a long shift before we drove to Cairnryan for the day's final ferry. We rested up on the sailing over to Belfast and then started the four-hour drive to Limerick. We made a couple of stops and grabbed something to eat, finally arriving at the ground around 6am. It had been a tiring night, but we needed plenty of energy for what was to come next.

The gates to the stadium's car park were still closed, but I went over and spoke to a security guard who was milling around. I told him I had arranged to meet with the Ukrainian side's coach and asked him when the team was due to arrive. He wouldn't tell me anything.

This was a problem, because I had been calling Oleg's number and it was switched off. Months had passed since our brief phone call, when I wasn't sure if he'd properly understood me, and I hadn't spoken to him since. I couldn't even be sure he was on the trip or was still the team's coach.

There was only one thing for it, we decided, and that was to try all of the hotels in the area. If it was uncertain that we would be granted access to him at the ground, we would have to find him before he reached it. We looked up the addresses online and began visiting them one by one. Some refused to tell us anything, while others confirmed the Ukrainians weren't staying at their establishment. We tried 14 hotels in total. In one, I saw what I presumed was the Irish team, young guys who looked to be footballers wearing Ireland tracksuits. I walked up to one and asked if he knew where the Ukrainian side was staying, but he said he had no idea. I tried calling Paul's number, but it didn't ring. In one of the last hotels we visited, the receptionist was very helpful and began calling round a number of other hotels. We had probably been to them already, but perhaps she would have more luck gleaning information.

Unfortunately she didn't, so we returned to the stadium, becoming increasingly anxious and weary. By this time it was afternoon and there were more people gathering, but still the gates to the officials' car park remained closed. We got chatting with one of the security guards, and he said the Ukrainian team bus was running an hour late, but was expected to arrive at 3.30pm. Maybe they hadn't been staying locally after all. We waited around, not moving far from the gates. This wasn't the best place to be standing with a Rangers shirt in my hand, a fact I didn't need reminding of as more and more fans wearing green-and-white scarves descended upon the ground.

I looked at my watch. It was after 3pm, so I went back over to the gates and spoke to the official on the other side. 'Look, I've been here since 6am and all I need is two minutes when the bus comes.' I hoped he would be reasonable. Just then, a coach came round the corner and the guard pulled the gates open. 'On you go,' he said to us.

Andy and I waited beside the bus as it came to a halt. The players slowly made their way off. Please let him be here, I muttered, as I watched each head emerge from the darkness. Finally, I spotted a familiar blond perm. It was Oleg!

I approached him as he stepped off and said, 'I'm John, I spoke to you on the phone.' I held the Rangers shirt and a pen in my hands. He smiled and nodded, and signed the shirt. I had Andy take a picture, but he was looking anxious. 'Come on, John, hurry up,' he hissed.

I didn't know what was wrong with him, but before I could let Oleg go I had another two shirts for him to sign that I planned to auction off to help pay for my final trips. Once he'd signed them I asked if he would mind posing for a picture alongside Andy. I felt it was the least I could do for my nephew, since he had paid for the trip and travelled all this way. Before I had the chance to ask Oleg if he knew Salenko's whereabouts, he said he had to go and rushed off to catch up with his squad. It was only when I turned round, three Rangers tops draped over my arms, that I saw what was causing Andy to be uptight. There was a fairly large crowd of Ireland fans on the other side of the fence and they had clocked me with the shirts. The natives were looking restless.

'Let's get out of here,' Andy said firmly. I stuffed the tops back into my bag and we put our heads down and walked briskly back to the car. We made the long drive back to Belfast, taking one or two wrong turns along the way and ending up on back roads with little fuel in the car, and breathed a sigh of relief when we made it back to the ferry terminal in one piece.

It had been a long, tiring day, but, against the odds, I had finally found Kuznetsov. One Oleg down, one Oleg to go. Where were you, Salenko?

Stuart Munro and Ian Ferguson

THE PROSPECT of travelling to Australia was weighing heavily on my mind.

The journey to America had been about as much as I could take, so I couldn't begin to imagine flying to the other side of the world. I was worried I wouldn't come back home alive, as I just didn't believe my health was up to it.

Ian Ferguson, one of the genuine legends of the nine-in-a-row campaign, and former left-back Stuart Munro were both Down Under. I knew I had to make contact to find out if there was any chance they might be coming home for a visit sometime soon. If they said it was unlikely, it looked like I would have to make the dreaded trip.

Fergie and Stuart had been working together until shortly before I got in touch. Ian was boss of Perth Glory and Stuart was his assistant, but after a poor run of games they left the club by mutual consent in February 2013.

I contacted Glory and explained my project, and they gave me Stuart's number. I called him, and he unfortunately told me he didn't envision returning to Scotland at any point in the near future. He had just started a new job in Melbourne coaching women's football. He was happy to meet me if I decided to come to Australia, but I told him I would need to speak to Fergie first to find out if there was any chance he was coming home. Stuart gave me hope, as well as his old teammate's number, when he said he thought Fergie might be back in Glasgow. That would be a result.

I called Ian, hoping he would say he was round the corner visiting Ibrox, but it turned out he was still in Australia. In fact, he had moved north and when I said I was thinking of coming over, he explained that he was around 2,000 miles from Stuart and I would require two internal flights to visit them both. He said to give him a couple of weeks. I think he was unsure of what was coming next for him and he wanted to wait for things to settle before advising me.

A couple of weeks passed and I didn't hear from him, so I gave him a call. There was no answer, so I left a message. I tried a couple of other times over the next few weeks, but he didn't respond. I wasn't sure what had happened, but I couldn't justify the expense and burden of that long trip for just one signature, so I went back to Stuart and said I would have to delay the visit. I had other players to meet in the meantime, so I focused on them and concluded that Fergie and Stuart would likely be the final names on my list.

That seemed to be the way it was heading until I received a Facebook message one evening from my friend Brian Campbell. Brian was the gentleman who drove all the way from Orange County in California to Arizona just to welcome a fellow Rangers fan to America. He explained that Fergie was coming to the States for a fans' convention and, if I wanted, I could give Brian the jersey and he would have Ian sign it. One of Brian's friends from the Motherwell Supporters' Club bus was travelling over, so I could deliver the shirt to him and he would take it across.

I had to think about this long and hard. I had never given the strip to anyone before – it had barely been out of my sight. I hadn't met this person, but Brian was a stand-up guy and he told me his pal was trustworthy. I felt I could rely on what Brian said, so I decided to do it. I met his mate, Scott MacKinnon, and handed it over and then spent the next two weeks praying nothing would happen to it!

I could feel the tension easing when I was sent a picture on Facebook of Ian holding the jersey, having just signed it. A few days later I met Scott in the Louden Tavern at Ibrox and had the strip returned to me. Lo and behold, just a short time later it was announced that Fergie was coming home for a visit and he would be taking part in a Q&A at the Louden – I couldn't believe it!

I'm not sure why I never heard back from Fergie a couple of years previously. Perhaps he had changed his number, or his time was consumed with his new coaching role with Northern Fury in Queensland. I know he wouldn't have snubbed me, because he's a genuine guy. That was one of the traits that made Ian Ferguson so special as a Rangers player – he was just a working-class bloke who had the chance to live his dream and appreciated every second of his 12 glory-laden years at Ibrox.

The future Hall of Famer's professional career began at Clyde, where he spent two seasons from 1984 to 1986, before being signed by St Mirren. He famously scored in every round of the Scottish Cup in 1987 as the Paisley underdogs went all the way to the final, smashing home the winner against Dundee United and lifting the famous old trophy. That was the first of many major winners' medals he would collect. Fergie's form had been noticed by Graeme Souness, and he signed the midfielder for £850,000 in February 1988, with add-ons taking the fee to £1m.

His first full season was also the first of the nine-in-a-row era and he played a massive part, starting 30 league games and scoring six goals in the race to the title. While Fergie would develop into more of a holding midfielder later in his career and be known for his no-nonsense tackling, he was also a skilful player with a great eye for a pass and, as the number of goals he scored from outside the box attests, a sweet right foot.

He made 204 appearances during nine-in-a-row, but that figure would have been so much higher had he not been plagued by injuries and ill health. He only managed ten starts during three-in-a-row and 12 the following season as a mystery virus laid him low, but he was back to his best for five- and six-in-a-row, playing 30 and 35 games respectively.

With his trademark right shirt side pulled out of his shorts, Fergie covered every blade of grass and would play wherever was required. He was deployed as a striker, attacking midfielder and defensive midfielder during his time at Rangers. In fact, he even stepped into goal for a short time during a game against his old club St Mirren in 1989, when Chris Woods went off injured.

For someone who grew up in the shadow of Parkhead, Ian was never more passionate than when he was up against Celtic, and he served up some memorable moments against them. There was the time he celebrated his goal in front of the away support when he scored at Ibrox in the New Year's game during seven-in-a-row, and the piledriver free kick that Pat Bonner couldn't hold during a 2–1 win at Celtic's ground on April Fools' Day in 1989. The ball spun up in the air and, as it was crossing the line, Ally McCoist put his head on it just to make sure. And then there was the time when the Gers all but clinched nine-in-a-row with a win at Parkhead and Italian hothead Paolo Di Canio completely lost the plot with Fergie and signalled he was going to snap him in two. Fergie calmly told him he would see him up the tunnel, but suffice to say Di Canio was nowhere to be seen. Fergie got showered and dressed and then went to the Celtic players' lounge, flanked by two teammates, but Di Canio wasn't there either. Clearly all mouth, he had fled the ground before Fergie could get near him.

Ian was one of the elite band of players to earn all nine league title medals in the campaign. After winning the ninth, he was out of contract and due to meet Atletico Madrid officials for signing talks, but instead he decided to stay and agreed a new deal. He was one of the few from that era to be kept on by new manager Dick Advocaat and was awarded a testimonial in 1999 (the last active player to receive such an honour). He won even more medals before finally leaving in January 2000, signing a deal with Dunfermline. He played at East End Park for two-and-a-half seasons before deciding to start a new life with his family in Australia. His last game in Scotland was against Rangers, appropriately, and he was given a standing ovation from all corners of the ground.

In his new home, he played for Northern Spirit and Central Coast Mariners until his retirement in 2006, when he moved into coaching and management, first with North Queensland Fury and then with the aforementioned Perth Glory and Northern Fury.

He'll forever be regarded as a Rangers legend and one of the most decorated players in our history. Fergie was a teetotaller in his playing days and said he only had a drink when Rangers won something – he was rarely sober, he joked. His passion and devotion made him a true blue.

Now that Fergie's name was ticked off the list, although not in the manner I had hoped, that left just Stuart Munro in Australia. I just could not afford to travel that distance, so I gave him a call and asked if he would be happy for me to post the shirt to his home. He said he would sign it, take a picture with it and then return it to me in the mail. Early in 2016 I packaged up the shirt, took it to the post office and inquired about their most secure, safest mode of delivery. My life wouldn't be worth living if I was to reveal just how much it cost, but let's just say the flights Down Under weren't looking quite so expensive any more! But it was a price worth paying if it was going to remain safe. A couple of weeks later, I received a message from Stuart saying the package had arrived.

Just like in his playing days, Stuart proved reliable and dependable. Originally from Falkirk, the left-back came to Rangers in the dark days of 1984, when the team was at a low ebb. Unlike most of that era, though, Stuart showed enough to be retained by Graeme Souness when he arrived two years later and was a solid player in his position, seeing off others to maintain his first-team status when big names were beating a path to Edmiston Drive. He was bought from Alloa, where he made an impression after failing to make the breakthrough at his first club, St Mirren.

During the nine-in-a-row years he made 81 starts, appeared once as a substitute and scored three goals. He said in an interview years after he left Ibrox that he was happy to sign short-term contracts under Souness because he was up for the battle. He certainly had plenty of fight and dig, and in the first season of the campaign he featured 22 times and scored crucial goals away to Aberdeen in a 2–1 win and in a 1–1 draw with Dundee United.

The following year, he was an ever-present with 36 starts and he crossed the ball for Trevor Steven to score the goal that clinched the title. He capped a tremendous season by scoring in the final match against Hearts, which finished 1–1 at Tynecastle.

Three-in-a-row proved to be his last season for the club, making 14 starts, and he was sold to Blackburn in August 1991 by Walter Smith. He was injured soon after, a broken bone in his ankle requiring surgery and 18 months of rehabilitation. It meant he only played one game at Ewood Park before dropping down to Bristol City, where he enjoyed four years, and then came back north to Falkirk and St Mirren, the club who had let him go 15 years previously.

Stuart met his wife on a pre-season tour of Australia with Rangers soon after signing, and promised they would return to her home country once he had finished playing. He emigrated even sooner, having a brief spell with Blacktown City and then Sydney United, before hanging up his boots in 1998. Since then he's had more than ten management jobs throughout Australia, including that aforementioned time as Fergie's assistant. He had just been appointed the inaugural manager of newly founded Women's NPL Victoria club Southern United, when I contacted him about sending the strip.

He sent me a picture on Facebook of him posing with the shirt in his sun-kissed garden and let me know when he had put it back in the post for its epic return journey. I don't think I was ever as nervous during this whole affair as I was while I waited on the jersey to come home.

At least when I was overseas I had some control, but now it was in the lap of the gods and I just had to hope it didn't go missing or become damaged in transit. Every morning I watched for the post, stalking to and from the front door and incessantly looking out of the windows to see if I could spot the postie approaching. And every morning I was disappointed. This went on for about three weeks.

I was becoming concerned. I was terrified something had happened to it. All that effort and it might be lying at the bottom of a container in a mail depot in Melbourne. The one morning I failed to look was the day it was shoved unceremoniously through my letterbox. It didn't quite fit, so the packaging was ripped, but thankfully it didn't cause any damage to the shirt. I pulled away the remainder of the wrapping and unfolded the strip, examining its latest signature.

The Australia problem had been taken care of, and I was on the home straight with only two more players to meet. However, there was just one problem – I had no idea where either of them were or how to track them down. No one said this was going to be easy, and I wasn't prepared to stop now. Next in my sights – if I could ever lay eyes on him – was French defender Basile Boli.

Basile Boli

BY THE spring of 2016 I had just two players to track down.

I was tantalisingly close to the end, but it felt like it was destined to be a case of so near yet so far, because I had been attempting to find these final two Bears for years.

One of them was Basile Boli, the French international who joined Rangers from Marseille in 1994.

After he retired in 1997, aged just 30, he set up a humanitarian organisation, Undertaking to Direct Africa, of which he became president. He was also involved in politics and was a supporter of future French president Nicolas Sarkozy, which led to him being appointed national secretary for co-development with the politician's UMP party in 2007, a position he held for two years. He also founded two companies – in television production and sports marketing – and was a pundit for the France 3 TV channel's football coverage. He appeared to be very busy, but all of this came before I began my nine-in-a-row mission.

In November 2009, he was arrested on embezzlement allegations reported to be related to Undertaking to Direct Africa, and he seemed to fall out of the spotlight afterwards. I regularly searched his name on the internet and even set up a Google alert, so that I would receive a notification any time he was mentioned in an English-speaking publication. I tracked his whereabouts as best I could, but for a long time it seemed like he had gone to ground. The months and eventually years rolled by, and I was becoming increasingly worried that I was never going to find him.

Boli came to France from the Ivory Coast as a boy and joined Auxerre when he was just 17. He played with the club for nine years and in 1989 was named French Player of the Year. He joined Marseille at the turn of the decade and played against Rangers in those famous group games in the first Champions League, where both matches ended in draws. Marseille made the final, and Boli scored the winning goal against AC Milan to lift the cup.

Amid match-fixing allegations, the club was relegated in 1994 and Boli moved to Rangers in a £2.7m deal. He'd previously been best known in the UK for headbutting Stuart Pearce during a France versus England international, but now he was joining one of the biggest clubs in Britain and he aimed to lift the Champions League trophy for a second time, saying he signed because he believed we could win the competition. Unfortunately that season we were knocked out early doors by AEK Athens.

Truth be told, Boli never seemed to fit in at Rangers. Although he was sometimes played out of position at right-back, he showed none of the attributes you would expect from a Champions League winner. During a break in France, Boli was reported to have said Walter's tactics were poor and complained about being played at right-back. He was recalled early to explain himself and it looked like his career with Rangers might be over, but he claimed his comments were misinterpreted and so he continued to be picked. Even when he was played in his natural centre-back position, he still didn't cover himself in glory, such as in the 2–1 defeat to Motherwell. He played 28 games in the seven-in-a-row season and scored two goals, in a 2–0 win away to Falkirk on 17 September and a 2–1 loss at Hibs on 8 October.

At the end of the season, he expressed a desire to leave, and the club didn't stand in his way. He went to Monaco in a £2m deal, but only lasted a season there as well. One scary incident during his time at the club came in a European match against Leeds, when he collided with another player and swallowed his tongue, leading to convulsions. Thankfully he recovered, and moved to Urawa Reds in Japan for what turned out to be his final campaign, 1996/97.

As I continued to search for him, I asked ex-players if they knew of his whereabouts, but none had kept in touch. I also spoke to sports journalists in the hope someone might have a contact. The trail was completely cold. Then I received an alert from Google, flagging up an article about his participation in a promotional leg of the Tour de France with other French celebrities. The article said there would be a chance to ride alongside the famous names. My eyes lit up. Not that I was planning on cycling – that would have killed me – but I thought

I might be able to get close enough to him to ask for his signature. I began pricing hotels in the area, but quickly realised this was going to be way beyond my budget. Because of the race, the mark-ups on the room prices were 200 and 300 per cent. With flights at that time of year also coming in at astronomical prices, it just wasn't possible. I also came to the conclusion that I probably wouldn't have got near him anyway. There would be thousands of people around, security would be tight and there's a good chance I would have wasted my money.

In September 2015, he was made ambassador for Marseille FC. This, surely, was my opportunity. I called the club, but no one seemed to speak English. I was passed from one person to another, but no one could understand me. I tried emailing instead, but received no replies to my numerous messages. I asked around my friends and family, but none of them spoke enough French to feel confident about attempting a conversation over the phone. I continued to check online, and it appeared he was attending most of the club's matches. In January 2016, he was finally acquitted at the Court of Appeal at Versailles of the allegations brought in 2009. And after Marseille's coach was sacked in April 2016, Basile was appointed the club's sports co-ordinator.

I knew this was it. I spoke to my nephew, Andy, and he agreed. But I had no money to make the trip. Andy insisted he would cover it again, so I quickly set about making the arrangements after checking the date of their next home game.

When the travel day arrived, I was up at the crack of dawn and drove to my daughter's house in Leeds. From there I took the bus to London, then caught a train to Stansted and flew to Marseille. I made my way into the city, dropped my bag off at the accommodation and then took the metro to the stadium. The game was kicking off at 9pm. I followed the crowds and saw the magnificent Stade Velodrome shining brightly, but as I drew closer I spotted high security fences up ahead. I had never seen anything like this.

By the time I reached the front of the queue, I realised I was not passing the guards without a ticket. I explained I was trying to meet Basile Boli and brought out the shirt to hopefully explain, but I was just waved away. I didn't know what to do. If I wasn't able to reach the stadium, how was I supposed to find Boli? I followed the fence around until I reached the next ticket checkpoint, and tried to speak to the guards there, but again they had no clue what I was saying, or if they did, they had no intention of helping. I kept walking, my heart rate rising as I panicked about the trip being pointless and wasting Andy's money.

I stopped any passing security or officials and appealed in vain for their assistance, but it was only when I spotted an official-looking gentleman at one of the security points that I made a breakthrough. He was suited and booted, and reminded me of the commissionaire at Ibrox's front door. I prayed he had more authority than those I had approached so far. I could have hugged him when he told me he understood English, so I explained I had flown over from Britain earlier in the day to have Basile sign a shirt that more than 80 players around the world had autographed. I asked if it would be possible for Boli to take a moment to add his name.

The guard seemed to take an age to ponder my request. Finally, he said OK and took the shirt from me. I walked after him but he stopped and said I would have to wait. 'But I need a photo of him with the shirt,' I pleaded. It was a firm 'no'.

Was I happy to let a stranger take the almost-completed shirt from me and into a football stadium with thousands of people around? No, but in that split second I decided I had no other choice, so I watched as he disappeared into the distance, my heart in my mouth.

I paced back and forth and smoked a cigarette while I waited, trying to keep my nerves at bay. The fans continued to queue up at the gates to have their tickets checked. Five minutes passed. I continually checked the time and looked for the man returning. The butterflies were fluttering. I started to think about what I would do if he never came back with the shirt. Ten minutes passed. Just then, I spotted him returning with the shirt in his hand.

'Did he sign it?' I asked.

He nodded his head as he handed the top to me. I held the shirt up and looked for the new signature. There it was. I thanked the guard and made my way back along the street, pushing my way against the tide of supporters. I returned to the metro but I wasn't ready to go back to the city centre just yet. I went to a food stand and bought something to eat, and once I finished I made my way to the toilets, which were an absolute disgrace. I've rarely been in toilets so disgusting, and, to add to the insult, it cost a euro to enter. I went outside for some fresh air, sat down and waited. I was determined to get a picture of Basile with the strip, so I decided I would walk back along to the stadium in time for the final whistle and wait for him to come out.

It was around 11pm by the time the match finished, so it was already late and I was tired after an early start and lots of travelling. I went back to where the helpful official had been earlier, hoping his well-turned-out appearance was an indication that he had been manning the executive entrance. I stood for a long time, hoping to catch a glimpse of Boli.

The fans were long gone, but still I waited. If there was one thing I had developed over the past few years, it was good patience. By 1am even I decided it was a lost cause. He must have left by another exit because there was no way he would still be in the stadium at that time. I was also concerned the metro might soon be closing down for the night. I made my way back to the station, slightly deflated, and returned to my accommodation.

I only squeezed in a few hours' sleep because my flight home was early. That was on schedule, but frustratingly I then had a two-hour wait for a coach into the centre of London, and from there I boarded a bus north. We had been on the road for more than an hour when I noticed we were passing places I had seen earlier. We were driving back to London! Just then, the driver made an announcement. He had forgotten to pick up the second driver, who was waiting at Luton, so had to go back for him.

It all kicked off on the bus. A lot of the passengers went crazy, giving the driver all sorts of abuse. It was a complete rammy, folk shouting over the top of each other and losing the plot. Some of them were going too far with the insults towards the driver, which made other passengers react in kind to them. It was threatening to explode, and the driver announced he would call the police and pull over if it didn't halt. That seemed to calm the situation down, but there was a prickly atmosphere for the rest of the drawn-out journey.

By the time we finally pulled into Leeds, the local bus service was off, so the coach company had to call and pay for a taxi to take me back to my daughter's house. I'm not sure how I found the strength to drive home to Pontefract. It was between two and three in the morning when I stepped through the door, meaning I had been on the move for about 21 hours. I was completely knackered and it took me three or four days to recover.

It was worth it, though. Considering I had gone over on a hope and a prayer, I was thrilled to have secured Boli's signature. It was the end of a long search for the Frenchman, but I couldn't help but feel disappointment at failing to actually meet him face-to-face and ask for a photograph.

On a positive note, I now had only one player left to track down, and I told myself I had to do it soon, because it was all becoming too much for my health.

I knew what this meant. A trip back to the scene of the worst experience of all the journeys, the worst trip of my life. Ukraine. If that wasn't bad enough, I had no idea how to contact the final name. But I was determined I wasn't going to fail now, even if it turned out to be the last thing I did.

Oleg Salenko, I was coming to get you.

Oleg Salenko

FINDING OLEG Salenko became an obsession. It was all I could think about.

I had done what had seemed unimaginable a few years earlier and collected 84 of the nine-in-a-row legends' autographs, enjoying some amazing times in countries around the world. Never could I have dreamed where this project would take me. But it would mean nothing if I couldn't nail the final signature.

Time was of the essence. Not only did I want to complete my challenge before the 20th anniversary of nine-in-a-row in May 2017, but my health was continuing to deteriorate. I was having breathing issues, a lifetime of smoking finally catching up with me, and I wasn't confident of how much longer I would be fit enough to undertake a flight to Ukraine and all the hassles a visit to that country might entail.

But the first thing I had to do was find Oleg.

I spent a long time trawling the internet, searching for scraps of information about where he was. The newest information I could find was from March 2013, when he fainted on live television while working as a football pundit. After that, the trail ran cold. I checked with some of the ex-players whose details I had, but they hadn't kept in touch with Oleg. My next idea was to go to the press and see if they could publicise my search. The *Sunday Post* did a great article in May 2016 explaining that I was down to the final player and how desperate I was to find him. It received a few responses from people making suggestions about how to track him down, which I began to follow up.

I was sent a link to a YouTube video and an accompanying match report for a group of Wales fans playing Ukraine's All-Stars in Kiev a few years back. Salenko was part of the Ukrainian team. I emailed the Welsh supporter who wrote the report and asked if he had contact details for anyone in the All-Stars side. He replied within minutes and said he didn't, but understood that Salenko lived in Kiev and added that the man who acted as master of ceremonies at the game was the press liaison officer for the Ukraine Football Federation. I found an email address for their media division and sent a message.

In the meantime, another person suggested I contact a British journalist called Neil Billingham, who had interviewed Salenko two years earlier for a football magazine. Neil told me he had spoken to Salenko in Kiev and he assumed he was still there, which backed up the first bloke. Neil was back working in the UK, but suggested I contact a freelance journalist in Kiev called Oleg Zadernovsky.

Eleven days passed without reply from Zadernovsky, and I thought it was another lost cause, but then he wrote back to say it would be no problem to set up a meeting with Salenko. All I had to do was tell him when I would like to come over and where I wanted to meet. I couldn't believe it! This was great news and all seemed so simple. As usual with me, life wasn't straightforward and the email arrived while I was in hospital, waiting to speak to a surgeon about a procedure. I was going to have to delay the trip.

Weeks passed. I told Oleg Z I would be in touch as soon as I felt I was returning to full strength. In the first week of July, I received a message from him, asking when I would be going over and confirming he had talked to Salenko, who was willing to meet me at Kiev Airport. Unfortunately it looked like I was going into hospital again for an operation the following month. Mr Zadernovsky seemed fine with that and wished me good health.

It was early September before I felt ready to attempt the journey. I emailed Oleg Z in Kiev and said I was ready to come over. Andy had once again kindly offered to cover the costs of the flights and accommodation. He knew how much it meant to me to finish what I'd started, and he was also invested in it, having accompanied me on trips and helped out whenever he could.

A few days went by without reply, so I contacted Zadernovsky again. Still there was no word. I left it a week and sent him one more email, explaining that time was short. I couldn't handle going to Ukraine in the dead of winter in sub-zero temperatures and with snow up to my knees. I decided the end of October was my cut-off point for travelling. After that, it would have to be the spring, and quite frankly I didn't know what shape I would be in by then.

When visiting the Ukraine Football Federation's website months earlier to contact their press department, I had stumbled across a photo of Oleg Salenko in the staff section, so I knew he worked with them in some capacity. I emailed the press office again and explained my story, providing a link to previous media stories about my project, and asked if they could connect me with Oleg. There was no reply. The following week I tried again, but I was blanked once more.

I had no idea how else to make contact with Oleg. Then my co-author mentioned a man called Jim Gillies, a kind-hearted grandfather from Cumbernauld in Lanarkshire who had devoted much of the past 30 years to delivering aid to children affected by the Chernobyl nuclear disaster fallout. Jim had no links to Ukraine, but felt passionate about doing whatever he could to help those forgotten souls living on the periphery of the Exclusion Zone. He began making annual trips to Ukraine, taking medical supplies, clothes and money to a children's ward in a run-down hospital. He was an angel to the kids, but little did I know he was also about to become my guardian angel.

We contacted Jim and asked if he knew of anyone in Kiev who could track down Salenko. There were a few that might be able to help, Jim said, and he made some calls. A couple of days later, he confirmed that unfortunately they had been unable to help. But there was one other person Jim thought might be able to track down Oleg. His name was Anatoli, a journalist Jim had been friends with for many years, but their relationship had become strained and they hadn't talked in a long time. Jim emailed him, but wasn't convinced his old pal would respond.

He did – and he was confident he could source a phone number for Oleg. This was great news. I had my eyes on a flight to Kiev in the middle of October, now just a couple of weeks away, and I was eager to book it before the prices went up. A few days later, Jim was back in touch. Anatoli had located a number for Oleg! I felt I was now within touching distance of setting the meeting up. Anatoli wanted to be the go-between, but he began talking about bringing along television cameras and was becoming quarrelsome, so we asked if he would mind passing the number on. He did, but it seemed to create a wedge between him and Jim once again, which I felt bad about.

Jim asked some of his other Ukrainian-speaking friends if they would mind calling the number and explaining who I was, but for reasons unknown to me none of them would do it. Time was becoming a real issue, so one morning I dialled the number and hoped he could remember some English.

The phone began to ring, which was a good start, and a man answered.

'Is that Oleg Salenko?'

'Yes.'

Thank God. I explained as succinctly as I could about what I was doing, but he told me he already knew about me. I wasn't sure if it was Anatoli or Oleg Zadernovsky months earlier, perhaps both, but he was up to speed and said he would be happy to meet. I told him I was planning on coming over on the evening of Thursday, 6 October. He confirmed he would be in Kiev at that time and I should call him when I arrived to arrange where to meet. I hung up and immediately called Andy and asked him to book the flights and a hotel near the airport. In less than two weeks, I would finally meet Oleg, but I couldn't help feeling nervous about returning to Ukraine.

By sheer coincidence, Jim was travelling to the country on his annual humanitarian trip at the same time. He was taking the bus, an epic three-day trek from Glasgow to Kiev, which allowed him to take medical supplies that he wouldn't have been able to push through airport security. Jim has ten years on me, but you would never know it from looking at him. He was arriving in the Ukrainian capital the day before I flew in and said he would come to the airport to meet me. I thought Jim and I might go for a pint when I arrived, but little did I know just how much he would help.

So just who is Oleg Salenko?

Born in Leningrad in October 1969, his first professional club was Zenit Leningrad (later Zenit St Petersburg), where he played from 1986 to 1988. He moved on to Dynamo Kiev for three years and then moved to Spain, turning out for Logrones and Valencia, before Walter made a £2.5m bid in July 1995. Salenko had come to global attention in the World Cup in America the previous summer. Having earned one cap for Ukraine in 1992, he was now picked for Russia and made a stunning impact at the tournament. Previously top scorer at the under-20s World Cup in 1989, when he represented the USSR, he achieved that accolade again in 1994, this time with the full team. Oleg scored an incredible five goals against Cameroon in an amazing display. He followed that up with a penalty against Sweden, giving him six goals for the tournament. Russia were knocked out at the group stage, but Oleg shared the Golden Boot award for top scorer with Bulgaria's Hristo Stoichkov, who played four games more. Strangely, Oleg never played international football again after that World Cup.

He was a substitute in the opening game of the eight-in-a-row season, a 1–0 win over Kilmarnock, and scored his first goal in the third game, a 2–0 win at Falkirk on 16 September. He put in a great performance in another 2–0 win, this time at Parkhead on 30 September, and struck a double at home to Hearts in a 4–1 victory on 21 October. He also scored away to Killie and at home to Aberdeen in the space of three days in November, and struck yet again versus Kilmarnock in the 3–0 Boxing Day match. His last goal was in the 7–0 rout of Hibs on 30 December at Ibrox, and his final appearance was at Falkirk, the scene of his first goal, on 6 January in a 4–0 win. Despite scoring seven goals from 14 starts and two substitute appearances, Salenko was deemed surplus to requirements and moved on to Turkish side Istanbulspor in a swap deal with Peter Van Vossen. He didn't play much in his time there and became embroiled in a contract dispute. He moved to Cordoba in Spain in 1999 and Pogon Szczecin in Poland the following year, but barely pulled on his boots due to injuries and left after just one appearance. He retired afterwards.

I'd never had travel insurance on any of my previous trips, and it wasn't something I was usually concerned about, but this time I was worried. With my list of ailments it would cost me a fortune to get cover, so it wasn't an option, but I feared I might need it. I had been in and out of hospital in the previous months, and the thought of falling ill and being stuck in Ukraine was preying on my mind. I tried to convince myself it would be fine, but my nerves were on edge as I flew from Leeds to London. My connecting flight to Kiev departed on time, and I attempted to keep calm while we were in the air.

I had never met Jim before, but he described what he looked like and, sure enough, he was waiting when I came through arrivals. He was staying at a budget hostel in the centre of Kiev. The airport was a considerable distance from the city, so I was grateful he had come to meet me when he must have been exhausted after three days on a cramped bus. We warmly shook hands and Jim introduced me to a man he had brought with him. They met at the hostel earlier in the day, and Jim asked if he would come along since he was fluent in Ukrainian and Russian.

We found a quiet spot in the airport and made the call. Thankfully Oleg picked up. Once I introduced myself again I passed the phone to the hostel man and they chatted for a few minutes. When he hung up, he told me Oleg wanted to meet at a café bar in the city the following day. I hoped I wouldn't have to venture into the centre, but if that's what it took then I would need to handle it. We made our way to my hotel and I ordered a drink to try to calm my nerves. We chatted for a couple of hours and polished off a bottle of whisky between us. That didn't make me feel any calmer. Truth be told, I wasn't feeling at all well. It had been a long day, so maybe I just needed some sleep. Jim said he would meet me in the city the next morning and explained which metro line I had to take.

The guys made their way back to the hostel while I tried to get comfortable in the hotel room, but it was no use. I lay all night, wide awake. I sweated profusely and my heart raced. It became so bad at one point in the early hours that I genuinely thought I was having a bad turn. I was feeling nauseous, I was dripping wet and I struggled to catch a breath. That only made me panic more as I worried about being rushed to hospital with no insurance and, even worse, potentially missing my meeting with Oleg.

With no chance of sleep, I was up and out early to make sure I made it into the city in time. I was still burning up, so I didn't have a jacket on, despite it being October in Ukraine. Everyone else was walking around wrapped up in winter jackets, scarves, gloves and hats, and here I was wearing a T-shirt. Not that it stopped the sweats. I met Jim at Independence Square train station. He looked at me and asked if I was OK, and I told him about my night. We had a couple of hours before we were due to meet Oleg, so we went for a meal at one of the food places in the station, but I couldn't eat much. Instead I drank glass after glass of bottled water to try to cool down. I saw the look of concern on Jim's face.

Afterwards, we made our way to the café bar where Oleg wanted to meet. I sat down pensively and made sure I was facing the door so I wouldn't miss him arriving. If he arrived. I was so nervous I had convinced myself the wrong Oleg was going to turn up. What if I had been given the number for Kuznetsov and he was going to come walking in? It was ridiculous, but I wasn't thinking straight. I kept looking at my watch and then to the door.

I caught a glimpse of a familiar-looking figure approaching the bar. Then I spotted the Ukrainian football crest on his jacket and knew it was him. He opened the door and, spotting my football shirt, smiled and came over to our table. I stood up and immediately felt a heavy weight lift off my shoulders. Jim said later he saw an instant change in me when Oleg arrived. The colour returned to my face and the sweating stopped. I think my horrible experience the night before had simply been nerves. I was so close to the end of my mission, and it had all become too much.

I greeted Oleg like an old friend, and we sat down and ordered a round of drinks. Oleg's English was better than I had anticipated, and we chatted about his experience at Rangers. Maybe it was the passing of time or because I had come all that way, but he spoke glowingly of his time at Ibrox and seemed to be regretful at having left so soon. Jim has absolutely no interest in football, so I was having to fill him in about some of the greats we were talking about. Oleg said he was on his way to work at the Ukrainian Football Federation, but he must have spent a couple of hours with us first. I told him about my previous trip to the country and the terrifying taxi ride, which raised a smile.

As Oleg finally signed the shirt, Jim took a series of pictures to preserve the moment. Then we went outside and took some more photos. I also had him autograph a special shirt I had printed for the occasion. My trip was tinged with sadness due to a tragic accident the weekend before. A Rangers supporters' club's bus travelling from Dumfries and Galloway to the game at Ibrox against Partick Thistle had overturned at a roundabout and killed a fan on board. His name was Ryan Baird, and as the news reports filtered through, I recognised his face. Ryan, originally from Larne, had purchased some of my signed memorabilia that I'd sold to pay for my trips. I met him outside Ibrox and we were friends on Facebook. Here I was, travelling all over the world for signatures, while Ryan left his house one Saturday morning to go the game and never came home. It was tragic. I had a T-shirt printed with Ryan's photo on the front and decided to dedicate the final signature to his memory. He had helped me, and I felt it was the least I could do to show my sympathy for his family's loss.

We said goodbye and Oleg went off to work. Jim gave me a quick tour of Kiev, places like Independence Square, which had seen so much conflict, protest, blood and tears over the years. Here I was, going around the city like a tourist when I had promised myself I would go no further than the hotel! I couldn't help but smile at the way it had turned out. I'm in no doubt that I would never have come this far without Jim. I most likely would never have located Oleg in the first place, but I certainly wouldn't have been able to navigate my way around the city alone.

After a momentous day, it was time to return to my hotel and catch some sleep before another early departure for the airport the next morning. Jim was going to be in Kiev for another two weeks, sleeping in a hostel, unable to speak the language and having to be on guard in what was a tough city. I didn't envy him – it was certainly more than I could ever do.

It was only when I was on the flight home that I had the chance to reflect on what had happened. After seven years, tens of thousands of miles, scary moments, amazing meetings and times of extreme tedium, it was all over. I didn't know how I felt about that. It was great to complete something unique, something that would never be replicated. But there was also a tinge of sadness that it was all over.

I had instructed my daughter, Debbi, to record me coming through the arrivals gate with the shirt. I had a little speech worked out in my head that I wanted to capture on camera, but as I came through the doors, the shirt proudly clutched in my hands, I was suddenly overcome with emotion. I couldn't force the words out, and instead I burst into tears, as Debbi hurriedly hit the stop button. I think it was the culmination of the effort, worry, hard work and strife bubbling to the surface, and I ended up trooping exhaustedly through the terminal trying to recompose myself.

What was I going to do now? Well, write this book for one thing, and hopefully you've had as much fun reading about my adventures with the nine-in-a-row heroes as I had meeting them.

And, people often ask me, what now for the shirt? Eventually it will be passed down to my great-niece, but it would be nice to first see it on display in the stadium. My ultimate dream for it, however, is to walk out on to the hallowed Ibrox turf with the shirt in front of a packed crowd and show it off to all my fellow Bears. I get goosebumps just thinking about it, and hopefully by the time you read this it will have become a reality.

As for me, it's just like the famous song says – anywhere, everywhere, we will follow on.

Davie Cooper

OF COURSE, there was one player I wasn't able to meet on my journey, and it breaks my heart to this day that he is no longer with us.

The 86th name on the list was Davie Cooper, taken from us far too soon on 23 March 1995 at the tragically young age of 39.

He was still playing at the time, back on the books of his first professional club, Clydebank, and he had so much more still to offer the game. He was making a kids' coaching video, *Shoot*, for STV with Charlie Nicholas and Tommy Craig in Cumbernauld when he collapsed with a brain haemorrhage. He passed away in hospital the following day.

The outpouring of grief from across the shocked football world was palpable, and the gates outside Ibrox became a massive memorial to one of the greatest talents to ever come out of Scotland. Ray Wilkins called him a Brazilian trapped in a Scotsman's body, and Ruud Gullit said he was one of the best footballers he had ever seen. No one who saw Coop in his prime would disagree. He was, quite simply, a genius.

Born in Hamilton, Lanarkshire, in February 1956, the skilfully left-footed Cooper played with Hamilton Avondale as a youth. He was rumoured to have turned down Rangers as a teenager because he didn't think he would break into the first team, and instead he joined Clydebank, but only after he had been working as an apprentice printer. The mild-mannered Davie accepted just a £300 signing-on fee, the takings from the club's social club the previous night, and quickly showed the close control and wizardry that turned him into a legendary figure. He played for the Bankies for three years until his childhood heroes came calling.

Jock Wallace signed him for £100,000 in June 1977, having been impressed with him when Rangers played Clydebank in the League

Cup earlier in the season. Coop had a dream first season. He made his league debut on 3 August 1977 and would go on to win the treble, and the following campaign he lifted both cups. It was bad luck that so much of Davie's time at Ibrox coincided with one of the worst on-field periods in Rangers' history, as the club went into freefall, first under John Greig and then in Jock Wallace's second spell in charge.

He and Rangers were revitalised when Graeme Souness arrived in 1986, and Coop played 42 times in the 1986/87 season as the club won the title for the first time in nine years. The following season he played 33 matches, and, on 9 August 1988, 5,000 fans were locked out of a sold-out testimonial against Bordeaux, which we won 3–2. The attendance showed in what high regard he was held by the supporters, not just for his amazing skills and commitment to the club through the tough times, but ultimately because he was one of us. He was nicknamed Moody Blue and Albert, after Albert Tatlock, a sullen character from Coronation Street, but to give him those monikers is to misunderstand him. Coop was simply unassuming and quiet, a homebody not interested in moving elsewhere to play his football or in attracting headlines.

His testimonial came at the start of the first nine-in-a-row season. He made nine starts and 14 substitute appearances in the league that campaign. He came off the bench in the first three games, including the 5–1 thrashing of Celtic, and then started the next three as the number nine; in the last of these, he scored against St Mirren in a 2–1 home win. He was a sub in the next four games, missed the following four and came on at home to Hamilton in a 3–1 victory on 16 November. He started five on the bounce until the 1–0 Ibrox win over Hibs on 17 December, made sub appearances in the 3–1 home victory over St Mirren on 25 February and the 2–1 away triumph at Parkhead on April Fools' Day, and then featured in the final five games – his only start of that run coming in the penultimate game away to Dundee on 6 May, in a 2–1 win.

At 33, Cooper's first-team appearances were diminishing, but he was still desperate to play, so Souness allowed him to move on. In an interview with the BBC in May 2016, the former manager admitted he regretted allowing Davie to leave. 'I did so because of our personal friendship,' Graeme said. 'He wanted to play regularly and I couldn't guarantee that and I did him a favour. But he could open doors as a player and I should have kept him. It was a big mistake. He was a fabulous player.'

Cooper played 540 times for the Gers and scored 75 goals. He won three titles, three Scottish Cups and seven League Cups. The big occasion brought out the best in him, and he scored four times in those seven League Cup victories. One of his greatest goals came in the classic League Cup Final victory against Aberdeen in 1987, when his thunderbolt free kick threatened to snap the stanchion as it shot into the top corner. But that goal was nothing compared with the piece of magic he produced against Celtic in the Drybrough Cup Final in 1979, when he flicked the ball over three Celtic defenders in their box before slotting it past the keeper. It was voted the best Rangers goal of all time, and will likely never be bettered.

Davie moved to Motherwell in a cut-price £50,000 deal in 1989 and rolled back the years, adding to his medal haul by helping the Lanarkshire side win the Scottish Cup in the 4–3 classic against Dundee United in 1991. His form for the Steelmen also saw him add two more international caps to his collection. For Coop to make just 22 appearances for the national team seems, quite frankly, ludicrous. When he was called upon, his contribution at times proved crucial. He scored the all-important goal, a nerve-jangling penalty against Wales in 1985, that ensured we would go on to the World Cup play-off against Australia. He also scored in that tie and helped the country to the finals.

Davie had such an impact during his time at Motherwell that the club later named a stand after him, but by 1993 it was time to move on again and he returned to Clydebank.

He's never been forgotten. The 2005 League Cup Final, an environment where he excelled, was to be contested between Rangers and Motherwell ten years after his death. In his honour it was renamed the Davie Cooper Final.

Before that, on 18 March 1999, a bronze statue depicting Davie was unveiled in Hamilton by Ally McCoist. His mum, brother and ex-wife, and past and present players from across Scottish football such as John Brown, Ian Ferguson, Paul McStay, Craig Brown, Jimmy Johnstone, Bobby Shearer and Billy Davies, all paid their respects.

There is one simple quote that sums him up – 'I played for the team I loved'. Every Rangers supporter will be forever grateful that you did, Davie, and you will never be forgotten.

I thought long and hard over the years about how I could include Coop in my project. He couldn't just be left out, as if his contribution didn't mean anything, but I wasn't sure how to mark it. I pondered over attempting to contact his brother and asking him to sign it on behalf of the Cooper family, but I finally decided to make a simple tribute instead. Once I had every other signature, I took the shirt to the statue in his home town and paid quiet respect to the great man. It seemed fitting, considering he didn't chase publicity.

The sun began to set behind Davie's statue as I gazed up at his likeness, just as it was setting on my long and incredible journey. I'm grateful to every one of the players for taking the time to sign the shirt, often going above and beyond to see me realise my crazy dream. They displayed Rangers class and proved they were worthy of being part of Rangers' history.

To all of the nine-in-a-row boys, thank you for the memories, on the pitch and, 20 years later, off the pitch. It's an experience I will never forget.